FLEA MARKET AMERICA

A Bargain-Hunter's Guide

FLEA MARKET AMERICA

A Bargain-Hunter's Guide

By Cree McCree

Illustrated by Betsy James

John Muir Publications

Cover Art by Isaac Abrams
Cover Design by Robert Wasserman
Illustrated by Betsy James

Copyright © 1983 Marcia McCree
Cover & Illustrations Copyright © 1983 John Muir Publications, Inc.
All rights reserved

Published by John Muir Publications, Inc.
          P.O. Box 613
          Santa Fe, New Mexico 87501

Library of Congress Catalogue Card No. 83-60096
ISBN 0-912528-31-1

First Edition April 1983

This book is for my teachers:

Rolf, master of tactics, who taught me to be a warrior

Isaac, master of strategy, who taught me to be an artist

Eve, master of light and motion, who taught me to be a witch

John, master of synthesis, who taught me something about all of it

ACKNOWLEDGEMENTS

A book is a living thing, the product of a collaborative process:

Isaac Abrams gave me the idea, set me to writing, lent his support and typewriter, and kept me on the right track.

Bob Wasserman was a continual source of editorial and design assistance. His enthusiasm and long hours were essential. He—together with Isaac's magic airbrush—wrapped it all up for me with a beautiful cover design.

Eve Muir helped me turn my motley assortment of file folders into a real manuscript.

Gerry Magill, Annie's mom, gave me a haven to complete the final draft. Both she, and my own mom, Millie McCree, helped make me believe it was all worthwhile.

Fima kept his Volkswagen alive and chauffeured me into fleadom, New Jersey style. And Leslie, Laura and Adrian Smith, guided me through their local markets in New Haven, Connecticut with friendly expertise.

Jane Nelson's help with the catalogue art when the deadline was yesterday was indispensible. John Scherman lent his design skills and boosted my spirits when the production jobs seemed endless. And Betsy James took on the heroic job of illustrating the entire book when it was practically on the way to the printer, adding the wit of her pen with astonishing rapidity.

Without these people and the staff at JMP—Ken, Lisa, Jeanne, Peter and the indomitable Stick—*Flea Market America* would still be on the drawing board.

To all of them, and to all the fleas who live in these pages: Thank you!

Contents

If everybody were living in the middle of a Doris Day movie, they wouldn't need to do this. It's not easy money. But it's direct money. You can get into this with very little capital. The capital is your flesh. The bank loan is your life.

It has to do with freedom.

—Joel Kaufman, owner
Canal St. Market, New York City

The flea market's always been around, even when the money was available. Now things is taking a gradual change, see, your main man in the office there has cut the money circulation down to a minimum. OK?

But the thing is, it's always been this way out here; always will be. You know? The market's always going to make it. It's just up to the individual, strictly basically up to the individual. You've got to be interested in sitting out here, being with people and making honest bucks. I always have, always will, get a kick out of this.

—Jerry Junk, vendor
Boulevard Market, New Haven

INTRODUCTION
Welcome to Fleadom

Flea Market America really *is* a country-within-a-country, a thriving underground economy I call 'fleadom.' Fleadom is populated by 'fleas' and has no geographic boundaries. It is a way of life.

We citizens of fleadom may have nothing in common during our weekday lives: we're old, young, hip, straight, every color and creed. But come the weekend, all this diversity becomes community. We're *fleas*. It is in our nature to be stubbornly independent, as opportunistic as Horatio Alger, with an ample supply of good old American ingenuity. We are not trapped by the burdens of inflation, taxation and corporate conglomeration, because we exist inbetween the lines of the system, and our community belongs to us.

Fleadom welcomes newcomers, and our economic survival strategy is open to anyone with the initiative to get out there and do it. As Jerry Junk says, "It's strictly, basically up to the individual." With open eyes, open ears and inner radar with antennae that are alway operative, you can learn to spot a bargain with the accuracy of a radar scope. The more you do it, the better you get, and fleadom is rich in rewards for the well-trained flea.

As a flea, you can have your own shop without being a shopkeeper. You can run your own show without lawyers, leases, bank loans, contracts, insurance or overhead. You answer to no one but yourself: no daily nine-to-fiving, no biannual inventories, no eviction notices, no threats from banks and utility companies. In fleadom, you control your own resources.

You also have complete access to the exchange of goods in the market-place. Sooner or later almost anything you're looking for—from a feather boa to a bathroom scale—is going to turn up at the market. Vigilant fleas rarely buy anything at retail prices—chopping expenses to the bone. Since it's a two-day work week (three at most, counting accumulating stock, but that's the *fun* part), fleadom offers a support system that both underwrites your cost of living and gives you time to live.

And you can take your act on the road. Fleadom is spreading throughout the land, and fleas can go almost anywhere in the United States and set up shop. At nearly any flea market you'll see older retired folks with tables set up outside their RVs, living the life of the gypsy as they follow the sun around the country. You, too, can 'retire'—and you don't have to wait until they give you the gold watch and shove you out the door.

There is a magic in fleadom that transcends the marketplace. It is living theatre, a folksy carnival with its own rituals, where anything can happen, any strange ikon be unearthed. If you stick in your thumb you might pull out a plum, and the promise of plums is the lifeblood of fleadom.

If you love surprises, if you're willing to dig and delve for buried treasure, if nothing makes your heart beat faster than a good old-fashioned bargain—you're already a flea. This book will help turn you into a pro. A pro like Jerry Junk who grins when he says, "I always have, always will, get a kick out of this."

Welcome to fleadom!

Flea Market America

Everybody trades, you trade your labor for money, you trade anything.
Everybody's a trader, I'm just more of a trader than most.
—Trader Jack Daniels, owner
Trader Jack's Market, Santa Fe, NM

1

Birth of a Flea

California, 1975. The year of the drought. Farmers gnash their teeth in barren fields, the lushest lawns are wilted brown. It was a bad year for business, unless you were hawking water-saving devices. Or selling at the flea market.

As the year of my entry into fleadom, it was perfect. No rain meant perfect sales days; no 5 AM weather checks or hauling in and out the plastic tarps. The 1975-76 flea season was a year-round operation, an extraordinary phenomenon for northern California. Occasional twinges of guilt over the plight of my fellow Californians were more than assuaged by the overwhelming success of what had begun as just talk: my outdoor store.

For years I had been a hardcore rummager, outfitting myself and my friends in the best cheap chic tradition. It was obvious my specialty was fashion. I found orange satin flapper dresses in the attics of abandoned farmhouses in southern Colorado, faithfully scoured St. Vincent de Paul's "everything for a nickle" afternoons for lacy nightgowns and lumberjack shirts, bargained at the flea markets of Paris and Amsterdam for old fur coats, prowled the open air markets of Afghanistan for Kuchi gypsy dresses.

Like many good ideas, this one had been staring me in the face forever. But it took a combination of financial desperation and the sharp-witted thinking of a couple close friends before I actually decided to flea for fun *and* profit.

I did my homework before I opened up shop. I talked to lots of vendors when I canvassed the various flea markets in the Bay Area where I then lived. I priced comparable merchandise, and got a sense of the general feeling of each different market. It soon became apparent that the Marin City flea market in Sausalito was *my* market. Smaller and more informal than its East Bay counterpart in Alameda, it had a colorful, carnival atmosphere I loved.

The Sausalito market is located in fashionable Marin County, just over the Golden Gate bridge from San Francisco. Marin County is both one of the wealthiest and one of the kinkiest counties in the country, making its flea market a treasure trove of unusual collectibles and cheap fashion-plate clothing. The market was only about 25% professional at the time I opened shop; most vendors were local amateurs out on a lark, drinking beer and catching rays while watching themselves being watched. This meant it was a great place to buy, as well as to sell.

And buy I did. Over the next few weeks I scavenged the market, thrift shops, rummage sales and garage sales until I had accumulated enough stock to have a gala opening. During this time I also collected display tools: an umbrella-style clothes drying rack for hanging goods, a couple of folding tables and chairs, suitcases to hold accessories, plenty of hangers, and a lightweight mirror. My shop was ready to open.

That original flea market store was straight out of the circus. Everything—stock, display tools, my partner Rolf and I—fit in and onto a VW bug. Thank god for the roof rack or we might never have managed it. When we unloaded our wares it looked like one of those circus acts where dozens of clowns keep appearing from inside a tiny automobile. But it worked.

The very first day we were swamped by the local pros immediately on arrival. I know I let merchandise go for much less than my market-wise self would today, but I still remember the astonishment when Rolf and I counted up our take at the end of the day. It was close to $300 and we still had good stuff left to sell. When we returned to the market the following day, we didn't set up until I had made my own buying rounds and could include new stock in the shop—a first-buy/then-sell routine I have followed ever since. That made me a pro.

We continued to sell regularly at the Sausalito market over the next couple years, commuting from the East Bay and later from Napa. The commute meant a super-early rising and an obligatory phone weather report before setting off. We could never be sure whether to go with or against the weather report, for while they were usually wrong, just every

so often they were right. So we learned, like our fellow fleas, to hope for the best, expect the worst, and be prepared for anything.

Whenever we travelled the open highway, for business or pleasure, we used the cross-county network of flea markets to underwrite our expenses. Operating out of a van, with its roof rack packed to the hilt, we were actually able to travel with two kids, the entire flea market stock and display tools, plus all our personal and camping gear—and still have room to breathe as well as to stash new bargains gathered along the way. Fleas, especially of the nomadic variety, must become expert packers. We passed the test.

Hungry for open space and fed up with California freeway madness, we scouted a move to Santa Fe, New Mexico in the late seventies. A major tactical consideration was whether the local flea market could give us the economic padding we knew we would need. We had become successful fleas in urban markets, but would our operation work in small-but-hip Santa Fe? The only way to find out was to try it.

We made an exploratory trip to Santa Fe, where we pulled into Trader Jack's market and set up shop—and did a brisk business. A second weekend confirmed our success as more than a fluke. We moved within the month, and Trader Jack's continued to be an important income source while we established our martial arts center. The flea market also helped us out by serving as an information network, yielding connections with more valuable implications than just the day's sales; many of our K'ang Jo Fu students were originally flea market customers.

It was in Santa Fe that we first opened a used book store as an adjunct to the boutique. I accumulated a large stock of good titles before the books made their debut, and organized them by categories in wire bakery baskets that served as both display and storage cases. The books were re-stocked as regularly as the clothing and we found the addition to be more than a modest success. It attracted a wider range of buyers to our stall and there were lots of cross-over customers. People might start by looking at the books and then discover the clothing—and vice-versa. The bookstore bred some spontaneous literary dialogues, and I found myself discussing Dostoevsky with one customer while selling a satin smoking jacket to another.

In the summer of 1981 I came alone to Manhattan, with no idea if New Yorkers even knew what a flea market was. The gods must have smiled on me, because I moved into a downtown loft building on Canal Street directly across from the liveliest flea market in town. Once again, my flea boutique brought in money while I juggled to get my other acts together.

It is here in New York that this book was born. I have broadened my own story by interviewing other pros with different wares and wiles, and I am indebted to the fellow fleas who shared their expertise with me to pass along to you.

The main thing is that you gotta be interested. You gotta learn something out of the deal. Otherwise, you're just wasting your time. Wasting your time.

—Jerry Junk, vendor
Boulevard Market, New Haven, CT

2

What Kind of Flea Are You?

There is an infinite variety of fleas; the only limit is your imagination. While the majority resell used merchandise, many sell new goods at bargain prices, operate food concessions, hawk handmade wares, and even sell their talents. One of the delightful things about fleadom is that there's *always* something new under the sun.

Successful fleas flourish because they combine a love for their merchandise with expertise in their field. Even if you are a flea of the weekend hobby variety, you must know the values of your wares to become a skilled bargain hunter. If you think a drill press is something your dentist uses to fill cavities, you shouldn't be dealing in tools. For unless you *know*, those who do will cheerfully clean you out. This is not malicious; it's simply the way of fleadom. You're expected to be sharp or winner takes all.

If you want to become a serious pro, you must not only know your wares; you must know your market, with all its local quirks and idiosyncrasies. In my years as a pro, I've seen all kinds of operations come and go. Some flourish, some flounder. Those that flounder usually sink because they're not appropriate for the local market (like punk shades in Enid, Oklahoma), or because the investment of time and money far exceeds the profit potential.

Be realistic. If you can knock off a couple of cords of firewood in an afternoon with your chainsaw and you haul your pickup load to the market when the leaves are turning and people are thinking winter, you'll probably do great. But if you only have a bow saw and those two cords represent a couple days of labor, or if you pick a sizzling Saturday in July to hawk your wood, you'll probably be disappointed. Anything goes. But what goes best is the right thing at the right time.

The heart of my own operation warrants an entire chapter of its own(see Chapter 5: *The Cheap Chic Flea Boutique*). The following is a survey of other major specialties, most of them described by long-time pros who are successful in their fields. These are some of the people who make it work.

JUNK

Junk dealers are the essence of flea markets. The best of these trash and treasure combos are almost mini-markets in themselves, with a little bit of everything thrown in. Junk dealers specialize in *not* specializing, and usually collect their oddly assortments for nothing or next to nothing. All they need is a reliable pickup truck and a little bit of hustle to get themselves in business.

Jerry Junk

I discovered Jerry Junk at the Boulevard flea market in New Haven, Connecticut, which has been operating in the parking lot of the Olympia Diner (next to Big Buy Supermarket) for the last ten years. The parking lot was jammed with buyers and vendors, many of whom rent dormant, weathered semi trailers from the management to store their goods during the week.

The Boulevard market is a little like a Mexican mercado. It has lots of produce vendors, offering everything from potatoes to live chickens and rabbits, plump and ready for the pot. There is a row of new merchandise sellers, and the rest of the market is a junk dealer's paradise.

Jerry Junk works during the week for the telephone company, but for several years he's been bringing in an extra income at the market. His hodge-podge display stood out from the others because almost everything he had, from aging baby dolls to a beautiful maple dresser, was really unique. He represents the best of this traditional breed.

They call me Jerry Junk. That's my alias name: Jerry Junk.

I find my stuff in alleys and cellars. See, I clean a lot of people's attics and cellars, and they let me take what I want. Plus I charge them. Can't beat it.

I collect antiques, but there's a lot of things that have antique value that I don't collect personally. Anything after the early 19th century, I generally sell. Like what you see here: flea market specialties. Big items were in demand at one time, but now people are looking for small items too. With small items, you can put 'em away, tuck 'em away; you can collect more when you pick up small items. Some people walk by me and say 'That guy's got a whole buncha junk.' And then there's other people who say 'Well, the stuff that this guy has is stuff that I sorta like.' Because I'm very particular.

The older stuff is, the better chance you have of making a buck. That's all there is to it, basically. Little things can bring you bucks: carpet bags, steamer trunks, hatracks, right? I could name so many things, you know, that I hate to get into it, it's a long sort of thing, right? But oak is in demand now. Mahogany furniture. Maple furniture. It all depends on who made it and how it was made. Was it made by hand?

A lot of people buy old homes, and they want to put old stuff in it. They feel that's the best place to put their money. See what I'm saying? They're afraid of banks now, so they buy something old. They put $100 or $200 into it, figuring it won't depreciate. They think the only thing it can do is escalate.

I didn't know too much when I started this. What got me going was that people would come by and buy things from me, and I would wonder why they would buy the old items. And I began to read books. I read and read, and finally I started stopping at shops to look at the prices they were getting on some of their things. After awhile, I began realizing that I was giving things away that were really worth something.

Now I know my business, and I keep up by reading the want ads. That's another way to determine what's moving; want ads. People don't realize that. Look in your newspaper. See what people are looking for, and find out how much they're willing to pay.

I've been down here for awhile now. When people get to recognize your face, they ask you about certain things. They ask me 'Can you locate this? Can you locate that?' So it's become a very interesting part-time thing for me. I get a lot of enjoyment out of it.

COLLECTIBLES

Collectibles includes everything from war medals and carnival glass to Coca Cola and vintage Mickey Mouse watches—anything that's old enough, or lovely enough, or loony enough to be quintessentially flea marketable.

Antique collectibles require impeccable expertise. You must know your merchandise well enough to recognize a bargain when you see it, and to discuss it knowledgeably with fellow fleas in your field. If you plan to sell as well as collect, remember that you'll need a moneyed market: an antique diamond brooch isn't an impulse buy. It's an investment.

George and Joyce

George and Joyce ran an antique business for years. In 1962 they sold their shop and began travelling the circuit of antique shows and flea markets with their small collectibles stashed in the trunk of their sedan. I interviewed them at the flea market in New Hope, Penna., which caters almost exclusively to buyers of high-priced collectibles. Their selection was most elegant, interesting and varied, and reflected their years of experience.

These folks know their stuff.

George: We've been all over the country—you name it. We do the Rosebowl in California, we go everywhere.

Joyce: You meet a lot of nice people in this line.

George: See that guy there in the picture with Reagan? I did business with him in Waldo, Florida. I got all these little pouches from World War II, they're something the soldiers sent to their girlfriends. Each one has a handkerchief in it. Believe it or not, this guy had a whole warehouse of these in Georgia. I bought a couple hundred from him.

Joyce: You've got to buy if you're going to resell.

George: What I like best is the old cards, advertising cards, postcards, all kinds of cards. These postcards here are really old; some of them date back to the early 1900s. The stamps make a difference to some people, to stamp collectors, but I'm not really into the stamps. I like the cards, and I like the messages people wrote on them. A lot of these cards have a whole history on the back.

   Now these cards here are very special. I'm from Brooklyn, and I'm making an album of all these old cards from Brooklyn and Coney Island. I don't sell them; I keep them. It's my hobby.

Joyce: Me, I like all the old dolls. I like jewelry, the art nouveau and the art deco. And I like glass. You've got to be able to point your finger at different types of glass, because they reproduce a lot. You have to know. But once you know, you know.

   These salt and pepper shakers are cut glass from the 20s and 30s. There are lots of different qualities of cut glass, even if it's old. See the difference in the cut of this one? It's much rougher. And see this one here? That's a signed Libby, so it's more expensive. Anything is more valuable if it's signed.

George: You gotta know what's what. This toy car here is an old one, from about 1920. It's rubber, American rubber. I picked it up for next to nothing at a flea market in Florida. That, I'm asking $20 for. And I'll get it, I'll get if from someone who knows.

   The Beatles thing next to it is a recent collectible. It's a model of the Yellow Submarine. See—it pops up. The Beatles stuff is getting out of hand. I've got a $50 price tag on that. Eventually, I'll get it.

   But most of our stuff is really old, like these photographs. Some of them are 80, 90 years old. You can't beat that photography, can you?

FOOD CONCESSIONS

Even when flea market shoppers aren't buying anything else they still want to eat. Prepared-food concessions may well be the biggest money makers of all, and many markets opt to control this turf by restricting food sales to operations run by the management. Other markets do rent space to food concessions but at a higher fee than they charge merchandise vendors. Why? It's probably a combination of the large sales volume of food concessions and the extra hassles management often experiences with food sellers.

Joel Kaufman, who operates the Canal Street market in downtown Manhattan, expresses his personal reasons for charging more: "Sure, I charge food concessions more; I charge them a space and a half. It's mostly because of the garbage. And because when they leave a spot, it's lubricated for life. There's nothing worse than extremely used oil." Of course, not all concessions specialize in the kind of fried foods that leave a trail of grease behind, but there's no question that the throwaway refuse of food operations adds a hefty share to daily clean-up. Conscientious concessions clean up after themselves, and this is a courtesy appreciated by management, buyers and other vendors alike.

If you already own and operate a mobile food concession of any kind, you may find the flea market a profitable new territory to set up shop and well worth the higher rental fee. But if all you have is this great idea to sell shish kebabs, remember that most food concessions require a substantial investment in equipment. To make your venture worthwhile you'll probably want to structure additional sales locations —such as auto repair garages and construction sites—during the week as well.

There is one other option, however, which requires minimal investment: you can become a sandwich man or cookie lady, selling goodies prepared at home which require no facilities to heat them up or cool them down. Most markets *do* allow these small-scale operations to rent space at the same fee as other vendors. Simple, well-prepared homemade food can bring you a steady income at the market, as well as provide dealers and shoppers with an alternative to corn dogs and fries. And you can sell between weekends at stores and offices, too, if you're looking for a steady trade.

The Sausalito sandwich lady with her basket of deliciously wholesome wares often saved me from starvation when the thought of one more chili dog was more than my stomach could bear. I'm sure many fleas are thankful for all the food concessions and vendors that have kept us well-fed. Food is a specialty that is also a service, and munchies that make the mouth water will always be welcome.

PRODUCE

Many flea markets evolved from farmers' markets, and produce continues to be an important specialty in fleadom. I've seen vendors successfully sell their own fruits and vegetables, honey, herbs gathered or cultivated, and seedlings in the spring. Even if you don't grow your own you can take your pickup to apple country at harvest time, load it up for next to nothing, and turn apples into dollars at your local market.

Marilyn

Marilyn is part of the venerable tradition of the farmer flea. I interviewed her at one of the biggest 'big daddies' of them all: the

Englishtown, N.J. flea market. On a day when threat of serious rain made for a relatively deserted market, Marilyn was doing a brisk business in late spring seedlings for the home gardener. The drizzle kept her seedlings and flowers happy while other vendors scurried frantically to cover their goods with plastic tarps.

Marilyn seems to know everything there is to know about growing things, and she cares not only about her flowers and produce but about her customers as well. I watched her ease a buyer's embarassment about breaking off the stem of a marigold with these words: "That's the trouble with marigolds. They break so damn easy. The best part is that when one breaks you can just tear it off and they come back."

And just like those marigolds, Marilyn's customers keep coming back. Coming back to buy good produce at good prices from a woman who knows about nurturing.

> I've been comin' to this market since I'm married to my husband. Twenty-two years. Him, all his life. He came when he was a kid, when the market was a horse auction. That's how it started back in the 30s. Once a week farmers would bring their horses and cattle to auction off, and a few farmers would bring produce.

We have a small truck farm, and we grow all our own vegetables. We only grow for retail; there's no money in wholesale. My husband stays home and does field work and hothouse. He's out plantin' tomatoes right now. Robert and I handle the business here.

Now it's garden plantin' time, so we're sellin' seedling plants and flowers. The flowers I buy; we don't have enough space in our greenhouse. Come June, all the nurseries will be unloading their flowers, and I'll go to the farmers' auctions to buy them. They're cheap; I'll get flowers for half of what I'm paying for them now. But just for June; after that, flower sales drop drastically.

Our first lettuce comes around the middle of June, and we go a couple of weeks on lettuce. When the lettuce fades out, we'll have beets; maybe some cabbage. Then we go into the summer, sellin' whatever is in season. Whenever people ask for somethin' a lot, like cherry tomatoes or basil, we start growin' it. By the end of summer, we have maybe thirty different items.

We only farm twelve acres, so sometimes we don't have our own corn every week. Then I go to the farmers' auctions and buy some. Even if you don't have a farm, you can work the auctions. You gotta have a good truck because you gotta buy in bulk. And you gotta know what you're doin'. Or else you might land with fifty bushels of somethin' when you wanted five! I went to the auctions with my husband for a couple years before I ever went by myself. It's just like any other business. You gotta learn the ropes, and then it's simple.

I have a stand in front of our house, but I only open for Halloween, for the pumpkins. I don't want to be tied down seven days a week. This is two days a week, and I'm done. I have no complaints. This is a crazy, beautiful market, the best market in the country. I wouldn't give up this place on Saturdays for anything in the world.

FURNITURE

Furniture requires brawn and a reliable truck. When you specialize in antique furniture, like Slim, you need expertise to find the bargains; if you want to go pro, you'll also need a moneyed market. Without affluent buyers, people may oo and ah over a hand-carved armoire, but that's about all they'll do. Other fleas, like Mary, deal in regular old furniture—maybe not the height of craftsmanship, but good in a pinch when you've just moved to town and have an apartment to furnish.

Furniture is a hefty specialty. Both Mary and Slim work alone, and Mary is grateful that she's never hurt her back. Slim confessed that occasional aches and pains are an occupational hazard.

But they both agreed it's worth it.

Slim—Antique Furniture

Slim looks like a prototypical good old boy. Like many fleas, Slim is now retired, and his laconic drawl and regulation cowboy hat belie his former existence as a production supervisor for Union Carbide. His antique furniture business began as a hobby: "The first thing you know, you've got a whole barn full of stuff and you've got to get rid of some of it."

I interviewed Slim at Trader Jack's market in Santa Fe, where he commutes every weekend from Albuquerque. During the week, he often sells to wholesealers, and he had just scored an entire truckload of goodies from a chance encounter with another dealer at a truck stop. The fellow was facing an expensive repair job on his broken-down rig and needed quick cash. Slim bailed him out and got a bargain basement price in return.

The ability to take advantage of whatever fate throws in your path is the mark of a bona fide flea, and Slim is as sharp as they come.

> I prefer oak, I know I can sell it. Oak is good wood; after 50 or 60 years, it's still in good shape. Highboy dressers, old iceboxes, any kind of dresser with a mirror. Mirrors are great sellers. And tables and chairs. If you've got four to six matching chairs, you can name your price.
>
> I also buy walnut and mahogany, but only if they're reasonable. Mahogany I can't always sell. Wicker from the 30s is a big seller, like that little wicker desk there. I buy mostly stuff from the 20s and 30s, but we're starting to run out. We're going to be into the 40s soon.
>
> Read a few books before you start out would be my suggestion. You've got to study a little bit, make sure you're buying old furniture and not reproductions. Go to auctions to see approxi-

mately what things are worth. You'll get a pretty good idea of what dealers are paying, and you know they've got to make a profit.

And then I'd go to farm sales; that intrigues me a lot more than auctions. Go to auctions to find out top dollar prices, but go to farm sales to buy. That cuts the middle man out, and you're dealing direct with the people. I'm on a mailing list that tells me about farm sales. Some of them are in the newspapers, but the best idea is to talk to some auctioneers and get on a mailing list.

You've got to buy cheap if you're going to sell. But that's not happening much any more; it's all high. Sometimes I buy pieces and turn them over right away and make fifteen or twenty dollars. I try to move it in and out, to go for high turnover. Last Saturday I sold out, had to go home.

You can't go out and bring back two or three pieces. You've gotta have a load to make money. I got a 35-foot rig, and I go out in that for buying. You've gotta buy from someone you trust, who won't rip you off, and you gotta buy a load if you're going to do it as a business. Everything you see here is mine, bought and paid for.

You gotta know what you're looking for.

Mary—Household Furniture

Mary is now a successful real estate agent in Santa Fe, New Mexico. Until a year ago, she made her living buying and selling furniture out of a shop during the week and at the flea market on weekends. Mary never dealt in antiques; she sold good used, useable furniture and new mattresses commissioned and bought by her from a wholesaler. I was interviewing Slim when she walked up and joined us, and her comments expand the realm of furniture dealing beyond the specialized antique market.

I bought things people really, really need, like for young couples who move into town and rent an unfurnished apartment. They need a mattress, they need a sofa, they need a table and chairs. It wasn't bad looking furniture, but not antiques. I'd sell them maybe two, three hundred dollars of furniture as a lot, and that would be enough to furnish an entire apartment.

And I used to order truckloads of inexpensive mattresses from a wholesaler. They were real hard foam mattresses, and they were the best seller I ever had. I sold a truckload a week. People are always moving in here, and they want a nice place to sleep—they don't want a dirty old mattress. Sometimes I had arrangements with summer people to sell them mattresses and buy them back at the end of the summer. I knew they weren't going to be used much, and then I could sell them again.

I got the furniture out of a big apartment complex when they turned it into condos; I'd buy it as they vacated the apartments. It's a good business. Everyone who gets into this starts to go into antiques, they don't want to be bothered with the other stuff. That's what the people I sold to did—and now they're not doing as well.

BOOKS

When you're moving an entire household, books are just so much dead weight. I can usually pick up paperbacks for a dime or a quarter and hardbacks for not much more. I sell my paperbacks for about half original cover price, which means a ten-cent investment turns into a dollar return.

With hardbacks and rare editions, the profit margins get even prettier. I found the first English language edition of *Mein Kampf* (1940) at a flea market for a dollar. Eventually, I sold it to a collector for $20, and he raved about what an exceptional bargain it was. Maybe I could have gotten more, but I was more than satisfied. 2000% profit isn't bad.

The success of my own book operation is based on a wide range of quality books, mostly paperbacks, categorized conveniently for the buyer. I include current hot items, whether or not they have great literary value. But the bulk of my stock is comprised of timeless classics and what I believe to be the best of contemporary literature and non-fiction. In short, I buy books *I* want to read.

I look for books in good condition, and because I can usually buy them ridiculously cheap, I'm able to keep my prices remarkably low. The most I ever charge for a book is half the cover price; usually the price is even lower than that, which pleases my customers and keeps my cash flow optimal.

TOOLS

The tool dealers of the market are a special breed. Harder-nosed than most, tool vendors know the absolute values of their wares and rarely bargain. This may be because tools are functional, and much of fleadom caters to luxury. You can pass up a red feather boa, much as you covet it, when you're pinching your pennies. But when you need a ratchet, you need a ratchet. Nobody expects to get a good hammer for 25¢, and Marcel is very aware that this makes tools a profitable specialty.

Marcel

I interviewed Marcel at the Boulevard market in New Haven where I talked to Jerry Junk. According to Marcel, it's the oldest market in the area, and existed in another location on Lafayette St. back when he was kid. That was quite some time ago.

Now in his mid-fifties, Marcel works during the week but has been dealing his tools on weekends for the past ten years. He and his young partner, Ralph (who uses the market as his sole source of income), rent two of the empty semi trailers in the Boulevard parking lot to store their goods during the week. They have an impressive selection of antique, used, and new tools, as well as sturdy kitchenware such as cast iron pots and pans.

Marcel is shrewd and totally knowledgeable about his wares. During our interview, he explained the function of a variety of tools, new and used, that were only objets d'art to me. ("There's a heavy duty screwdriver. Why is it square? Reason for it. You can put a wrench on the shaft.") He told me his name at the very end of our interview, and it was a wonderful non sequitor for me. I had, of course, been expecting a 'Harry' or 'Bud.' With a name like Marcel, he could be a hairdresser; instead, he's the quintessential tool man.

> Tools are something I know and I stick with them. Tools seem to go pretty good—they're something everybody's looking for. Some people are addicted to tools. A lot of men can't pass by a good tool; they've just gotta buy it. The price of tools today has been going right out of this world. My prices are good, so people keep coming back for more.
>
> I have some new tools here, but I don't get them from a wholesaler. I buy them from people who never used them and finally decided to get rid of them. Let's say a machinist is retiring, and he has some specialty tools that he can't use around his house. Or the husband passes away, and the wife gets rid of his stuff. Things like that.

Most of my tools are used. I go around to lots of sales, and sometimes I pick up antique tools. Some people collect antique tools. These tools all have their use, but they're slowly becoming obsolete. Like that pipe threader there. Today most of the plumbing work in houses is done with copper tubing or plastic, so the old cast iron is going out of style. But some people just like old tools. They hang them around the house for display, they add a little decoration to their basements.

A lot of these tools have machinist's marks on them. You don't drill or do machine work on tools unless there is a reason for it. A tool and die maker doesn't work for two dollars an hour you know, so you don't have him scratch marks on something that don't mean nothing. Every mark means something: it tells you what was done to the tool. When you get to know tools, you understand the marks.

I sell a lot of pots and pans, too. Good pots and pans. Because today, see, you go to the store to buy a small saucepan and you're talking five, six dollars. And you take that pan, and you can squeeze it like that in your hand. It's all light-weight material. The stuff I buy is always heavy gauge. I get good prices, because everything is in tip-top shape.

Last week, for instance, I had a lobster pot, real good-sized, that sells for $45 in any store. Heavy gauge, real good shape, almost brand new. So I asked $15 for it and it sold right away. People figure what the heck? They can't pay that kind of money in a store, so they come here and get that same pot. I don't have any pots and pans right now, because I already sold off what I had this morning. People that need 'em come down early and pick 'em up. That's the way it goes.

The only problem with tools is that if they get wet, they're going to rust. We've got to watch out for the weather. We've got plastic and there are some things that we cover up. And if they do get wet, we clean them before they start to rust.

It's like anything else. You gotta use precaution.

HANDMADE ARTS & CRAFTS

Fleadom is bargain hunters' turf, and it can often be discouraging for craftspeople. I've seen many a fine craftsman wilt in the midday sun, reaping nothing but appreciative words from customers while the junk dealer across the way is cleaning up, selling broken tricycles and cracked mirrors. Which is not that amusing when you've put in money for materials and many hours of loving labor to prepare for your trip to the market.

The flea market is not the place to sell handwoven silk caftans or sculptured gold jewelry. If you need high price tags to bring the return your worksmanship deserves, you're better off doing the crafts fairs. You can, however, build a good flea business selling handmade items which require a minimum investment of money and time. This is what Andy has done, successfully enough to support himself solely with his flea market earnings.

Andy

I discovered Andy's wooden toys at the bustling roadside market in Lahaska, Pa., and practically pounced on the poor guy with my enthusiasm. His display was exactly what I had been looking for: an example of someone selling handmade goods that are both fun to make, and cheap enough to be affordable for the average flea market buyer.

Andy's bear chairs immediately caught my eye. These child-sized chairs feature a grinning bear, and are a delightful extension of *The Three Bears*. Andy completed a Papa Bear chair for himself a week before our interview, and has a Mama Bear chair in the works. They're real winners.

Andy also has some traditional favorites in his stock, like trains and trucks and rocking horses. But even more fun to discover were his own innovations, like the dragons and whales who have holes in their backs to serve as crayon holders. And his notched wooden square with dowels set in to hold two colors of wooden doughnuts: it's a three-dimensional tic-tac-toe game.

I bought presents for the 2 young boys in my life: a crayon holder for the four-year-old, and a tic-tac-toe game for the seven-year-old. They loved them, and *I* loved Andy's phenomenally low prices: 75¢ for the crayon holder, $1 for the game. The bear chairs sell for $14, which is a downright steal.

Andy loves to work with wood, and I think he enjoys the special magic of being a toymaker. He works quickly enough to sell his toys at rockbottom prices and still make a living, and is a fine example of how to turn a hobby into a successful flea market enterprise.

I've sold my wooden toys at this market for six years. The first four years I starved. But the past couple of years I've been making a living doing this.

I have a wood shop in my garage, and do most of the cuts on a bandsaw. I buy my lumber, but I use construction lumber instead of first-rate lumber. That way, I keep my costs down and my prices low. My toys are unfinished; that is, they're unpainted and people have to do some work on them, like fine sanding. I think I actually sell more because they *are* unfinished. People are willing to do a little extra work in exchange for a low price, and they like to add their own touch by painting them.

For a long time I had seen wooden toys—at crafts fairs and mall shows, mostly—and they were all selling for really high prices. Expensive toys don't sell that well, except maybe at Christmas. I didn't want to rip off the public, and I also wanted to make a living. That's why there's nothing fancy about my toys; they're all plain and simple. People like them, and they buy them.

I started out making trains, but most of these designs are new. A lot has evolved in the past two years, and it keeps evolving. The bear chairs have become one of my biggest sellers, and that design just came out of the air. Almost every new design I come up with is a 'mistake'; I screw something up and then it turns out better than I wanted it to. I think every artist who's honest enough to tell you would say he works like that.

This flea market is my only sales outlet. I come here every weekend from the middle of February until Christmas. It gets cold as hell in the winter, but I have the right equipment. February through May is real good. Then in June and July, my business drops off. We get lots of people, tourists mostly, but they browse a lot more than they buy. From August to Christmas sales build up, and I always sell the most just before Christmas. I use the month of January to design new stuff.

Lots of toymakers go to shows, but I don't do any shows at all—not even at Christmas. I won't do mall shows because they all have Muzak. I refuse to listen to that twelve hours a day. Also, this market is real convenient, and I'm basically a lazy person. Here I sign up for the month, I know where I'm going to be, I don't have to hassle about parking or anything. And I can use the time during the week to work in the shop. I have to make a lot of toys to make money, and that takes time.

I figure that by now I could become relatively rich doing this. But I have no yearning to do that. I think that running a factory would be just as bad as working in one. I don't have any helpers, because I really don't want to make a living off someone else's labors. I refuse to do that. I also have no interest in having a career. I'm going to take this as far as I think I can take it. Then, at a certain point, I'll just forget it.

I like selling things that make people smile. But it's weird. I'm selling more now, but the smiles have dwindled in the past three years. Maybe they've lost their sense of humor. A lot of people come through here who think they know everything. Most of them have probably never touched a saw. But they're buying, so I guess I can't complain.

There's one new thing that interests me. Last year, a day care center asked me to design eight different animals for them—everything from skunks to elephants. I did the designs and outlines, and they painted the details. That was incredible. I've never gone to anybody to get work, but if someone comes to me, like from a school, I like to design. That's a direction I can see myself going in.

Meanwhile, I'm here, and I'm making a living. Other toymakers have tried to sell here, but they can't touch my prices. One guy set up here in the winter thinking 'Boy, look at that guy, I can make a bundle here.' But his stuff was really expensive and it just sat there. He got so fed up he said 'I'm going to sell junk from now on.'

So I'm not too worried about competition. I like what I'm doing, and I know I can always make a living.

For now, that's enough.

FANTASIES AND FORTUNE-TELLING

You don't necessarily have to sell goods at the market; you can sometimes sell your talents as well. I've known card readers and palmists who did a brisk business out of colorful tents; make-up artists who decorated the delighted faces of kids and grownups alike; and even a flea

37

shrink who brought in extra bucks with bargain basement psychiatry in between hawking such exotica as aardvark capes. These people help to give the flea market a special charm, a charm that evokes the feeling of a renaissance fair. Whether you can do this successfully depends on the character of your local market.

Entertainers can take their mime and music to the market, for fleadom is rich in street theatre potential. While this is not exactly a direct route to stardom and wealth, being a tips-only situation, you can make a little money and have an instant audience. If you're doing a local perform-ance, the market can also be a good place to drum up business. Tantalize them with tunes that set their feet tapping, then pass out flyers announc-ing where they can catch your whole act. It's a test market and advertis-ing gimmick rolled into one.

There are also fantasy saleables, such as helium balloons, pinwheels, magic tricks, disguises, kites. Fleaing is usually a family affair, and grownups are often happy to appease their brood, grown weary from dragging through aisle after aisle, with a balloon or a colorful kite. This variety of fantasy flea will find business is good almost everywhere, and helps keep the rest of us smiling thru the bad day blues.

NEW MERCHANDISE

"New" has its own mystique, especially at the flea market where second-hand has traditionally reigned. For some buyers, bargains have an extra appeal precisely because they're NEW. Never been used.

New merchandise is also a controversial specialty in fleadom because there is a growing trend toward goods that are as chintzy as they are cheap. Many long-time fleas resent the intrusion of K-Mart conscious-ness on their turf, and flea market owner Joel Kaufmann is one of them:

"New merchandise is the crisis of flea markets. It's a real cancer. That's because a lot of the people who sell new stuff have absolutely zip imagination. They just go to a distributor, pick up their stuff, come to the market and dump it, and go home. That's boring. There're no surprises."

Having plowed through row after row of the same selections of chintzy clothing, handbags and "novelties" at some flea markets, I tend to agree with Joel about the danger of this trend. It is also one of the main targets for the tax types, who are sparked into action by rightfully outraged discount retailers. Retailers resent fleas who sell exactly what they sell, and who escape the burdens of overhead, insurance, and—most importantly—taxes.

There are two types of new merchandise which I feel are an appropriate addition to fleadom. The first are goods which serve a utilitarian function, like cassette tapes, tools, sunglasses and such. The other is goods that are unique or interesting enough to give buyers real bargains on quality merchandise. These include high quality imports, seconds or samples from brand name or designer manufacturers, and specialty goods not easily available elsewhere.

Harold and Catherine

Harold and Catherine fall into this final category of 'new,' and sell an extensive selection of knives and weaponry. As a martial artist, I appreciated such exotica as 'shuriken'—star-shaped discs with sharp edges that are deadly throwing weapons if you know how to use them.

I interviewed Harold and Catherine at the Lahaska market in historical Bucks County, Pa. In a market that features old-timey collectibles, they are a bit of an anomaly, but the cluster of buyers around their stall testified to the success of their operation.

It's anything but boring.

Harold: We started out selling rocks and minerals, but they got hard to get and the prices went up. And we got tired of all that wrapping and unwrapping. Rocks and minerals are the same as glassware; they're very fragile. We were looking for an easier way to do this, and that's when I got into knives.

Catherine: We handle all new knives, every type of knife from hunting knives, pocket knives, novelty knives, dress knives, anything you can think of.

Harold: We buy all our knives from the manufacturers, and I have suppliers all over the country—and other countries, too. That knife with the elephant head is from Bangkok. We don't handle old knives because there aren't that many available, and they're also very high-priced. We couldn't afford to do it as a hobby thing. With the new knives, we can keep our prices low so we have a lot of turnover.

Catherine: Harold makes all our display cases. He's very handy that way. He even makes his own belt buckles—like those, see, with the buffalo head nickles. They're very attractive, don't you think? And we don't have to charge a lot because we can still get buffalo head nickles at a good price.

Harold: I also make up the horse shoe buckles. Those I sell all year 'round. Last week, somebody bought six of them.

Catherine: We sell a lot of these throwing knives too. See, they even adjust—just push a button and it'll balance it.

Harold: And see these—the star-shaped things? They're called shuri-ken. They're throwing weapons, but lots of people buy them to wear around their necks. Sometimes girls into martial arts buy them to put in their rooms for decor.

Catherine: You'd be surprised what sells—even the handcuffs!

Harold: The second pair of those I sold was to a 65-year-old woman.

Catherine: A little old lady! To this day, we don't know what she was going to do with them.

Harold: They come with a key, sure. But sometimes someone will stand here kidding with their wife about handcuffs, and I'll say "I sell them without the key too, if you want."

Catherine: See that sign that says "no switchblade knives"? We don't sell switchblades because they're against the law. We try to make it real clear. But people still come up and ask us about them.

Harold: About 45 people a day! We sell them these switchblade combs instead.

Catherine: The kids love 'em! A lot of our business is the teenage trade. They come back with their friends, and we do a lot of repeat business.

SPECIALTY LIST

The following list of popular flea specialties and sub-specialties adds to the survey of options we've explored in depth. The list is not complete, and will never really be complete. There's always room for another good idea in fleadom, and almost any good idea can potentially evolve into a profitable enterprise.

If you want to become a serious pro, just remember these basic guidelines: know your merchandise, and choose a specialty you enjoy. This appreciative expertise will yield an ongoing dialogue with fellow afficionados that can broaden your knowledge and help your business thrive. Otherwise, as Jerry Junk says, "you're just wasting your time."

What kind of flea are you? Only you can answer that question. But, as Joyce observes, "once you know, you know." The *knowing* determines your strategy as you begin to build an ongoing operation.

The rest is tactics.

Popular Flea Specialties and Sub-specialties

Books (new and used)
Furniture (used and antique)
Food (stand or produce specialty)
Clothes (new & used)
Tools (new, used & antique)
Arts & crafts
Kitchenware (new and used)
Linens and fabrics (new and used)
Firewood
Crystals (the lead glass ones from Austria)
Stationery and office supplies (mostly new)
Pets (from free kittens to pedigreed pups)
Tapes and records (new and used)
Posters and prints (new and used)
Bicycles (mostly used, plus parts, pieces, accessories)
Collectible dolls
Collectible clocks
Camping gear (new and used)
Sunglasses (mostly new, sometimes old collectibles)
Cutlery (mostly new, sometimes old collectibles)
Collectible coins
Knives (as weaponry, both collectibles and useables)
Guns (mostly used, both collectibles and useables; often subject to local regulations)
Collectible toys
Toys (new and used)

Automobile parts and accessories (mostly used)
TVs and radios (mostly used, sometimes collectibles)
Small appliances (mostly used, like blenders, toasters, etc.)
Large appliances (mostly used, like washing machines and stoves)
Luggage (mostly new, sometimes old collectibles)
Make-up and perfume (new)
Shoes (as specialty, mostly new)
Gloves, hats, scarves, socks (as specialty, mostly new)
Musical instruments (mostly used, sometimes collectibles)
Cameras and photographic equipment (mostly used, sometimes
    collectibles)
Sporting goods (new and used, like tennis rackets, hockey sticks, etc.)
Automobiles (used, one at a time)
Drug paraphernalia (usually new, like rolling papers, pipes, etc.)
Lamps (as specialty, mostly used, sometimes collectibles)
Hi-fi's and tape machines (new and used)
Handbags (as specialty, usually new)
Electronic parts (new and used)
Picture frames (new and used, sometimes collectibles)
Plumbing fixtures (mostly used, sometimes collectibles)
Mirrors (as specialty, mostly collectibles)

_____ Trader Jack _____

Trader Jack's flea market was my stomping ground for three years in Santa Fe, New Mexico. During the time Rolf and I sold there we always felt part of a special community; we knew that owners Jack and Caggie cared about us, and we cared about them.

Once—just once—we did a test run at the gigantic Albuquerque State Fairgrounds market, sixty miles away. Everything there was a battle, from the interminable check-in lines (where we waited from 6:00 to 8:00 AM to get our space), to rip-offs, to an unrelenting sun which is at least ten degrees hotter than in Santa Fe. The huge Albuquerque market once was king. Now many dealers actually commute to Santa Fe from Albuquerque. At Trader Jack's they find a profitable buyer/seller ratio (up to 10,000 buyers for a few hundred dealers). They also find a home.

During the course of my interview with Jack and Caggie we were continually interrupted by vendors, buyers, friends and acquaintances. Some had questions, some merely wanted to pass the time of day. It was like sitting on the front porch of an old general store, chewing the fat, letting time wend a leisurely course through a summer afternoon.

To me, Trader Jack and Caggie are the heart of all that is finest in fleadom: the living pulse of an America which blesses us with hope against all odds.

Jack: *Before I opened this flea market, I had never set foot in a flea market. Never.*

        That drive-in movie market was there for six years before I opened this, and it went just about as far as it could possibly go. It was behind a wall; hell, you had to know it was there. Then you'd go in and they wanted 50¢ a head to shop. That's what hurt it more than anything.

Caggie: *God, Cree, some of these people can't even afford a loaf of bread. And they figure they can come out to the flea market and just look. One of the reasons this market has been so successful is that it gives people something to do. It's an outing, it's a togetherness thing. I would never charge people to come in and shop.*

Jack: *It all goes back to the fact that you can't get too greedy. You've got to leave something for somebody else. If you get too greedy, someone's going to come along and hurt you. They're going to put you out of business.*

    If that other market hadn't gotten too greedy, I would never have opened this place. We went down there, see, and they wanted 50¢. Well, I backed up. I didn't give them the 50¢. And I said to Caggie, "Hey, I'm going to open a flea market." And she said "How do you do that?" And I said "I don't know."

Caggie: *He hadn't decided to go into the antique business until he opened an antique store either. I said "Jack, we don't know anything about antiques." And he said "We'll just have to learn quick."*

Jack: *I opened an antique store on Cerrillos Road. But then I got tired of sitting in the store.*

Caggie: *That's when we started the flea market. We figured maybe it could be a source for the antique store.*

Jack: *And we had a heckuva source—for about a year.*

Caggie: *Then everybody got smart.*

Jack: *Everybody became dealers!*

Caggie: *When we first started we were in that little lot. Cree, there was eight of us, and we parked in a horseshoe. It was so small that the shoppers would come in, drive around, and come up through the middle. They could see everything from the car.*

Jack: *And we sold Coke from quart bottles.*

Caggie: *We had one of those old red Coke boxes, and we'd pack it with ice, and haul it in and out of the station wagon.*

Jack: *We sold maybe a case a weekend. Now we sell 2000, 2500 Cokes a weekend. Now we're the second biggest flea market in New Mexico.*

Caggie: *We've been listed in flea market directories all over the country and I don't guess we've ever turned it in. I think that happy vendors that have been here travelin' turn it in.*

Jack: *This market is getting to the point that I hope it never gets any bigger. It's the perfect size right now. Big but not too big. We know everybody, everybody knows us.*

Caggie: *We just kind of grew up with the market. We started small, and everybody learned as we went along. We got feedback from people who had done this for years, and they'd say this market does this and that market does that. But we always had to keep Santa Fe in mind.*

      See, in a small town where people aren't big city minded, it takes a while to get started. We lost money for two years before we got this market going. You've got to have lots of patience.

Jack: *We're all out here trying to make a living. I make a helluva living!*

Caggie: *Several other markets have tried to open here, but people just aren't prepared to work hard enough.*

Jack: *That's what it takes. A lot of hard work. We could have hired a manager several years back and just turned it over to them. But if you don't take care of your own business, nobody's going to take care of it for you.*

Caggie: *If we hired a manager, this would just be a source of income. And that takes all the fun out of it. Money is great, it certainly is important, but knowing people, being friends and all that— that's more rewarding. We've met so many people and know so many people by name in this town. Because of the flea market. Cree, I was walking down through here one morning, and this guy behind me walked up and said "You know what, ma'am? Following you is just like following Reagan out on a spring walk. Shakin' hands and kissin' babies!" He said, "I have never in my life seen anybody call so many people by their first names."*

Jack: *You know, one of the local commissioners wants to close this place down because of "too much traffic." Now that's an awfully good way for a politician to lose a whole lot of votes. He'd be dead politically. Hell, you're lookin' at ten thousand votes out here.*

Caggie: *We go around town and we see our friends all over. We've made these friendships through the flea market. To me that's the good part. We feel part of the community.*

You gotta buy if you're gonna resell. You have to know what's what. But once you know, you know.

—Joyce, vendor
New Hope, PA Market

3

The Bargain Hunter's Guide

You can't sell at the flea market until you've got an inventory, so the successful flea is always hot on the trail of the nearest available bargain. I back up my flea market buying with conscientious scouring of local sales and whatever lucrative private deals come my way. Like the broker who wouldn't dream of missing the latest Dow Jones averages, the flea must keep abreast of the current action.

Start by doing your homework. Buy a copy of every local paper that has classifieds; Thursday, Friday and Saturday's classifieds are required reading. Check the listings under "Garage Sales," which usually include rummage sale notices and special thrift shop sales. Scan the used merchandise categories of your specialty; most classifieds list used merchandise and garage sale ads near each other.

Especially valuable resources are the weekly buy/sell papers that have been proliferating everywhere. They advertise used merchandise for sale and trade, and usually have good listings of rummage and garage sales. Check your local supermarkets, which are the major distribution centers for these papers. They are usually free, and have names like "Thrifty Nickel" and "Swapshop." Read them as thoroughly as you would the text for tomorrow's exam. Many of these papers are unclassified, so you've got to search carefully for what you want. Get the paper the day it comes out. If there are any private ads that list merchandise you want, call the seller immediately. Don't wait until tomorrow or your bargain may be long gone.

Clip all ads announcing relevant sales and auctions and post them in plain sight as reminders (I put them on my refrigerator). Also watch for signs in laundromats and supermarkets advertising auctions and rummage sales. Write the information down so you won't forget, and post it next to the ads. Sometimes posters are the sole advertising for a sale, so an ongoing poster alertness should back up your classified homework.

There's also the "I brake for garage sales" alertness. Unless you're in the middle of a real-life emergency, when you see a sign that says "Garage Sale," pull over. Some folks never place an ad or even post a pre-sale poster; they simply put up a sign and haul out their stuff. You never really know when you might score like a bandit, and it's often worth checking out.

As we travel through bargain hunter's country, we'll go first to the flea market. Here you'll learn bargaining skills that will serve you well everywhere in fleadom. Then we'll hone you into a ruthless rummager, and help you buy your way through a typical weekend maze of garage sales. We'll also discuss the art of thrift shopping, and pay respects to the auction.

Because I want to tell you how to buy when the buying is good, my anecdotes focus on days of super-successful buying. But do remember there will also be buying forays that yield only minimal bargains or that are a complete bust. There are few sure bets in fleadom, and buying—like selling—has its ups and downs.

Don't get discouraged. There's always a bargain waiting around the next corner, and the only way to find the bargains is to keep hunting. Your vigilance will be rewarded, but you'll have to live with the uncertainty of just when and where you'll get your reward. That's just part of life, and part of being a flea.

Happy hunting!

BARGAINING FOR BUYS AT THE FLEA MARKET

Serious flea market buying has one main imperative: get there EARLY. What's early? That all depends on the customs of your local market. Early in Sausalito means no later than 7AM; early in Santa Fe means no later than 9 AM. While treasures may still be found late in the day, for the best bargains you should get there when the pros do. That way you're ready to greet one-time amateurs as they begin to unload.

Bring along a large shopping bag or fold-up shopping cart with wheels to stash your purchases in. No need to struggle with an armload of goods that may leave a trail of trinkets behind you. Keep your money in your pockets, and *be sure to have plenty of singles and small change*. Many amateurs arrive unprepared to make change, and having correct change will both help their predicament and speed up your rounds. It can drive you nuts to watch a nearby arrival unpack an incredible deco lamp while you're cooling your heels waiting for someone to scrounge up the change for your 50¢ purchase.

You can't be everywhere at once, so begin to train your eyes to spot the most likely treasure troves for what you want. I watch for fashion-conscious young women, usually in pairs, unpacking boxes and bags of clothing from small foreign vehicles. A furniture dealer looks for pickup trucks loaded with lamps, rocking chairs and drop-leaf tables. You want to cover as many new arrivals as possible, so don't waste time watching people unload hi-fi equipment if you're looking for kitchenware.

Be as thorough as possible at each stop on your rounds, but be quick to move on once you've made your purchases or decided there's nothing for you. You'll be competing with experienced pros who know exactly what they're looking for, so you must learn to be both speedy and sharp. In fleadom, it's first come, first served; there are rarely any second chances. Check out the merchandise for flaws so you know what you're getting, but don't linger.

Later in the day you can afford to be more leisurely, especially after the pros have stopped buying and started setting up. As the day wears on, there will be fewer bargains, but those you find are likely to have price tags that are more negotiable. If you had to take the kids to the dentist in the morning don't let that keep you from the flea market. One-timers are anxious to sell as much as they can, and the pewter platter that was a firm twenty bucks in the morning may well be had for ten by the middle afternoon. Amateurs are rarely prepared for a day in the sun and often begin wilting early. Prices may drop rapidly even before noon.

Bargaining is a combination of intuition, know-how, and that indefinable quality we call "art." You must first, of course, know the value of your merchandise. If you do not yet have an insider's expertise, hang around the pros that do. The regulars love to talk shop, and you'll be amazed how much information you can garner in a single afternoon. Do your research late in the day, when business is slack; most sellers are not territorial and will welcome you.

Once you know what does—and what does not—constitute a bargain, you've done your scales. Now its time to learn the dance, with all its subtle nuances. This is difficult to teach, for only experience will transform you into a Baryshnikov of bargaining. The best I can do is take you along on my own buying rounds so you can experience the inner calculations that make this flea tick.

Although I write in the language of my particular specialty, the essence of the bargaining exchange is universal. The rips I find in the silver fox jacket that allow me to shave down the price could just as well be nicks in depression glass, or a wobbly leg on an old oak chair.

"How much is the jacket?" I'm drooling inside over a lovely 30s silver fox hanging next to the polyester pants suit. I carefully contain my covetousness.

"Twenty bucks."

My heart races faster now. Twenty bucks is a great deal; it's an easy turnover at seventy-five and a "star" (attention-getter) to boot. But I do not allow myself to jump.

"May I try it on?"

"Help yourself, lady."

I slip it off the hanger, checking it over carefully for flaws. Old furs are particularly vulnerable to disintegration, and if it's really starting to go only a furrier can tackle it, which means a high repair bill. I find a small separation of skins on the right sleeve, making sure the seller notes my discovery. I calculate the damage. No problem, it's on a seam, and well within my limited abilities as a seamstress.

"Looks like it's starting to go." I ease into the jacket, pausing to inspect a rip in the lining. "You have a mirror?"

"Just the rear view."

I opt for the reflection in the window of his station wagon. Magnificent. Beautifully styled, flattering lines. The try-on is essential for me to determine this, for that is precisely what my customers will do. And furs are funny. Some may be fine specimens of the animal, but fail to transform the wearer. Can make you look positively dowdy. Ah, but this particular silver fox is hot. Very sexy, very decadent. Still I do not jump.

"Looks good on you." The old man grins, sensing a sale.

"I'm not sure." I've taken the jacket off, and am busy inspecting its various weak points. "Looks like it needs a lot of repair." And it *does* need repair, but it's a half hour of my time at most and more than worth it. I finally make my move. "Listen, would you take fifteen for it?"

"I dunno, lady, twenty bucks is a good price."

"It's a lovely fur, but it needs a lot of work, and I'm just not sure if I can sell it. Not this time of year, anyway," I add, looking up at the blazing sun.

He begins to see a sale slipping through his fingers; he counters.

"Tell you what. You can have it for eighteen. But that's my final price."

"Seventeen?" I soften my eyes.

"Nope. Eighteen." He is standing firm. I bow to his figure.

"All right. Sold. Got change for a twenty?"

With the fox clutched lovingly under my arm I move on to the next vendor, where I promptly spend the two bucks change on a lavender silk blouse I can easily sell for ten.

Do I sound chintzy? I am. One of the world's great chintzes. I get away with whatever I can; every dollar or two I shave off here I can spend there.

Now, if the old man had stood pat at twenty, of course I would have snapped it up anyway. The point is it never hurts to try, even when the item in question is a good buy to begin with. The less you spend on any one item the more you have to spend on others. It's that simple.

Chintziness does have its point of diminishing marginal returns, however. There is a point beyond which even I will not go. When being offered a beaded evening bag for a dollar which I can easily sell for ten, I do not try to get it for 50¢. That's an insult to the seller, to me, and to the dignity of bargaining.

Be chintzy, but be honorable.

Bargaining over an individual item, like the silver fox, is pretty straightforward. The seller names a price. You counter with a lower figure, generally no less than 50% or more than 75% of the quoted price. The seller either accepts your offer (if you're lucky), counters with a second figure mid-way between the two, or stands firm. When the counter offer is reasonable, and you really want the item, go for it. If the dealer stands firm, and especially if you plan to resell the piece, you must make some calculations:

Is the price as it stands low enough for you to make your profit margin? Profit margins vary with different specialties, but I generally don't buy anything I'm not sure that I can sell for 3 times what I paid.

Is the item in good condition? Except for junk dealers, most specialists buy damaged goods only if they are super cheap. When an item is only slightly damaged, like the silver fox, I'll pay more, but only when it'll give me a high return on a minimal investment of repair time.

Is the item a "star"—a lure to draw people to your stall? I'll sometimes pay more for stars with true pizazz because I know I can keep their price tags high until the right buyer comes along. Meanwhile, my stars attract customers, who often stick around to make more modest purchases. But I only pay more if I absolutely have to.

Multiple purchases make the bargaining even more interesting and more profitable. You can do very well, if you play it right—especially when you're buying from one-timers whose main goal is, after all, to get rid of the stuff.

I approach a couple of Marin county lovelies at the Sausalito market. They're just unloading the VW, and already I spy a silk nightie poking out of a shopping bag. I decide to stick around, being sure to hang on tightly to my finds; already several of my competitors are making a beeline to the new arrivals. I ask a couple of prices to get an idea of what these ladies are changing.

"How much for the nightgown?"

"Let's see. Mary, how much do you want for your nightgown?"

"Gosh, I don't know . . . what do you think? . . .how's five dollars?"

Not bad at all. It can go for fifteen. I know now that they're not in the 25¢ category, but they're also obvious novices and they've got a carload of good stuff. I keep digging, and am rewarded with a Japanese kimono, a couple of Danskins, some silk scarves, a great 40s frock, several pieces of costume jewelry, and a fine linen blazer.

"Can you give me some prices on these?" I lug my armful of goodies over to Mary.

"Okay. Well, the kimono is ten dollars."

A little high for me, but if I throw it in with all the rest of the stuff, I bet I can shave off three or four bucks. I put it aside. "And the leotards?"

"Oh, a dollar each."

Excellent. I keep going. "The scarves?"

"Fifty cents each." Great. Many people price small accessories like throwaways. Properly displayed, I'll get $3 to $5 for each of the scarves.

"And this jewelry?"

"Oh, you can have all of that for three dollars."

This is really getting good. I've got at least $25 worth of great old costume jewelry in my hand.

"The dress?"

"Three dollars."

Nice. A $15 turnover. I hold up my final prize. "And this jacket?"

"You can have that for three dollars too."

Fantastic. The linen is spotless, the lines classical. Twenty bucks, no problem. "So what's this all add up to?"

Mary tallies. "OK, the nightgown was $5, the kimono's $10, that's $15; $3 for the dress, that's $18; $3 for the blazer, that's $21; $1 each for the Danskins, that $24; another $3 for the jewelry, that's $27; and six scarves is $3 more, so it comes to $30." Mary's eyes are shining. Thirty dollars is a lot for a bunch of stuff she was bored with anyway.

"Listen, would you take twenty for all of it?"

Mary pauses to consider. She's not about to be made a fool of, but she's eager to sell. "No, but I'd take $25."

"Sold." I hand her the money and trundle off with my purchases, followed by the jealous eyes of my competitors who got there just a little too late.

I review my good luck. Loathe to spend $10 on the kimono, I succeeded in shaving its price down by combining it with the other items that were already within my profit margin specs. Mary probably wouldn't have come down much on the kimono if that was all I was buying, but in combination with my other purchases she hardly realized it was gone.

Quantity discounts are always a great way to go. Whenever you luck into a treasure trove of good stuff, stick around until you've accumulated the cream of the crop. Almost always, the more you buy, the cheaper each piece gets.

RUTHLESS RUMMAGING

If you're looking for clothes, books, bric-a-brac or a little bit of everything, rummage sales are top priority. You'll get more for less than almost anywhere else, and the selection of merchandise is often enormous. Only the largest rummage sales, however, include furniture and major appliances. For these, your chances will be considerably better at private garage sales.

Rummage sales usually stick to their scheduled opening times and keep the growing throng of buyers in a state of high-pitched excitement until the doors open on the dot of the designated hour. To be on the safe side, however, you should arrive at a sale at least fifteen minutes early. I hate arriving five minutes ahead of schedule only to find the doors opened ten minutes ago and I've been beaten to the draw.

Let's go to one of those huge rummage sales in San Francisco's Hall of Flowers so you can learn my tactics first hand. I'm stalking my usual cheap chic clothing, but the techniques I use are universal. If you're hunting for memorabilia, make a beeline to the bric-a-brac tables instead of to the stacks of lingerie.

It's only 8:30 AM and already the crowd of rummagers pressing toward the doors is getting antsy. Doors are scheduled to open at nine. Meanwhile, we jockey for position, peering through the windows to spot our prey. We're a motley assortment: white-gloved old ladies out for

their morning sport, grim professionals pacing and ready to pounce, hopeful hippies toting babies and backpacks, housewifely regulars nervously chatting.

I spot at least twenty of my competitors from the Sausalito market in the crowd. We acknowledge each other, exchange glances and nods, gear up for battle. Once those doors open, it's every man for himself. We're ready. I'm there with my standard rummaging gear: one huge straw shopping bag I can stuff to the brim. That's it. No purse, it only gets in the way. Just a couple of twenties stuffed in my back pocket. More than adequate for even the most rewarding sale.

Ten to nine. You can feel the adrenalin surge as the minutes tick past. My heart is pumping furiously, and I take a few deep breaths while I wait for the doors to open. I've already spotted the lingerie table, and will make that my first target. Love those sexy silks, and my customers love them too.

Nine o'clock. We're off! The doors swing open, and the throng begins to funnel its mass through the opening. I snake in and out, becoming a front-line runner. Dashing to the lingerie table, I begin to demolish the carefully folded piles of slips and nighties with eager hands. I'm going for fabrics at this point, searching for silk and rayon and lace with my fingers as well as my eyes.

I don't take even a split second to check for the size or condition of my finds. Later for that. I'm trying to accumulate as many pieces as I can, and I've only begun. On my way to the men's shirts, I pass my eyes and hands along the racks of hanging clothes. Again, I'm checking for fabrics. I whisk a deerskin jacket into my bag, a slinky 30s crepe, a couple of bright cotton summer frocks. Oops, almost missed that two-piece gabardine suit. Into the bag it goes.

Elbowing my way into the action at the men's table, I begin to sort and grab again. Anything with cowboy snaps, whoosh, in the bag, and those rayon Hawaiian numbers when they surface, and those fine cotton dress shirts and the garish bowling shirts and . . .

So it goes, through all the piles of blouses, skirts, accessories and shoes. Soon my bag is bulging beyond its limits, so I begin to fill a cardboard box with treasures. I have to shove the box around with my feet as I continue my rounds, and guard it fiercely: "Sorry, that's my box." I hang on tight to my finds, or they'll be gobbled up instantly.

Now I am an honorable rummager. I'm fast and I'm ruthless but I'm fair. I never grab a garment already clasped in another's hand, nor do I sneak out goodies from someone else's stash. But be aware that there are some who do. Keep a sharp eye on your boxes and bags. You've earned your bargains; they are rightfully yours.

I take advantage of the time when the masses are standing in wearisome long lines at the check-out table to relax and re-sort. Now I carefully consider each individual item: that's a great silk blouse, but those armpit stains look indelible. I toss it aside. Ditto for the wonderful crepe gown that will only fit a size 42. I have no desire to accumulate merchandise that will wind up in a 50¢ box. An excess of repair projects can drown you in your own bargains, even if you're only buying for yourself (see The Overload Factor in Chapter 4).

Once I've eliminated the dross I'm ready to check out. By this time the lines have died down, and I breeze through. Most rummage sales have set prices for various categories of merchandise: 50¢ for blouses, $1 for dresses, etc. This is what makes them such terrific hunting ground. But many sales price hanging goods higher than those on the tables, and occasionally you'll get a very sharp check-out clerk. Be ready to bargain when your turn comes, and try to get a reduction on the total tally rather than hassling over each individual item. Rummage sales make their money by turning over a mass of merchandise in a single day, so they

want to keep it moving out the door. My pile comes to $23. Betcha anything I can get it for twenty—and I do.

Leaving a successful sale is a delightful high for me. The cutting edge of combat has left me exhilarated, and the fact that my twenty-dollar purchase will mushroom into a two-hundred-dollar return leaves me with the warm inner glow of a job well done.

Rummage sales are the single richest vein of gold for those of us in the rag game. If you're hunting for cheap chic, you must never, never miss out on a rummage sale. I owe my favorite black garter belt to the Methodists.

GARAGE SALE SAFARIS

Successful garage sale buying requires almost as much organization and planning as running your own sale. The number of garage sales on a sunny spring weekend can be overwhelming. Once you've clipped the garage sale listings from the want-ads and checked the posters, how do you choose which sales to hit? How do you make it to as many sales as possible?

The juiciest sales are the ones with several families participating, and those listing a wide spectrum of goods that includes items you want. Sometimes sales with come-on ads are a bust, but normally they live up to expectation. You also want to consider distances; I never drive to faraway sales unless they *really* sound good.

You must plan your buying days with precision, organizing times and distances as efficiently as possible. If you don't already own a good map of your town, get one. Make sure it includes a comprehensive street directory. You don't want to wind up driving around in circles in unfamiliar parts of town, knowing full well the early birds are beating you to the bargains.

When you've picked the sales that sound the most attractive, make a list that includes addresses and opening times. Mark the locations on your map in pencil. Give priority to those areas with large clusters of sales, unless you know there's an absolute don't-miss outside of the cluster groups. You can't be everywhere at once; you've got to hit the biggies first and hope for good leftovers at the sales you scavenge after the initial rush.

Plot your course through clusters that will yield the most sales for the least driving. This gets tricky, because you need to juggle sale times with the geography. Sales can start anytime from 8 AM to noon, but the majority will fall into the 9 AM to 10 AM range. Fortunately, garage sale opening times are more flexible than rummage sales, so you can often arrive early and scoop up bargains before the masses descend. It's fair to arrive up to an hour before schedule, unless the sale ad specifically stated "no early sales, please." I always respect this request, and suggest you do too.

Some early buyers can be truly predatory when skimming the cream off family sales. Sellers are often disorganized and flustered, vulnerable to fast-talking pros. While I always go for the early bargains, I never intentionally take advantage of a seller's set-up jitters. I don't grab and shout and ask prices for every trinket I pick out. I go about my shopping calmly and unobtrusively, waiting for the seller to have a moment's respite before I begin to bargain for my finds.

I do not screech "How much for the shawl?" while the seller is balanced precariously on a ladder hanging a clothes line for display. As much as I love a good deal, the human exchange is as important to me as my profit margin. I treat my buying sources with the same respect I treat my customers. Never do I look a gift horse in the mouth, but neither do I attempt to create a gift horse out of a seller's nervousness and inexperience. Good-karma fleas have more fun and more friends.

If you arrive early as a customer rather than a predator most people will welcome your business. Early sales start the day off on a high note and boost the spirits of the sellers.

Let's take a typical spring Saturday in a medium-sized town and start making our rounds:

You definitely want to hit the big multi-family sale that starts at 9 AM, arriving at least fifteen minutes early. It's on the west side of town. Are there any super-early sales in that general area? 8 AM sales aren't common, but with luck there may be at least one you can cruise en route. Be as speedy and sharp scouring garage sales as you are in your early morning flea market buying. Be thorough enough to get what you want and know what you're getting, but don't linger. If that 8 AM sale is obviously no treasure trove, it's better to arrive even earlier at the 9 AM sale than to chat over coffee with the 8 AM sellers, pleasant as that might be.

Allow yourself up to an hour at the big 9 AM sale, especially if it's sponsored by a civic organization or charity. Such sales are often equivalent to rummage sales in the vast amount of goods available, and you may need that time to really do a thorough job of hunting. Your next destination after leaving the 9 AM sale at, say, 9:45, will be the nearest cluster of 10 AM sales you can hit. If there's only one 10 AM in that general neighborhood, and it doesn't sound that hot, hightail it over to the south side of town, where you've marked a big cluster of 10 AM sales. Hit as many of these as possible, always giving priority to multi-family sales and those with the juiciest listings in their ads.

After you make these rounds, you can continue on to other clusters which make a convenient route. With luck, there may be some 11 AM or noon sales in these clusters that can still allow you first pick. When this is true, give priority to clusters that include such late morning sales. By noon, almost all sales will be well under way, but even if you're not an early bird you can often find bargains that others missed, or which the sellers just got around to unpacking.

If you plan to become a regular vendor at the flea market, you'll need to coordinate your garage sale rounds with your own Saturday sales and set-up. You can opt to forget the garage sales and do your buying at the market, but sometimes there will be a super garage sale or rummage sale on Saturday you don't want to miss.

Some options: if your market allows you to reserve space by the month and arrive whenever you please, you can do your rounds before you go to the market. Some markets, however, have a cut-off time as early as 10 AM for you to arrive without forfeiting your space, even if you do reserve. If you're part of a team, your partner can arrive early at the market to set up while you're busy doing the sales. If you're working solo, you can arrive early at the market and secure your spot by leaving your display gear in your space. Never leave merchandise unattended, but display tools are usually safe, with or without the surveillance of a neighboring vendor. Then hop in your car, do the sales, and return with your scores to set up and sell.

THE ART OF THRIFT SHOPPING

When you make your regular rounds of local shops, or explore unknown turf on the road, your thrift shopping must develop into a fine art. Once again, your job is to be as thorough as possible without investing an excessive amount of time and energy.

Most of your weekday buying will be from thrift shops and second-hand stores. If you don't yet know where your local shops are, ask around. Consult the yellow pages, which usually list such shops under "Thrift Shops" or "Secondhand Stores." Check under the proper headings for particular specialties. "Furniture, Used" and "Clothing, Used" will often follow listings of retail stores.

Also check the white pages for common thrift store chains: Goodwill, Salvation Army, Volunteers of America, Disabled American Veterans, St. Vincent de Paul. Sometimes shops will have either white or yellow page listings, but not both. It's a good idea to call these shops first. Their hours are often irregular, with odd days off. It's not much fun to drive all the way across town to the Volunteers store only to discover it's closed on Tuesdays (and it's Tuesday) or it closes at 3:00 (and it's 3:45).

Some shops can be eliminated virtually out front. In general, the more streamlined the operation, the higher the price tags. Goodwills across the country have gone almost entirely in this direction. If you enter a Salvation Army and find color-coded racks, dressing rooms marked "three garments only, please," bright flourescent lights and Muzak, you can almost turn right around and walk out. This ain't bargain hunter's territory; it's the Sally (jargon for Salvation Army) gone suburban. Ditto for the fancy little resale shops run by do-good socialites.

Even in high-priced shops it sometimes pays to make one quick round. There are occasional slip-ups in the pricing room you can take advantage of. And because these shops are so tidy and well laid out, you can canvas the whole scene in about five minutes by merely eyeballing the racks and tables, stopping only occasionally to inspect an item that looks of interest. Always check out the accessories and small bric-a-brac. Even in the most expensive shops these are sometimes priced quite reasonably.

It's the funky, disorderly, underlit and overstocked shops where you can score like a bandit. To illustrate, we'll take a trip to one of my favorite thrift shops: the Santa Fe Sally. This is a classical middle-range shop, not nickel and dime land, but full of surprises and a continual influx of merchandise that make frequent visits pay off.

The Santa Fe Sally makes valiant attempts at order, and indeed many goods are racked and priced. But mountains of recent arrivals on the floor, in the hall, and in the back room are evidence that all attempts at order are nearly useless. There's a standing rule here that unpriced merchandise is not to be sold, but this mostly depends on the whims of the check-out people. Gloria sticks to the rules unless she's in a

really good mood, but Theresa doesn't give a hoot and will price anything off the top of her head.

Today Theresa is behind the counter, which is already cause for celebration. I give one thorough sweep of the shop with my eyes to spot any obvious treasure, like the grey fedora on top of the shelf with the suitcases. I hand it to Theresa to keep for me while I continue my rounds. Your rounds will depend on your prey, but the substance of the hunt is the same.

I make a pass at the rack of newly-priced items not yet hung in their various categories. Many shops have daily racks of new stock, and clothes horses should check these on arrival. Today I am rewarded with a gabardine cowboy shirt—perfect, with six pearly snaps per cuff, and a good buy at $3 that will bring me ten. I also find a satin bed jacket for $2 and a sweet cotton sun dress for only $1.50. All right! Off to a good start.

I begin to pass up and down the aisles of hanging clothes. How quickly I work depends on who's in the shop. When there are two chic Santa Fe beauties and a hip urban cowboy in punk shades making their own rounds, I work pretty fast. I know that they're going to be looking for what I'm looking for. When there's only me, a genial wino, and a couple of junior high school girls, I can afford to be more leisurely.

Today, I'm virtually alone in the shop. I work efficiently, but with no edge of frantic acquisition. I pass my eyes and hands over the racked items, feeling the fabrics and looking for colors and prints that attract me. In thrift shops where I buy without the time pressure of rummage sales I *do* gauge size and condition of my finds as I go along. A black velvet smoking jacket shows up in the men's section, but at $12 it's no bargain. I return it to the rack and pick up a 50s linen sport coat for $5, as well as a pale salmon cotton shirt that is pure elegance for a dollar.

I always check the kids' racks for the occasional mini-kimono or tiny fringed jacket that make a nice addition to my big people's clothes. I also look for larger boys' and girls' sizes that fit grownups. All kids' clothing is usually super cheap, and the size 14 rayon Hawaiian shirt for only 75¢ will fit a size 7 woman and sell for $10. Two bright cotton tank tops show up in the girls' section for 35¢ each. These are actually adult items, but got thrown into the girls' clothing by mistake. Things have a way of getting mixed up in an even moderately disorderly shop, so don't pass up a section of goods because you think it's not relevant.

Now it's dig and delve time, and here at the Santa Fe Sally I have some standard excavation sites. I dive into the lingerie barrels and find a lacy black slip; it's unpriced, but Theresa will charge me 50¢ at most. Then it's into the scarf and hat barrel, where I dig out a white silk dress scarf (75¢), a soft suede tam ($1), and two cotton print headscarves (25¢ each). Today I've got time so I scavenge through the mountains of unmatched shoes. It takes me five minutes to find the mate for the wonderfully tacky plastic sling-back, but at 75¢ it's worth the effort. I can sell those shoes for $5.

Now I diversify into non-clothing items (if you're not in the rag game, this is, of course, where you would start). The current dollar-a-bag book sale is a stroke of luck for my bookstore operation, and I've soon filled a grocery bag with a slew of good recent paperbacks, an 1897 edition of *Vanity Fair* and several copies of *Life* magazine circa 1950. Among the jumble of pictures and prints I unbury two gilt frames for $1 each. I browse the bric-a-brac, where a pewter candle snuffer shows up for $1.50. A final cruise through the linen rack to make sure I'm not missing a tapestry or 30s drapes (no such luck today) and I'm ready to check out.

Theresa tallies my purchases, which come to just under $24. You can rarely bargain at thrift shops, so you must make your profit margin decisions based on the marked prices as you go along. My $24 has not yielded the immense profit margins of my $20 expenditure at the rummage sale, but it represents in toto about $100 resale return. That's 4:1, and I'm delighted to have more new merchandise to add to my stock.

Theresa gives me a grin as she fills up two bags with my bargains.

"You find anything good today?"

"Oh, a couple things," I reply casually, returning her smile.

She knows, and I know she knows, that I'm a pro, but we have a tacit agreement to keep it under our hats. The Theresas of the world help keep us pros in business. A tip of my latest fedora to all of them.

AUCTIONS WITHOUT TEARS

Auctions are generally not good hunting ground for chintzy fleas like me. Which is fortunate, because at auctions I'm a disaster. As ruthless a rummager and shrewd a bargainer as I may be, drop me in the middle of breakneck speed competitive bidding and I fall apart.

For furniture, antique, and other specialty dealers, however, auctions are important events. They are advertised in the same classifieds, buy/

64

sell papers, and posters as the other sales, and usually announce preview times to view the merchandise.

To succeed at auctions, you must become an expert. Know your merchandise, *always* attend the previews to decide exactly which pieces you will bid on, and set yourself an absolute maximum price you are willing to pay for each item. If merchandise is being offered in large lots, determine how much of the lot is of real interest to you, and set your maximum bid based only on the total value of those particular pieces. Also decide whether the acquisition of a few potential money-makers is worth being saddled with a mass of damaged or unwanted goods of dubious resale value. Write all this information down to remind yourself of your sound good judgment when the heat of the bidding may tempt you to overstep your own bounds.

If you're a novice at auctions, you may find the auctioneer's droning, rapid cants to be nearly unintelligible. Auctioneering is an art form not dissimilar to square dance calling, and you must understand its codes and subtle inflections to compete successfully with those who know. I suggest you attend several auctions as an observer before you enter this domain as a serious bidder. You're learning what is essentially a foreign language, and a Berlitz course in auctionese will prepare you to enter the country as more than a bewildered tourist.

When you finally take the plunge, and the bidding begins, you must be quick on the draw and just as quick to drop out if you're over your head. Stick to the figures on the list you made up at the preview. Never open a bid, and remember that a sharp auctioneer can manipulate you into bidding against yourself. The slightest gesture can be interpreted by the auctioneer as a bid, so once you drop out you must assume instant rigor mortis. Otherwise you may find yourself carting home a lamp you knew was a bargain at fifty bucks and you wound up paying two hundred.

Good luck! And to those of you who learn to do this well, my heartfelt admiration and respect.

It's just like any other business. You've got to learn the ropes and then it's simple.

—Marilyn, vendor
Englishtown, NJ Market

4

The Professional Flea

If you've been cultivating the habits of a discriminating buyer and skillful bargainer you're well on your way to becoming a legitimate flea. Now it's time to cover the numerous pitfalls a novice vendor will want to avoid on the path to becoming a pro.

Rummage sales and garage sales cluster in the spring, and since summer is prime outdoor selling season, spring is a good time to begin your operation. You can enter fleadom throughout prime season, but if it's November when you're reading this and you live anywhere outside the sun belt, you'll probably need to wait until spring to start. Meanwhile, visit your local thrift shops faithfully, continue to read the classifieds, and stay alert to any bargains that fall in your path. You can certainly stockpile merchandise, even if snow and ice keep you from opening shop for a few months.

Start with as much merchandise as possible, selectively chosen to produce pleasure for your customers and profit for you. The more variety you have in your specialty, the greater the number of sales. Don't jump the gun and go to the market with a couple dozen items; wait until you've accumulated a substantial stock of goods. This will happen sooner than you think, especially if you're collecting during prime season from the market and various sales.

Remember, *the single most important key to successful selling is successful buying*. Buy with a sense of the tastes of your particular market, the tastes of the segment of population you're buying for, and a well-honed expertise in your specialty that tells you instinctively what is really a bargain.

Buy low, sell high. This is gospel. But be sure you know exactly what you're buying and selling. Understand thoroughly the value of your goods and the reality of their potential market. Otherwise the gospel is gibberish, and all the tips in the world about becoming a successful vendor won't mean a thing. Once you have developed a keen buyer's sense—if you're really and truly a flea—the rest is gravy.

That said, we'll take an insider's view of the many components that make up the life of the professional flea.

STARTING OUT

Even fleas must make a modest investment to enter the marketplace. How hefty a stake you need to start your business depends on your specialty.

Fortune tellers need only come up with the rent for their space at the market. Dealers of new merchandise generally make consignment arrangements with suppliers so that their only investment is in display tools. Food vendors' stakes range from substantial (the cost of equipment and vehicle to operate a mobile food concession) to modest (the cost of ingredients for five dozen avocado and sprout sandwiches). Since most produce dealers grow their own, and most crafts dealers make their own, their stakes are determined by the cost of their raw materials plus the value of their time and labor.

Stakes vary widely even among secondhand fleas. Enterprising junk dealers like Jerry Junk can actually get people to pay them for their stock by cleaning out basements and attics and keeping the cream of the discards to sell. Others, like Slim, need a fair amount of capital for openers. Slim advised that $2000 was the minimum investment to go into the antique furniture business.

If you've chosen a specialty that requires a big stake, you'll have to conjure up your own resources. You could begin by selling pieces on consignment until you've made sufficient profits to invest on your own, but consignments also mean more work and less money for you (see Consignment Sales, p. 102). Or maybe you'll just run lucky and be able to use that collection of cuckoo clocks you inherited from Grandpa to put you in business.

In between the no-stake and high-stake extremes are fleas like me, who sell used merchandise we pick up for a minimal investment by knowing where to look and how to buy. If you're among us, $200 can put you in business. And $200 is actually a generous stake.

I had to start my New York flea operation from scratch, because all my stock and display tools were stored in Santa Fe, two thousand miles away. Isaac (who also encouraged me to write this book) lent me $150 to begin an entirely new operation here. This was sufficient to cover the materials costs of my mobile stand (about $50) and the accumulation of a substantial stock (about $100).

Fine. But what if you have no guardian angels willing to stake you? From what magical source will the money appear? It helps to expect miracles, but you don't have to rely on magic.

HAVE A GARAGE SALE!

The garage sale (alias tag sale, yard sale, loft sale, lawn sale and god knows what else) is the grassroots heart of fleadom. Many a flea caught the bug by running a garage sale, for it's delightful to watch your discards turn into dollars. The garage sale teaches valuable lessons about buying and selling, and it is the classical initiation into the world of fleadom.

Start by dragging everything out you can possibly bear to part with. And that means everything, including useless junk, broken bric-a-brac, nuts and bolts. Those dimes and quarters pile up, and you'll be amazed what people will pounce on. You want a sheer mass of merchandise. The more, the better. Haul out the old toaster, the carpet remnants, that busted phonograph you were always going to fix, the tricycle your kid outgrew years ago. You'll have a wonderful sense of having purged all the unnecessary accumulation from your life, as well as the sheer joy of making money from things you no longer want (if you ever wanted them in the first place).

One note. If you're planning to go pro don't sell anything in the category of merchandise you've decided to make your specialty. If you're planning to sell memorabilia, hang on to your collection of campaign buttons; if you want to deal tools, don't sell the old drill press. This is valuable stock and should not go cheaply, for it will help get your business off the ground when you're ready to open shop. Use your garage sale to sell your discards, and invest the profits in your specialty.

Here are some pointers to make your sale a smashing success:

Whenever possible, combine forces with friends and neighbors. Group sales bring the buyers out in droves, and allow you to share the burden of organizational costs and jobs. The more, the merrier.

Advertise. Everywhere you can. Place ads in the local classifieds and buy/sell papers. Twenty to thirty dollars should cover the costs of thorough advertising almost anywhere in the country, and it's well worth it. If you've joined forces with friends you can split these costs and reduce your personal investment.

Don't chintz with your ads to save an extra dollar. If you're selling in prime season (spring/summer) you may be competing with dozens of local sales, and you want your ad to catch the eye and interest of potential buyers. If you opt to save two bucks by simply listing the date, time and location of your sale, you may be disappointed in the results. You want to tantalize and tease them into deciding *yours* is the sale not to miss that weekend.

A sample ad:

Multi-family garage sale. Fifty years accumulation of everything imaginable. Furniture, finery, rare books, sporting goods, ping-pong table, appliances, butter churn, cut glass, baby stuff, art prints, much more. Saturday, May 17, 10-4. 667 Babylon Dr. (just off Maiden Lane). 221-6033.

This list of goods has managed to appeal to just about everyone, from antiquers to sportsters to newlyweds to literati to housewives to art collectors to just plain bargain hunters. They'll be there. Listing choice goodies that hit as broad a spectrum of buyers as possible is always worth the additional cost. It's also advisable to give at least minimal directions to your location, unless you live on a well-known street. This saves buyers the hassle of studying their maps and street directories to find you. Some can't be bothered, and you want maximum turnout.

The phone number listing is optional, and depends on whether you want to be bothered with pre-sale calls. This can often pay off, however, because specialty dealers will call about items that interest them and you may well be able to sell the cut glass to an antique dealer on Friday for a good price.

Ads for Saturday sales should appear in both Thursday and Friday classifieds; Sunday or two-day sales will want to include Saturday listings as well. Be sure to check with your local papers about classified deadlines. Don't walk into the newspaper office on the Thursday before the sale only to find out your ad won't appear until Saturday.

GOLDEN APPLE TRANSFERS PRESENTS:

THE

MULTIMEDIA LIBERATION

PSYCHEDELIC RETROSPECTIVE

LOFT SALE

BARGAIN BUYS
FROM BYGONE DAYS OF FUTURE PAST

XENON 16mm PROJECTOR • LIGHTS & STANDS
EKTAGRAPHIC SLIDE PROJECTORS • SPEAKERS
REAR PROJECTION

"ANG JO FU ASSOCIATION

RUMMAGE SALE

EVERYONE, BIG BARGAINS!
GAMES, BOOKS, HOUSEHOLD,
CHOTCHKES. BIGGIES:
MOTTECHIA 10-SPEED.
SEPTEMBER
19-20 10-4 AM PM
(SUNDAY'S REMAINS)
CONQUISTADORA

MEXICO OR BUST

MULTI
FLEA

OLD & NEW FASHIONS

SKI EQUIPMENT

RARE BOOK

KITCHEN WARE

CHOTCHKAS

526 GALISTEO (CORNER PASEO
SUNDAY, JAN.11, 10-4

CREE'S LIQUIDATION SALE

GETTING DOWN TO BARE ESSENTIALS

MOVING! EVERYTHING MUST GO!

FLEA MKT. STOCK
(INCLUDING NEW IMPORTS)
COSTUMES, ACCESSORIES,
PERSONAL WARDROBE

SAT/SUN SEPTEMBER 19-20 10-4 AM PM
1826 PASEO DE LA CONQUISTADORA
(TAKE CAMINO ALIRE OFF AGUA FRIA OR W. ALAMEDA)
INFO: 982-2396

Back up your newspaper ads with a thorough postering campaign. These posters should be real eyecatchers. If graphic art is not your strong point, find a friend who can help you out. I've included copies of sample posters that resulted in successful sales. Have fun creating your own.

In a medium-sized city (50,000-100,000) fifty such posters should be sufficient; ditto for large metropolitan areas, where you can concentrate postering in the most immediate neighborhoods or suburbs. Don't make 200 copies of your poster or you'll only feel obligated to put them all up. No need for overkill.

Copy your posters on any good copying machine. Offset printing doesn't make sense for such small quantities and will end up costing more. If you're lucky, you'll find an accommodating friend to copy them on an office machine. If not, the most you'll need to spend is 10¢ a copy; large commercial copy services usually charge much less.

Your signs need not be posted until early in the week previous to the sale, for bargain hunters don't plan ahead. If you're doing a group sale, divide up the postering job with your cohorts. If you're working alone, spread your postering out over two or three days to avoid the burnout factor. I *hate* postering, but it's a necessary ingredient for maximizing garage sale turnouts so I try to make it as painless as possible.

I try to avoid the discouragement of "no-posters" policies by sticking to locations which are the best candidates. Supermarkets and laundromats are prime targets, as are public libraries and universities. Record stores, health food shops, bookstores and food co-ops generally have bulletin boards or poster space. Shops which are already displaying at least one poster are usually the most receptive, although you may still find that while posters announcing cultural events are permissible, those announcing garage sales are not. Most small shops and the majority of restaurants won't take posters, and this is also true of most large shopping malls.

Your community may have several standard areas for public notices. Take advantage of these, but do not poster indiscriminately in public places like telephone poles and windows of defunct stores, unless you are certain this is permitted by local ordinance. In Santa Fe, for instance, a recent ordinance prohibited all posters in public places. This is unfortunate, but that doesn't change the reality of having twenty choicely placed signs removed in less than 24 hours.

Divide up your postering runs into geographic clusters for a minimum of driving hassle. And be sure to carry whatever you'll need to affix your

signs to a variety of surfaces. I bring scotch tape for windows, thumb tacks for bulletin boards, duct tape for metal surfaces, and a staple gun for wooden walls and posts (staple guns are also good for bulletin boards if they don't use heavy duty staples). That way, I'm prepared for anything.

Once you've placed your ads and postered the town, your pre-sale advertising is essentially complete. Early morning on the day of the sale, you may want to post a few signs at well-trafficked intersections in your neighborhood to point people to your house. You'll probably pull in a few "I brake for garage sales" impulse buyers along with the folks who are already headed your way. The only other ingredient is word-of-mouth, sometimes the most effective of all. Tell everyone—friends, acquaintances, checkout clerks, gas station attendants—about your sale and the fantastic bargains that await them.

When you've recovered from postering, sort out and organize your wares. Separate the items in good condition which are highly saleable from the soiled clothes, busted toys and trinkets (being sure not to mistake a small gold pin for a bubble gum prize). If you have goods which you feel may have substantial value but are unsure of your ground, recruit a knowledgeable friend to help you with your pricing decisions.

Remember you're trying to do two things: to sell as much of your stuff as possible in one, or at most, two days; and to make the greatest profit you can from your sales.

Say you have what appears to be an expensive pair of skis and you're not a skiier yourself. You phone a friend who oos and ahs over the brand name, telling you they're $250 retail and maybe $100 used at a ski swap. This is good information, and you're glad you didn't follow your original guess and price them at $10. On the other hand, you may not necessarily want to hold out for top dollar. It's May, and people are more likely to be thinking swimming pools than ski slopes.

So you price the skis at $50. This is a super bargain, enough of a bargain for a skier to put out the $50 now, knowing he or she will be grateful for this foresight next winter. A $100 price tag is probably a little too prohibitive for all but the most farsighted of the ski set. At the end of the sale, you'd still have the skis; better to have the cash in hand. You did well to avoid the giveaway of a $10 price tag, and you're $50 bucks richer.

If you research all items with potentially large price tags in this way, and weigh your knowledge of top dollar values against the realities of demand, season, and the limited time a weekend sale allots you, you should end up with fair return for your goods and plenty of satisfied bargain hunters.

Damaged discards and virtual throwaways can simply be dumped into 25¢ or 50¢ boxes. Don't bother with 5¢ and 10¢ boxes. If someone will give you a dime, they'll give you a quarter. Twenty-five cents can be your rock bottom price for anything. If every 10¢ item is sold instead for 25¢, that's an extra 15¢ per item. Which adds up, if you've got a lot of them.

The bulk of your garage sale merchandise will probably fall in between the extremes of the $50 ski boots and the 25¢ half-empty bottles of cologne. Price these items low enough to be legitimate bargains, but high enough to give you a decent return. A toaster in good working condition is a bargain at $5 for the buyer who needs a toaster; you don't have to sell it for $1 to make the sale. Think about how much you would be willing to pay for used merchandise in good condition, especially if the item in question were something you needed. That should give you a reliable guideline for pricing such goods.

Whether or not to use labels and price tags is up to you. If you're easily flustered under pressure you may want to tag your goods so you're not thrown into a tizzy by the early morning rush of buyers. Otherwise, as long as you've sorted your goods thoroughly to separate the wheat from the chaff, you don't need to add the job of marking dozens of individual items to your agenda. Do, however, have a firm idea of what prices you want to get for every item not in the 25¢ category.

The day before your sale, be sure to visit the bank and load up on change: plenty of singles, fives and quarters will streamline your operation when the mass of morning bargain hunters descend. The hard core pros may arrive up to an hour before your scheduled opening time, so be ready for them. It's best to set up as much of your sale the night before as possible, unless you're a pre-dawn riser. If your sale is listed to start at 10:00, have everything ready to go by 8:30.

These early morning sales are the big money makers. That's when the serious buyers appear, and they want to swoop down on you as quickly as possible so they can move on to the next sale. As a buyer, you'll probably be among them. As a seller, you can capitalize on their ready money and avoid the risk of random pricing amid chaos by having everything set to sell. These folks are sharp; they know if you're confused and disorganized, you're likely to underprice your goods simply because you can't deal with it all. Good organization avoids this pitfall, and the buyers will happily hand you cash for legitimate bargains even when they're not dirt cheap. If you're prepared for the onslaught everybody wins.

By the time early afternoon rolls around the hustle and bustle will have subsided. You'll probably have a slow but steady stream of customers who are looking for bargains but are not professionals or afficionados. There will be lulls when there are no customers at all. As the afternoon wears on you'll want to become more and more negotiable with your prices, only standing firm on items you're not all that sure you even want to sell. At this point, you want to milk potential cash flow for whatever you can, and see as much of your merchandise march off as possible.

When I have a garage sale I only run it for one day. Second day sales are usually so light it's not worth the hassle of sticking it out. People know the best stuff went the first day, so only hopeful scavengers will show up. A full-fledged sale can really be a wipeout; I suggest you run it on Saturday, make your bucks, and take Sunday off to bask in your earnings. The leftovers? Stash 'em for another sale, call one of the fleas who advertise hauling in the local classifieds (they'll do it free if you give them the goods), or schlepp the whole lot over to the Salvation Army.

What if it rains? Actually, there are a couple ways to nip this problem in the bud so it doesn't become a problem. First, when possible, try to have your sale at a time when local weather is unlikely to burst into thunderclouds; don't hope for the best during rainy season. But we all know there's nothing as unpredictable as the weather.

If you've got the space, try to keep as much of the sale indoors as you can, in the garage or breezeway or whatever, only using the lawn and driveway for really large pieces. If you organize like this, you may want to add the words "rain or shine" to your ads so people know you're open for business regardless of the weather. An alternative method is to schedule an "in the event of rain" day in advance, usually the following weekend, and include this information in your ad. You'll still want to run new ads the following weekend as well, but if you include the rain date on your poster, you needn't do another postering round.

The prudent garage saler will make it a practice to beat the weather by using one of these methods. I've usually been less than prudent, and I have yet to be rained out. Most garage sales during non-rainy seasons *won't* be rained out, but if you feel skittish about this, by all means buy yourself a little insurance.

An alternative to having your garage sale at home is to take it all to the flea market. This saves you the chores of advertising and postering, and lets you opt for another weekend if rain clouds squelch your plans. It also means packing up and hauling the stuff to the market, repacking it and taking it home. This is no big deal if you've got a moderate amount of goods, but is a big deal indeed if you've got a lifetime's accumulation that includes large pieces of furniture and a backlog of bikes. At the flea market you'll get a steady stream of potential buyers, but you'll also be competing with lots of other vendors.

There's no sure gauge to tell you whether you'll make more at the market or at home, so you need to juggle all the factors involved to decide which option makes the most sense for you. Generally I have found that a home garage sale, especially a group sale, brings the greatest amount of profit in a single day. This may be because a well-advertised sale attracts serious buyers who have taken the trouble to come to your sale because they want to buy, whereas the flea market clientele is full of browsers as well as buyers.

Garage sales have become an American tradition, both at home and as a family outing to the local flea market. Whatever route you choose, may the sun shine bright and your pockets bulge with the fruits of your labors.

PRICING YOUR WARES

Your pricing decisions as a professional vendor will be different from those at your family garage sale. At the garage sale, you kept your specialty goods aside and sold your discards cheaply enough to unload as much as possible in a single weekend. Now you've invested your profits in a selection of specialty merchandise and you're in business for real.

If you've done your research well, you should have a good idea of the going rates in your field. As a vendor you determine prices by how much you paid for an item, what condition it is in, and how much you think you can get for it as a knowledgeable pro at the flea market.

I price to give my customers a good deal and, whenever I can, I keep my prices lower than my competition. I always pass on my own savings to the customer. If I score a mint-condition gabardine cowboy shirt for $1, I sell it for $10, even though many competitors sell equivalent shirts for $15-20. I still make 1000% profit, my turnover is rapid, and my buyer gets the pleasure of having found a real score. If I buy the same shirt for $5, I charge $15. This is consistent with the going rate, and I still make my profit margin.

I also price my goods so there's built-in bargaining room. If I must make $6 for a skirt that cost me $2, I'll price it at $7.50. That way, I'm ready to bargain and still make my profit margin.

Some customers don't even think of bargaining. They like the skirt, the price is reasonable, and they're happy to give me $7.50. Fine. I got an extra $1.50 over what I needed. Other folks love to bargain and don't consider a proper flea exchange has taken place unless they've managed to shave the price a little. Fine. I respect this, it's all part of the game. So I let the bargainers have the skirt for $6. They're delighted to have pulled off a bargaining ploy; I still make my profit margin. Everybody's happy.

I always give quantity discounts when they're requested. If someone wants five items that total to $27, I'll let them go for $25. This makes satisfied customers, who love to come back and bring their friends. It's more than worth the two bucks, and my profit is covered by the built-in bargaining percentage anyway.

Always be willing to bargain, but don't offer to unless the customer asks you. If someone wants to pay full price, fine. Many do. Unless— and this is an important unless—the item in question is one of those old dogs you've carted around forever. Then for god's sake get off it, and offer it super-cheap to anyone who's interested. It's worth it not to have to look at it again. Careful buying usually avoids this, but there are always a few items I'm glad to say good riddance to.

In the world of secondhand, every rip or crack or chip offers the shrewd customer an opportunity to knock down the price. Most will at least be unwilling to pay the top dollar the piece would command if in impeccable conditon. I only buy merchandise in perfect or near-perfect condition, which usually eliminates this problem. But if you're selling stock in varying degrees of repair, don't expect to get top dollar for damaged goods. You may fool a few novices, but regular flea customers are pretty sharp, so it makes sense to price a damaged item lower in the first place.

Occasionally, a customer notices a flaw which I overlooked and I always reward such vigilance by offering to lower the price. How much I lower it depends on the extent of the damage. If the damage is slight and easily repaired, I offer only a modest discount. If the damage is substantial or unrepairable, I'll usually slash the price fairly dramatically. But most times my built-in bargaining percentage covers any discounts that arise from haggling over the condition of the merchandise.

Never forget you're a pro. Flea market vendors are essentially retail merchants, and there's no reason to offer wholesale prices to specialty dealers unless they're buying a really large amount of goods from you. Jerry Junk puts it this way:

> I don't sell nothing for a quarter or 50 cents. I did when I started, but now I try to stay in the range of two bucks and up. That's why dealers don't buy from me. They know that they have to pay the price if they're gonna buy from me. I'm not gonna give them the leeway on me where they're gonna make 99.5 percent profit off me, off of something I sell, you know?

To Tag or Not to Tag

Whether you price your goods with tags and labels is up to you. Some do, some don't. If you work with a partner, it's a good idea to use price tags, unless you are both completely aware of what you paid for each item and exactly how much you need to get to make your profit margin. Tagging saves the frustration and profit loss that results when a well-meaning but unknowing partner sells a lamp for $5 when you needed to get $15.

If you're working solo, tags and no-tags each have their advantages. Untagged goods give you absolute freedom to respond to the mood of the moment and gauge your customer's willingness and ability to pay. When an obviously well-heeled young matron is hot for your oak-framed mirror, you may well be able to ask $75 and get it (even though you really only needed $45, and would have tagged it at $50).

This same spontaneity of pricing can also leave you open to underpricing your wares on a day of sluggish sales (see Bad Day Blues, p. 111). Suddenly you're telling someone they can have the cream pitcher for $3, even though your business self knows better. You *paid* $3 for the pitcher, and in your desperation to make a sale—any sale—you gave it away. If you'd tagged it at $10, you could still have made the buyer grin by giving it to her for $7. You would have made a sale and made money too.

But if you're hardnosed enough not to allow the bad day blues undermine your profit structure, you may find you enjoy the freedom of untagged goods. There is an important advantage to doing it this way: it saves you time. Tagging goods means buying labels and price tags, and hands you the job of marking dozens of individual items. You'll be too busy in the morning at the market to do it there. Even when you're only marking new acquisitions, it means additional pre-market time. I always used tags when I worked with a partner, and I usually devoted a couple hours each week to the process.

Tagging also has its plusses, even when you work alone. If your prices are normally lower than your competition, the browser knows immediately there are bargains to be had at your stall. Some customers are terribly shy about asking prices because they're afraid that asking a price means they're ready and willing to purchase the item. They think the price may be too high, and that by opening the dialogue they'll get in over their heads. A reasonable price tag lets a buyer know there's nothing to fear.

You can avoid this problem with untagged goods simply by being sensitive to it. When you notice a shy young woman lovingly fondling a velvet gown, you can tell her "That's fifteen dollars. Nice velvet, isn't it?" Then she can decide whether she wants to pursue the purchase.

You can compromise by grouping goods together ("Everything in this box $2). You can also tag selectively, restricting yourself to high-priced "stars" or to super-reductions you want to hustle as "don't-miss-this-one'' bargains. I've often had special $1 sale racks, and end-of-season bargain racks. These require only attractive, legible signs, and usually result in brisk sales.

Try it both ways, or in any combination, and find out what works best for you.

DISPLAYING YOUR WARES

A tiny lady in lavender pauses at my accessories table to open an antique fan. She smiles sweetly behind the faded silk, twinkling eyes framed by snow white hair.

"I just want to tell you, dear, you have such lovely things."

"Thanks." I am genuinely flattered. "I enjoy collecting it all."

She moves closer for a confidential whisper. "You know, so many people have a lot of junk and everything's on the ground getting dirty. But your booth looks so pretty, just like a fancy shop."

I grin to myself as she walks away. No matter that she's bought nothing; her words are a confirmation of the care I take with my display. A care appreciated not only by the photographers who sometimes snap my set-up, but by my customers, regulars and newcomers alike. It lends my flea market operation true boutique credibility; this, combined with moderate prices, has always resulted in consistent sales.

The keys to successful display? Attractive visibility that allows maximum access to the merchandise. You're there to sell. Don't hide your wares, because your customers are essentially paying you for the selection process. Not everyone's a flea, and most people don't want to rummage through boxes and bags in search of buried treasure.

GOOD DISPLAY TOOLS ARE ESSENTIAL. You'll need to budget some of your initial stake for this equipment. The structure you design depends on your specialty, but display is an area you don't want to mickey mouse. Your gear must be lightweight and portable, enabling you to set up and tear down with a minimum of blood, sweat, and tears. I have seen fellow fleas spend up to an hour lugging it all out, and an equal amount of time hauling it all back in; time that could be much better spent buying and selling. Keep your operation as simple as possible.

Almost all vendors need several sturdy folding tables, unless these are provided by the market management. Your tables can be funky to look at since you can cover them with fabric, but they must be able to take the wear and tear of weekly outings to the market. You don't want to watch your collection of glass figurines get dumped when a careless customer bumps into your table and a leg collapses. Lightweight, yes; sturdy, yes. This combination is the basis of good design.

Card tables are standard, and fold-up rectangular metal tables work well too. If you're short on tables and need a large display surface, a hollow door is a good solution. It can be suspended between two card tables or saw horses, and gives you an instant giant table. You can cover it with fabric to unify it visually into a single surface.

You also need a folding chair (one for each if you're partnering). It's boring and hot to sit in your car all day, and it's unlikely you want to spend eight hours on your feet. True, you can sit on the trunk or hood of your vehicle, but that means sacrificing what are good additional display areas.

A canopy is optional but highly desirable. During a blazing summer afternoon, it's good to protect your merchandise from possible sun damage, and to provide welcome shade for yourself and your customers. If you're selling goods particularly vulnerable to the rays of the sun, like records or candles, a canopy is essential. Canopies can usually be rigged to attach from your vehicle, so only the front needs poles and staking, If your market has a dirt surface, poles can be driven into the ground. If the surface is asphalt, use concrete blocks or sandbags to stabilize the poles. Some vendors use beach umbrellas for shade.

You want to attract buyers to your booth, so whatever your specialty, make your display colorful and visible. A multi-colored canopy catches the eye better than drab olive green. Helium balloons and high-flying flags can attract customers even at a distance.

Make it colorful, but keep it simple. Don't get so enchanted by the artistry of your design that you forget the efficiency factor. A classic example is the beautiful octagonal dome a friend created to display his lead glass crystals. It was gorgeous: reminiscent of Turkish minarets, it featured open arches that sparkled with the rainbow refractions of the crystals. He had used it first at the Renaissance Fair, and for that it was perfect. But the Fair is a two-week event; the flea market requires you to set up and tear down in a single day. When he brought his crystals to the market he spent nearly all day assembling his rig. The result was a stunning display, but by the time he was ready to sell the sun was sinking in the west and his customers had all gone home.

With your inner radar alert you'll probably find most of your display tools in fleadom without having to pay retail prices. You may well have exactly what you need in your own basement. Scrounge whatever you can, but be willing to spend a little money if you have to. Your display rig is, in fact, your shop. A well-designed structure is both a boon to sales and a way to minimize the weekly wear and tear of setting up shop.

When it comes to set-up and display, many specialties have their own idiosyncrasies. You can do your own research in fleadom to see what works (and what *doesn't* work). But here's some advice about handling specific problems in a few major specialties.

Jewelry and Small Collectibles

When you're dealing jewelry or valuable small items of any type, you must take extra care with your display. Buy or build locking display cases to prevent rip-offs. Nothing is easier to pocket than a piece of jewelry, and the extra investment in well-made cases is an essential insurance policy. Rip-offs are as unfortunate a reality in fleadom as anywhere else, and there's no sense being a sitting duck for thieves.

Collectible Breakables

Fine breakables carry certain liabilities. There's the wind factor. I've seen a few heartbreaking crashes in my time, when a sudden gust of ornery wind totalled a display of fine china in one fell swoop. Some breakables dealers just hope for the best. Others find ingenious solutions like building tables with deep-set trays that provide a windbreak function. You may figure out a better solution, but do keep the wind factor in mind when designing a display for breakables.

Also remember that breakables are one of the more time-consuming specialties, in terms of the set-up and break-down of your display. Breakables require super-care in packing and unpacking, and each piece should be wrapped individually and handled with delicacy. Always stay alert to clumsy customers and their kids, and ask your buyers to handle the merchandise with care.

The profits they bring you will make it well worth the extra time it takes to treat this merchandise with proper respect.

Books

In my case, the perfect display tools inspired the addition of a bookstore to the boutique. For a long time Rolf and I had been interested in beginning a used book operation, but we always balked at the bulkiness the sheer weight of books implied. Until we found a bunch of wire baskets, presumably from a bakery, for a dollar apiece at—where else?—the fleamarket.

These baskets are ideal; they weigh next to nothing, stack easily for storage, and can be lifted in and out of the van with ease. They're also large enough—about one foot by two and a half feet—to work as organizing tools for a variety of book categories: fiction, how-to, religion and metaphysics, astrology, biography, poetry, science fiction, history, politics and economics, miscellaneous non-fiction, and rare books.

Almost all successful large-scale book dealers categorize their wares in similar ways, creating a flea facsimile of a book shop. Customers are happy to pay a little more for the privilege of browsing at their leisure without having to rummage their way through mountains of unclassified books. Organized categories also help you really know what you have.

Produce

I never realized how time-consuming the set-up and display of a produce dealer can be until I talked to Marilyn. She's been doing it for twenty-two years so she certainly knows all the shortcuts, and she has an able assistant in young Robert. Nevertheless, the following description of her daily market routine should make would-be produce dealers aware of just what they're getting into:

> We load the trays of young plants and seedlings on shelves in the truck, and we use a pole with a hook to pull them forward. It takes

about an hour and a half to set up. You gotta keep everything separate: one kind of tomato on this end, one kind on that end. We got one, two, three kinds of hot peppers and we got a frying pepper and a sweet banana pepper and we got your regular peppers. We put signs on everything. My husband, he could tell the difference, but they're easy to get mixed up. Someone wants bell peppers and you sell them hot cherry peppers by mistake. Oh Lord! It happens, though, even with us, it happens occasionally.

Vegetables take much longer to set up. We bring them down in big bushels, and put them out in measures like one-quart, two-quart, four-quart baskets. And stuff like cabbage we sell by the piece: lettuce is by the head, beets by the bunch, like that. We always weigh one measure or piece, because if Weights and Measures comes through, you gotta know what it weighs.

It takes a long time to set up. And take down at night.

Clothing

All clothing vendors need sturdy racks that won't collapse with the first gust of wind. Whether you use my designs or come up with your own, do avoid those portable aluminum racks made for home use. They're a disaster in the wind, and have to be staked so much to stabilize them it's not worth the effort. Even if you live in a windless clime, heavy garments and careless customers can dump these racks in record time.

You also need a plentiful stash of hangers. Wire hangers are OK for some garments, but especially useful are the plastic ones with notches to hold straps and keep wide-necked pieces from flying off the hangers. You'll also want skirt and pants hangers, and sturdy wooden ones for heavy garments. Multi-tiered skirt hangers with clips work well for displaying scarves, ties and belts.

Don't hang sweaters and knitted pieces; the hangers will stretch the garments along the neckline and this is hard to rectify once the damage is done. These goods are better displayed on tables or in bins, even if folding them again after customers plow through them is a hassle.

Long hours in direct sunlight can be harsh on clothing, especially of the vintage variety. A canopy to shade at least the more delicate items in your stock will save you the heartbreak of discovering your impeccable Chinese silk robe has a distinct fade line along the top of the hanger. All fragile and high-priced items should be carefully protected; keep your

Victorian lace wedding dress in a dry cleaner's bag. If someone is seriously interested in it, you can unveil it for inspection.

Suitcases, trunks and hatboxes make attractive display cases for small accessory items. They serve as self-contained storage units during the week and can be packed up quickly when the weather threatens to disagree.

Always be prepared for the possibility of an unexpected shower, even if there's not a cloud in the sky. When rain clouds move in, try to beat them to the punch and immediately protect your stock with heavy plastic tarps. It's important to keep your merchandise in good condition, even if it means losing a few last-minute sales. Even a few raindrops can damage your more delicate items. Don't take that chance.

A mirror is standard equipment. People love to preen, and most folks need a reflection to let them know if their instincts are right. Having a mirror means you'll sometimes be subjected to a parade of customers from other vendors who want to check out potential purchases, but in the long run this is a plus. In the course of their decision-making process they will often notice what a dynamite selection *you* have, and boost your sales accordingly. Dime-store mirrors usually distort in the direction of making the customer look long and lean; this is hardly a drawback.

Design #1: Working Out of a Vehicle

This design (see following page) came from the first van Rolf and I used as our flea market vehicle. It was an old Corvair camper, complete with canopy attachment that was supported by a rectangle of metal poles from the van. When we sold the Corvair we kept the pole structure and attached it to our Dodge van with C-clamps.

The rack is super-sturdy and requires no staking, even in areas with sudden high winds. You can construct such a rack yourself to attach to any rack or station wagon, based on this design. Use lightweight poles that disassemble as easily as they assemble. The structure itself provides stability, so you don't need heavy, and expensive, components.

Design #2: Self-Contained Mobile Display Rack

This design is useful for urban dwellers operating without a vehicle, and for vehicle vendors who can adapt the design to make it collapsible

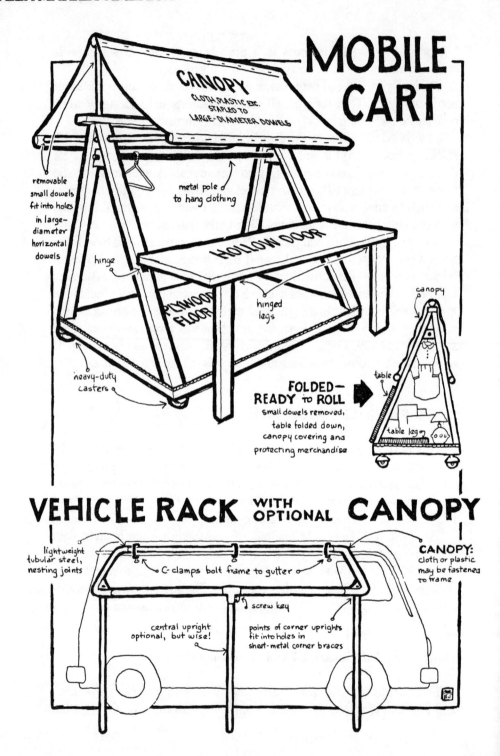

MOBILE CART

CANOPY
CLOTH PLASTIC ETC.
STAPLED TO
LARGE-DIAMETER DOWELS

removable
small dowels
fit into holes
in large-
diameter
horizontal
dowels

metal pole
to hang clothing

HOLLOW DOOR

hinge

PLYWOOD
FLOOR

hinged
legs

heavy-duty
casters

canopy

table

table leg

**FOLDED—
READY TO ROLL**
small dowels removed,
table folded down,
canopy covering and
protecting merchandise

VEHICLE RACK WITH OPTIONAL CANOPY

lightweight
tubular steel,
nesting joints

C-clamps bolt frame to gutter

CANOPY:
cloth or plastic
may be fastened
to frame

screw key

central upright
optional, but wise!

points of corner uprights
fit into holes in
sheet-metal corner braces

so you can assemble at the market. Designed for my Manhattan operation, this unit rolls into the elevator, out the door, and across the street to the market. If you are working without a vehicle, don't chintz on the casters. Get big heavy-duty casters, or you're courting a hernia. Large-diameter wheels also won't get hung-up in the inevitable cracks and potholes of city streets. With good wheels, this unit can be easily maneuvered by one person—which is how I do it.

It's basically a giant sawhorse with a floor, and includes a colorful canopy and fold-out table as well as a permanent rack for hanging clothes. During the week it is a self-contained storage unit that rolls into a vestibule, out of the way of household traffic.

If you have access to cheap metal poles you may want to use them instead of the two-by-fours I used. A pole structure would be lighter and easier to maneuver. I opted for wood construction only because metal poles were prohibitively expensive for me at the time and I was unable to scrounge any.

WHEN TO SELL

How long the flea season lasts depends on local climatic conditions. Most markets operate on a "weather permitting" basis, starting as early in the spring and running as late into the fall as they can. Others have set opening and closing days, which generally run from March to just before Christmas in areas where winter is indeed Winter. If you live in the sun belt you may be lucky enough to have a practically year-round operation, though the hottest summer days will be HOT.

Within these parameters you can count on a fairly consistent operation, broken up by occasional rain days. You may choose to become a diehard, which is what you have to be if the flea market is your only source of revenue. If your flea sales are also backed up by some other income, however, you can afford to pick and choose a little. I've done my diehard stretches, but when I can afford to sell only under the best of conditions I opt for comfort.

I try to avoid truly miserable weather, be it drizzly cold or torridly hot. There may be sales those days, and the diehards often do well simply because the ranks of vendors are so diminished. These decisions are up to you. But if you decide to battle the elements, at least be sure you're prepared for comfort. Andy, the Lahaska toy maker, bundles himself up in high mountain gear, and only takes January off. He makes sure he doesn't freeze to death in the process.

Many markets extend their usual two-day stints an extra day during holiday weekends such as July 4, Memorial Day and Labor Day. I've generally found that the tacked-on holiday extras just don't pay off; most folks are off doing a long family weekend and are unaware the market is open anyway. Holiday weekends in general tend to be slow, and Sunday sales on Easter and Mother's Day can be miserable.

The weekends just previous to major holidays can, however, be very lucrative, especially if you can capitalize on the coming holiday in some way. Once I did a brisk business in dried flower bouquets (seconds from a friend's stash) the day before Mother's Day. I sold out. On Mother's Day itself, I stayed home.

A major exception to the holiday slump is Halloween, a day for fleas to clean up. Last minute costume panic is in the air and if you can round up weirdo costume paraphernalia for the masqueraders bring it out in full force. Masks, wigs, feathers, funny hats, and strange clothes have their day on Halloween.

Pre-Christmas sales are great if you have the weather on your side. For

toymaker Andy, pre-Christmas sales represent 25-30% of his business. But, unlike most merchants, you can't always count on the Christmas season because your shop may be under two feet of snow by Thanksgiving. When you can, gear your operation for the Christmas market. Wreaths, poinsettias, Christmas trees, unusual gifts and stocking stuffers of any variety go well during the holidays. At Christmas most folks are eager to buy, so expand your normal stock to accommodate the holiday fever. Santa Fleas often ho-ho-ho themselves to the bank. You can too.

PREPARING FOR A DAY AT THE MARKET

You've got plenty of merchandise, good display tools, and a workable pricing structure. You're ready to open up shop and rarin' to go. If you can organize yourself well for the market the experience will yield maximum pleasure and minimum frustration.

It's a good idea to pack up your vehicle the night before. This is especially true if your market is one that demands a super early arrival.

It's heroic enough to arise at 5:30 in the morning so you can have breakfast, cover the miles, and get a good shot at the early bargains. God forbid you should have to set the alarm for 4:30 AM so you have time to pack your gear.

Pack your vehicle so that your display tools are completely accessible. Your structure is your first set-up job, and you don't want to dig under a mountain of merchandise to find your tables. Pack your goods to be organized in the way you'll eventually display them. Junk dealers are an exception to this rule, but specialists with organized displays need to keep the job as simple as possible.

Store everything in the cases or bins you'll use for display. A hodge-podge chaos which requires sorting at the market is an incredible waste of time. If you deal clothing, have all hanging garments already on hangers. I've seen vendors spend forever hanging up dozens of pieces after they arrive. You've got better things to do. Like *buy*. Once your merchandise is organized properly the system runs itself. You need only to add new stock to the proper categories. This can be done at the market, unless the amount of new stock is overwhelming.

Prepare for the vagaries of the weather. Heavy plastic drop cloths are essential to protect your stock if the rains come, unless you're in the desert or the middle of a bona fide drought. Don't be caught tarpless when that impeccable blue sky suddenly develops black clouds in the afternoon. *Always* be prepared for rain, no matter what the weather report says or what your instincts tell you. You just never know.

If you live in an area where frequent high winds blow in without warning (as they do in Sausalito), have plenty of staking tools on hand to secure your display rig and ensure that your colorful canopy doesn't become a wind sail that carries your merchandise to the land of Oz. And if you deal in breakables, be prepared to pack them up at a moment's notice. Have your boxes and containers readily available so you're not digging them out of the back of the van while the wind is cheerfully demolishing your antique cut glass.

Summer sun is *hot*, especially when you're exposed to it for several hours. Unless you're a born Arab, include a sun hat, sunglasses, and possibly sunscreen, as part of your standard gear. Pack a cooler of cold beverages of your choice and carry a water jug. Don't wilt under a July sun with nothing to quench your thirst.

Conversely, prepare for a chilly drizzle when appropriate. In some climates, temperatures rise and fall erratically. You may have to prepare for early morning fog and mid-afternoon sunstroke. And if you're easing into a fall chill in any climate, have plenty of warmies and a thermos of hot coffee or tea to see you through. Gear yourself for the weather patterns and seasons of your environment.

Many flea markets have a good selection of food concessions, so you may not need to pack a lunch. But if you're working alone, or if the market concessions are limited to the hot dog variety and you prefer something healthier or more substantial, bring along some provisions. No point in starving if you don't have to.

You might also want to bring along your favorite intoxicants to boost your spirits on days when sales are slow. If you're easily bored, pack a good book to keep you going through the inevitable lulls that occur even on boom days. Or your knitting, or a deck of cards, or your backgammon set, or whatever serves to amuse you when the customers are few and the sun seems to be getting hotter by the minute. Let your friends know you're a regular at the market and encourage them to come by and visit. The flea market is a delightful place to socialize as well as to do business. You can make new friends and keep the old.

Be sure you're prepared to make change and come armed with plenty of singles, fives and quarters. This may mean a trip to the bank Friday afternoon, but it's worth it. More than one potential sale has been stymied by a vendor frantically running around to hustle up change for a twenty while the buyer loses interest. Keep coins and small bills readily accessible in deep, secure pockets or a change apron. I use different pockets of my clothing (often overalls) to stash ones, fives, tens and coins where I can reach them quickly.

In short, try to be prepared for all the possibilities an open air market naturally engenders. The more you do it, the more you'll learn the idiosyncrasies of your particular market and how to best equip yourself to handle whatever storms may come your way.

THE OLD SOFT SELL

Some of these guys, they're fly-by-nights. They'll sell you the moon if you pick it up before the sun comes out.
—Marcel, vendor
Boulevard Market, New Haven, CT

"What do you think?" The lithe California-brown blond buttons a gabardine jacket over her running shorts, eyes herself critically in the mirror.

"I think it's a little big; that kind of jacket should fit snugly over your body lines." I pinch the material into darts with my fingers. "Like this." Her breasts become more sharply defined under the maroon fabric.

"Yeah, I see what you mean."

"You could have it tailored."

"I could, but if I know me, it'll hang in the back of my closet for months before I get around to it."

"I know, I'm the same way. One more project. So don't buy it, some nice size 9 will come along and it'll fit her perfectly. You're what? A five? Seven?"

"Well, big five, small seven."

"Right, it's a size or so too big."

"Too bad." She sighs, hanging the jacket back on the rack with longing eyes. "I really wanted it to fit . . . hey, what's this caftan, that's nice."

"It's a designer silk, hand-dyed."

"How much?"

"Twenty bucks."

"Yeah? That's a good price. Let me slip this baby on."

The silk billows in diaphanous waves, transforming her into an ethereal goddess. "I love it! It's perfect, I must wear it for Randy tonight."

"It's stunning on you." I hand her change for a fifty.

"Thanks. You here every weekend?"

"Weather permitting."

"Well, you've got great stuff. I'll be back."

And I knew she would be back, along with many others, regulars and semi-regulars who always check my display when they're out for a flea day. My flea market store is like any other business: its success grows from the process of building satisfied clientele who return with their friends, not just catching one-timers for impulse buys.

There are some high-pressure fleas around. I've hardly picked up a small china figurine, and already I'm hearing,

"Now that's a real deal, only a couple of chips, a gift from my wife's aunt, real Belgian china, I'm gonna give you a chance to own that for only fifteen bucks, you know what those things go for in an antique store, fifty, sixty bucks, listen, for another five bucks I'll throw in that little cream pitcher . . ."

By this time, I'm about three stalls down, and he's still following me with his rap. All right already. Now there may be folks for whom this approach works, but for me, and the vast majority of customers, nothing is a greater turn-off from buying than a hardsell sales rap. I never pressure a customer. I let people take their time, make their own discoveries. Only when I strongly feel a particular item is just perfect for a potential buyer do I even make a suggestion. And even then, I drop the subject immediately if the customer isn't interested.

I do most of my selling with my buying. With careful buying and good display, the merchandise sells itself. Your job is to display your wares as attractively and accessibly as possible, then allow people to browse through your goods at their leisure. Catch their eyes with colors and well-placed "stars" to pique their interest. Once they're in your shop they'll discover a whole variety of quality goods at reasonable prices. From that point on the selling happens almost organically.

I treat my customers well, with honesty and tact. If that's really the wrong shade of pink for the redhead, when she asks my opinion I tell her. And when book customers want my opinion of a recent novel I give it. Maybe these customers will buy something else from me today; maybe not. But they'll remember me and come back to my spot another day.

All established professional fleas share a belief in the right and proper exchange of an honest business deal. Cheating the customer does nothing but belittle the vendor and turn his or her business into a ticket to nowhere. No customer ever returns to a vendor who's sold her a bunch of malarkey, unless she intends to try out her mean left hook. Honesty is always the best policy. As Trader Jack Daniels says, "If you get too greedy, someone's going to come along and hurt you. They're going to put you out of business."

Every vendor I interviewed expressed this same adherence to a code of honorable business, either in their words to me or in their exchanges with customers. When a scrupulous customer told Marilyn he wanted to be sure she had added in all his numerous purchases so he wouldn't short her, she commented that she understood what he meant. She'd sometimes run after customers with 15¢ in change they forgot to pick up.

Slim says, "You only want to do business with people you trust," and Andy keeps his prices low so he "doesn't rip the public." Jerry Junk talks about "making honest bucks," and Marcel, the tool man, talks at length about honest deals—especially when you're selling electrical appliances. These are usually sold on the dealer's word alone, for many markets have no electrical facilities.

"I don't sell any electrical stuff unless I know it works. I always check it out first. That way, I can tell people, 'I know it works.' Even then, some people are leery, and I can't blame them for being leery.

"So when someone is leery, I tell them, 'this works, but if you're not sure—don't buy it. That way you won't get stuck.' What else can I say?"

Keeping Records

Let me first tell you this about keeping records: I don't. I never have and I never will. Because even though I often find myself searching for my keys when they're right in front of my eyes, my inner flea has an impeccable memory. I'm not sure exactly why this is because I never cultivated it. But I've talked to a lot of other fleas who share this ability to remember precisely what they paid for their goods, even if they have hundreds of different items. I not only remember how much each item cost, I even remember *where* I bought it (oh yeah, I got that shirt at a thrift shop in Bristol, Tennessee for a dollar).

If your inner flea is not yet this sharp in the memory department you may want to keep track of what you buy and sell: how much each item cost, and what you sold it for. That way you'll know how much profit you're making and how fast various goods are moving. Keeping records can be simple if you organize it right.

The best way is to eliminate any ledger type of accounting altogether. When business is booming, it's a hassle to start writing everything down. Do it instead with your price tags, in much the same way as you would with consigned goods. Write a short description of the item on the back of the tag, and underneath it write a code that tells you how much you paid. So if the cut glass salt shaker cost you $2.50, your tag would read: Cut glass salt shaker, 550250 or whatever. Any code will do.

On the front of the tag, write the selling price. The only time you'll need to do anything else is when you sell an item for less than marked price, in which case you should correct the tag accordingly. Other than that, just save the tags, put them in a good stash place like a cigar box, and forget about it till the end of the day. Then, at your leisure, add up total sales and total costs. Subtract costs from sales, and then subtract from that figure any other expenses like flea market rent and gas. That's your profit.

Included in the survey of publications at the end of this book is the *Flea Market Handbook* by Robert Miner. Though limited in scope, it's a good guide for people interested in dealing early American antique furniture and collectibles, which are Miner's forte. He also devotes at least a quarter of his book to record-keeping, and approaches it like an accountant with a ten-year plan. While this is the antithesis of the way I do things, if you're itching to play with figures read his book. He'll tell you how to treat your flea business like it was a multi-national corporation. He's been making money in this game for years and he knows of what he speaks.

As always, figure out through trial and error what approach works best for you. Cultivate the memory of your inner flea, keep it simple with a tag system, or go all out and get into double entry bookkeeping. There are no rights or wrongs. Only what works.

Whatever method you use, may your records show you solidly in the black!

RED TAPE

According to the Sales Tax Office, 1982 will be the year of the salmon; not pink, orange or polka dot. Think Salmon, get your new sales tax cards as soon as you can. Get it over with. And be confident that somewhere out in the vast reaches of our state government you have made some bureaucrat very happy.

—Joel Kaufman, *The Canal Street Flea Market Newsletter* (12/81)

Fleadom is refreshingly free of red tape, but regulation is beginning to encroach upon even this hallowed territory.

How official you need to be vis-a-vis the tax types depends on where you're doing business. Many flea markets have no tax regulation whatsoever; others require everything from an honor-system envelope contribution at the end of the business day to the filing of forms and securing of vendors' licenses.

Generally, the large urban markets have the tightest regulation. Many California markets require all vendors to file forms every business day which list all merchandise with serial numbers for their records. The listing of merchandise is primarily to prevent the sale of stolen goods, but these forms also ask vendors to report sales and deduct taxes from the day's revenues.

These daily tax bites, whether accompanied by forms or simply dropped into sealed envelopes provided by the management, are similar to the honor-code taxation of tips and gratuities. Obviously, there's plenty of room to fudge, but it's a good idea to abide by the local tax regulations if you're a regular vendor. Chances are the IRS will never get around to investigating your flea market income, but, just in case, it would certainly look suspicious if you sell at the flea market week after week and never make *any* money.

I asked Andy, the toymaker at the Lakaska, Pennsylvania market, about local regulations:

There's a Pennsylvania regulation that everybody's supposed to put up sales tax. But usually nobody does. Well, sometimes once in a while an agent will come around. Normally they hand you the forms, and you fill them out and send it in. Then they check back later.

I think that maybe they're going to crack down soon, because there are so many people now who make a living at the flea market. They're going to start to think they're losing a lot of money. I heard, but I don't know, that there's a bill in Harrisburg now. They want to make the owners of these places charge a set fee that would somehow go into the tax ante. Maybe that's an efficient way of doing it, but it's probably not very fair. Not very fair at all.

Joel Kaufmann runs his flea market in Manhattan, where he is subject to a hierarchy of regulatory bureaucracies:

In terms of what they require of you, the feds are the easiest, the state is the next easiest, and the city's the worst. You go down through the bureaucracy and it just gets more complicated. The regulations governing flea markets in the City of New York were written in the 20s and 30s, and they're a shambles; there's no semblance of reality to them. They waste my time. That's the best thing they do.

Most fleas will have less red tape to untangle than Joel, but the important job is to keep the tax types happy. Bureaucracy thrives on sameness, so give them sameness. Always fill in their forms exactly according to directions. If you give them a perfect form they can process without thinking, the chances are you'll never be strangled with their red tape.

Good Luck!

RESTOCKING YOUR MERCHANDISE

If you keep going back to the market and you don't have enough stuff, you reach a point of diminishing marginal returns.
—Joel, Canal St., NYC

How often do you restock? As often as possible. Never turn off the radar, and never stop looking for new merchandise.

Begin each visit to the flea market with a round of buying from early morning arrivals. You can well afford a later setup; your real customers are probably still dozing and breakfasting, while only the hardcore flea buyers are out looking for bargains. You can often sell an item at noon purchased earlier in the morning, if it's ready to go. Which much merchandise is. Buy it and display it. No need to wait until next week, and lose a possible quick sale.

Make sure you continue to make every relevant garage sale, rummage sale and auction you can. Read the classifieds and buy/sell papers faithfully, and stay alert to any private deals that come your way through friends, flea market connections, and the papers. Follow up leads like a hardboiled sleuther, because you never know when you're going to stumble into a gold mine.

Once your friends and acquaintances know you're a flea, you'll be amazed how many of them will feed you juicy information like, "Hey, my aunt Bessie has this whole attic full of stuff and she's been at me for years to come over and help her sort through it." If you're a true flea, you'll be paying Aunt Bessie a call before your next market day.

You may also want to advertise yourself in the same buy/sell papers and classifieds you use as resources. I've done this from time to time. When I ran an ad that read "Wanted to buy: Vintage clothing 1920-1950" in Napa, California, I was rewarded with a call from a farm wife who let me go nuts in her attic. She wanted only twenty bucks for the

bushel load of treasures I found. I insisted on giving her twenty-five, knowing that my scores were going to bring me close to $300. We had tea, and chatted, and she was delighted to have me give her the chance to reclaim a little storage space. I didn't even have to feel guilty.

I usually figure on reinvesting about a third of my weekly profits on new merchandise. But that's no hard and fast rule, just a rough estimate of average expenditures. It varies with different specialties.

Never pass up a good buy, even on days when sales are slow. You'll kick yourself later for not snapping up items that would go like hotcakes on a day of brisk sales. Buying is the single most important key to selling, and your regular customers will be delighted to find new merchandise every time they pay you a visit.

Keep 'em happy. They're your bread and butter.

RESTORATION AND REPAIR

If you're running an ongoing garage sale at the market, restoration is not an issue. Everything is sold "as is" and it's up to your customers to decide whether they want to breathe new life into a damaged piece.

If, however, you're a specialist who's opted for top-dollar prices for used merchandise in mint condition, there will be times you'll have to weigh the decision whether or not to restore a piece for resale. Each specialty offers its own restoration problems, but there are some general guidelines to follow in making your decisions.

Any potential candidate for repair work must first and foremost be a super-cheap buy. That way, if it winds up costing far more in labor or materials than you anticipated—or if it simply becomes a rainy day project that gathers dust in the basement—at least it's not a lot of money down the drain.

Even if the item in question is really cheap (or even *free*), you must still decide if your investment in restoration is worth it. First you need to figure what, if any, materials the repair work requires, how much they cost, and how available they are. Perhaps the job requires only minimal investment in materials. Fine. You're halfway home. But don't forget that time is money, too. If it takes three hours of labor to turn a 25¢ purchase into a $5 sale, you're getting about $1.60/hour for your labor. By this you make a living?

I learned this lesson the hard way. When I started out in this business I was continually buying 25¢ pieces which, restored to good condition, might bring me a top of $5. I wound up spending hours each week mending these "great scores"—and I hate mending! My investment of labor simply wasn't worth it. All I got was a few extra bucks and a lot of nasty needle pricks for my efforts.

At a certain point I realized this was insanity. I began to restrict my buying to goods that were either in mint condition to begin with, or which required only the most minimal repair. Small rips in seams and a missing button or two I can handle, but that's about it. Even then, I can't be bothered unless I'm going to get a really hefty return on my investment. I'm willing to put up to an hour of time repairing a mink jacket I bought for $15 and will sell for $75, but I don't put even five minutes into an Indian cotton blouse that will bring me $2.

The same is true for other specialties. The rickety oak chair with two coats of blue paint may seem like a bargain at $10, but by the time you've spent the better part of two days stripping it and mending the leg, the $50 you get for it hardly justifies your expense of energy. Unless you've got nothing better to do and find the process itself is its own reward. That's your decision.

If, on the other hand, that $10 chair was already stripped, and you're super handy so it took less than an hour to fix the wobbly leg, the $50 you get for it next market day makes it well worth your while. Understand your own limits of tolerance and expertise vis-a-vis your specialty and combine that with your know-how about the value of the merchandise.

Expertise really pays off when it comes to restoration. When you know how to gauge the extent of the damage to determine how much time and money a repair job will take, you'll be able to make a reasonable decision whether or not a particular job is worth it. Once these decisions become obvious, you'll only be undertaking restoration work that results in maximum profit for minimum expense of your time, money and energy.

CONSIGNMENT SALES

Whatever your specialty, you may sometimes want to round out your stock with merchandise on consignment from individuals and shops.

You can often make arrangements with retail stores to sell seconds, samples and storeroom leftovers at the market. Friends and acquaintances may also have discards they would like to sell without making the trip to the market themselves.

Consignment sales can be a profitable and attractive addition to your regular stock, but you must be discriminating in choosing the right merchandise. The goods should be appropriate to your specialty and eminently saleable. When a friend asks if I will sell some wide-track tires for her, the answer is no. Tires don't make sense in my bookstore/ boutique combination; they're dirty and a pain in the neck to haul in and out. But if you sell tools or automotive equipment or run an ongoing garage sale the tires would probably be a nice addition to your wares and make you some extra money.

While I welcome consignments of goods which reflect my usual merchandise, I'm not interested in becoming the broker for a gross of size 5 rain boots. Someone else's dogs are unlikely to become hot sellers for you, unless the owner of the goods fails to recognize their worth. If someone offers me ten dozen 1950s cat eye sunglasses, now in heavy demand by the New Wave set, it's an offer I can't refuse. Just restrict yourself to consignment goods that enhance your display and are in demand and you'll find it's a good way to boost your sales.

I follow the same standard rule for both shops and individuals: a straight 50/50 split. For a long time I gave consigners 60% and kept only 40%, but experience has taught me that equal shares are fairest to all concerned. Not only are you, as the vendor, paying rent on your space, the consigner reaps the benefit of your accumulated "good will" and its resultant regular customers. Consignment sales also mean bookwork and inventory tallies for you. To make this extra time pay off you need to make enough on such sales to make it worthwhile.

Whether or not you tag your own merchandise with prices, you *must* do this with consignments (unless you're dealing with just one or two large pieces). You must know exactly how much the consigner wants to get for the merchandise, and adjust your pricing to accommodate this. Even if the consigner leaves pricing decisions up to you, you must keep track of all sales. This can get confusing, especially when a customer is buying some of your regular stock and some consignment goods.

I've found the simplest method for dealing with a number of items from several consigners is to tag each piece with the price and name of the consigner. That way I don't have to keep writing everything down at the time of sale. I simply remove the tags on consigned goods and tally the totals of each consigner's tags at the end of my sales day. If I deviate from the marked price and sell an item for less than it was marked, I write the actual figure on the tag so I don't forget. That's my bookkeeping.

If it's important to a consigner to know exactly what items were sold and for what price, I write a brief description of each item on the back of the tag when I price it. I hand over all tags to the consigner so there's no confusion. When the consigner only cares about the amount of total sales I eliminate this step.

Keeping track is different when you're dealing with large numbers of the same item at a standard, mutually agreeable price. If I take fifty scarves from a consigner who wants a dollar apiece for them, I just make chicken marks on a slip of paper every time I sell a scarf. An alternative method is to put a dollar bill aside each time a sale is made (in my case, usually in one of the many pockets of my overalls which I designate for this purpose). Do whatever is easiest for you.

Whenever possible pay off your consigners at the end of each sales weekend. That way you don't start to think of the money as "yours," nor do you have to become an accountant and bank for the consigner.

Consignment sales mean more work, but they also mean more profit and can help fill out a depleted stock during times when your buying isn't restocking your wares as quickly as you'd like.

THE OVERLOAD FACTOR

Where do we store stuff? In the house. Our whole house is a flea market!
—Caggie Daniels, owner
Trader Jack's Market, Santa Fe

The first thing you know you got a whole barn full of stuff and you've got to get rid of it.
—Slim, furniture vendor, Santa Fe

Overload is not an issue for junk dealers who have plenty of storage space and a big truck. But for many of us dealing in specialty items, it can indeed become a problem. And, as Caggie's comment indicates, flea market owners are by no means immune to the overload factor.

Once all your friends and acquaintances know you're a professional flea you may be deluged with well-meaning offers. Many people have a surplus of household goods they're dying to get out of their basements and attics. With the best of intentions, they'll offer to give it all to you, gratis, to sell at the market. Learning how to refuse these offers—or to take advantage of them only to the extent of selecting the merchandise you really want—can be a real lesson in diplomacy.

If you accept all these offers indiscriminately, you may soon find your house or apartment overflowing with the discards of your friends. What was once your den has suddenly become the intake room of St. Vincent de Paul. As usual, I had to learn this one the hard way. Fearing to offend, I allowed my home to become a dumping ground for a while. No more.

The obvious point is to nip this trend in the bud at the outset. These days when I'm approached with such offers, I thank my friends cordially and tell them I might be interested in sorting through their discards. I let them know immediately, however, that I sell a specialized selection of merchandise, and that I'm only interested in those items relevant to my specialties or of such intrinsic value that they stand on their own (like a handsome cutlery set I can obviously make money on and that would make a provocative counterpoint to my suitcase of silk lingerie).

I then sort through their discards, take only what I really want, and do one of two things. If I find next to nothing for me in their stash, I thank them, and suggest they take it all to the Salvation Army. If I find a number of great scores, I take the remainder of their goods to the Salvation Army myself as a gesture of gratitude. This seems to be a fair exchange.

My reaction is the same when other fleas or shopowners approach me with large quantities of merchandise as a lot for one set price. Even if the price is low I tell them I'm only interested if I can sort through the goods and take my pick. I'd rather pay $20 for six pieces I really want than $20 for a mountain of goods that will only yield those six pieces. Otherwise, I'd soon be drowning in my own stock.

I love being a flea, but during the week I like to live my life to accommodate the rest of my many personae. If you share this point of view, you'll continually be alert to the overload factor and eliminate it before it becomes a problem.

PARTNERING

I started this market together with my wife, but then she started losing interest and it was either dump it or take it over. So I took it over, and with the last four years of growth, I've really launched myself into it.

But I get lonely out here—you know, when you're by yourself? I get infinitely lonely.

—Joel, Canal St., New York City

There's nothing like a good partner to make your entire flea market operation simpler, more efficient, and more fun. It means there's someone to help you set up and tear down, someone to cover the action while you're out buying at local sales or at the market itself. It means you don't have to have a heroic bladder or starve if you forgot to pack a lunch. It means you've got someone to bitch and moan with over approaching storm clouds, someone to help pull up stakes when the rains come. Someone to share a bottle of wine with after a satisfying day, someone to empathize with when sales are slow and your metabolism even slower.

For several years Rolf and I worked as a flea team, and we had our operation down pat. We knew what our jobs were and divided the labor to best advantage. I was always the buyer because Rolf never did learn to tell silks from synthetics. But he had a knack for the soft-sell that kept those dollars coming in while I roamed the market for scores. I priced all the merchandise with tags and followed standard guidelines with him for the bargaining margin (never less than 80% of marked price).

When we arrived at the market Rolf would immediately begin the structural set-up while I scouted the early morning bargains. When he had the display set-up rigged, I returned to put out the merchandise while he made his own rounds (usually hot on the trail of ankle weights, boxing gloves, and the perfect knife). When I had the stock ready to go he checked in again and I would go off to continue buying while he manned the shop.

Throughout the rest of the day we spelled each other, making food runs and bathroom calls as needed. Then we both tore it all down, packed up, and counted the day's take. Good days or bad, we'd always go out for

dinner and a couple beers before winding down and settling in for the evening. A day at the market—even a boom day—is almost always a wipe-out. If you plan to generate energy for a social evening afterwards it's a good idea to give yourself time for a nap and a bath; you'll probably need them both.

If you have a partner with buying expertise, so much the better. I tried to combine forces with a couple of potential buying partners, but they didn't meet my specs. Finding someone whose buying specs and tastes are compatible with your own is difficult but possible. I've certainly known teams who worked beautifully together in acquiring merchandise.

In any case, a flea team only needs one buyer; someone covers home base while the other buys. What's most important in team work is that the jobs be clearly defined so you know just who's doing what. Work out a routine that becomes second nature; don't get stuck arguing about whose job it is to hoist the canopy. Make sure you both understand the pricing and bargaining allowances. Unless you both absolutely know correct prices, tag *everything* to avoid those "How could you have sold that bowl for a dollar?" confrontations. Good flea teams work together, not against one another.

I'm a lone flea now, soloing in Manhattan, and I can frankly say that I miss having a partner. I make do by asking neighboring vendors to watch my goods while I make a quick dash to the bathroom, but it's always a risk to leave my stall. Even the most well-intentioned neighbors can be side-tracked by their own customers, so excursions must be kept to a minimum to avoid rip-offs. In my buying, I'm restricted to the closest neighboring vendors, and must keep a vigilant eye on my display while I scour my neighbors' wares.

So if you can, partner. If you can't, make the best of it. Pack your own lunch and liquids so you're not overcome by starvation and thirst. Develop the bladder tolerance of a yogi. Keep your journeys beyond your stall to a minimum, and confine them to slow periods when your neighbors can keep a careful eye on your goods. Tell all your friends to come by to bring supplies, stimulants, and good cheer. Get to know your neighbors and chat with your customers to keep boredom at bay. Keep your operation simple enough to readily handle your set-up alone, without undue wear and tear on the body and psyche. And keep your eyes and ears open for potential partners, because partnering with the right person is the ideal way to go.

RIP-OFFS

Stores have elaborate search systems and they still get ripped off. The best thing we can do is to prevent rip-offs from happening. What we have going for us is that we have so many eyes. The vendors watch out for each other.

—Joel, Canal St., New York City

Theft is a fact of life, and fleadom is a happy hunting ground for thieves. Know this, and be aware of it continually.

Some things are obvious: valuables, such as fine jewelry, should always be in a case, preferably a locked case. Don't leave valuables lying around loose on the tables, no matter how vigilant you think you're being. There's always a moment of sudden customer flurry when you simply can't be on top of the whole scene, and this is when things disappear.

Design your display so you have maximum visibility of your stock, being careful not to create blind spots. Keep your money on your person in deep, secure pockets or lock it inside your vehicle: don't tempt thieves with cigar box cash registers in public view. Stay alert.

No matter how many precautions you take, you'll probably be ripped off at one time or another. If you do get ripped off, sound the alarm to your neighbors. Fleas really pull together, and occasionally a thief is spotted and pursued. But, most likely, you'll have to kiss the item goodbye. I take a few deep breaths, clear my head, and get back to business as usual. I know that somewhere, sometime, the thief is gonna have some karmic debts to deal with. Small solace, but that's the way of the world.

Bad checks are another kind of ripoff, a slow lingering death as opposed to the quick kill. Like most fleas, I have a no-checks policy. Period. I would rather take a deposit on an expensive item to be picked up later that day or during the week than to accept payment in full by checks which may end up bouncing as high as the current unemployment rate.

Just watch it. Because you can at least save yourself the additional agony of self-beratement over the gold watch you left lying on the picnic table.

Which is something.

BEATING THE BAD DAY BLUES

Yup, there are going to be some low days, when nobody's buying and everybody's chintzy, and you're just about ready to pack it in for good and get out of this lousy business. Fleadom, like any other domain, has its ups and downs, is its own casino.

I have found there is absolutely no predictable pattern of sales, no sure-fire method of really knowing what the weekend will bring. Weather is obviously a factor; no one feels much like buying in a stultifying heat wave or on a cold, drizzly day. Still, there can be days of awful weather with a high volume of sales, and days of perfect balmy sunshine that crunch you.

Sure, the old flea maxim about people being out of spending money before the fifteenth and at the end of the month has a grain of truth to it. But I've seen 'em gobble up the goods on March 31 and pass up everything cold on May 3.

One thing I do know: there is some weird, collective buying energy on any particular day that seems to pervade the entire market. There are some days when everyone's buying, there's a kind of fever in the air, cash flows and goods change hands. There are also days when nothing is good enough or cheap enough for anyone, when everyone is just browsing, reluctant to part with their cash. If you can figure out a coherent pattern to all this, please let me know. I'd like to be initiated.

A couple of pointers for the bad day blues:

Don't sell cheap. Avoid the desperation complex that would have you sell the pewter bowl for five bucks because nothing's coming in. You know perfectly well on another day it's an easy fifteen. Maybe come down a little to sweeten the pot on days when everyone's feeling chintzy. But sell it for twelve, not five or eight. All you'll do by selling cheap is cut your profit margin and deplete your stock. It isn't worth it. There will be other days.

Don't pass up buying just because money is not flowing in. Slow days usually pervade the entire market, and you can take advantage of this by scooping up bargains from fellow fleas who got the bad day blues too.

Pack up early if it's really getting you down. It's unlikely that any miracle is going to turn the tide. Pack it in, cruise the market for last-minute buys, go out and have a couple drinks, and forget about it till next weekend. By then everything will have changed, and often feast follows famine. I expect at least one bad day a month, maybe two. The rest of the days will be average, with a couple of big boom days to recharge the spirit and the pocketbook.

Bad day blues? Beat 'em and buy. This too will pass.

MAKING IT THROUGH THE WINTER

What to do when winter finally settles in? If you want to continue to flea while the snow falls, you've got a few options. There may even be a year-round, indoor flea market in your area.

You can consign to shops that deal in your specialty. With valuable antique pieces, this can be quite worthwhile—providing you know the value of your merchandise and can work out an equitable deal with the shopkeeper. In my used clothing and book business I've found that consignment to shops simply isn't profitable, and I've yet to find a shop which will allow me a large enough profit margin to make it worthwhile. But check it out in your area as shop consignments may vary with your specialty and your geography.

You can also make a spare room of your house into an informal store, relying on friends and word-of-mouth to make it known you're open for business. This works quite well if you've got a lot of traffic flowing through your life already. I've always sold a lot of merchandise to friends, even during regular flea season; they like to get their pick before it goes out to the general public. And regular market customers often ask me to locate specific items. I keep a list of these people with their phone numbers so I can alert them to any new acquisitions that may be of interest.

It's pushing your luck and the zoning laws a bit to operate a formal shop out of your home, but you can run advertisements in the local classifieds that announce you've got goods to sell. Keep the ad informal, simply listing what you've got and your home phone number. Don't represent yourself as a shop, just an ongoing private sale.

You can also organize advertised one-day sales during the winter. Toward the end of each flea season I keep a sign-up list at my stall for customers who want to be informed about winter sales. Nearly all of them do, and I usually compile a hefty mailing list. I've always run a pre-Christmas indoor sale, often joining forces with other friends— fleas, artisans and craftspeople—to create a bazaar. In addition to my mailings, I advertise in the papers and poster the town. These Christmas sales have always been mobbed and well worth the organizational time.

Indoor sales in January and February have been less successful. People are bought-out after Christmas and the winter doldrums have set in. But, in a pinch, even dead-of-winter sales have produced enough profit to keep the landlord away from my door.

Use your own home for such sales or make arrangements with a friend who has suitable space. Remember, it's an indoor flea market and not a garage sale, so arrange your wares with the same care you take at the market. If everything's in heaps on the floor people aren't going to pay more than rummage sale prices. Heaps are okay if you're a trash-and-treasure type, but with specialty merchandise display brings better prices.

The golden rule is to buy as if you were buying for your own wardrobe.
—Cree

5

The Cheap Chic Flea Boutique

Even those of us in the rag game are a varied lot. Many vendors specialize in one type of clothing, like jeans, which they organize and mark according to waist and length measurements. Others specialize in military surplus clothes culled from various government surplus sales. Some deal exclusively in baby and children's clothes, which are usually available super-cheap from all sources and always in demand.

Lots of fleas offer a diversified spectrum of clothing of all varieties, and there's as much of a market for polyester as there is for crepe. My own prejudices determine my buying selections, and by no means do I want to discourage clothing vendors from selling whatever works best for them.

I'm a typical flea: I love my merchandise and I know it up, down and sideways. My flea boutique gives me a state-of-the-art wardrobe that is continually changing; what I tire of today, I sell tomorrow. But there is also an important economic reason why I peddle rags. I was able to go into business on a shoestring—and a chintzy shoestring at that—because of something Rolf dubbed the "float factor": the ability to float dimes into dollars so that a minimal investment yields a maximum profit.

In our throwaway culture, certain used merchandise has tremendous float potential. Clothing is a 'high floater.' People often know the approximate value of their great aunt's china, or Dad's portable deco radio, but they'll blithely sell their wardrobe discards for dimes. Many a time I've dug a silk blouse out of a 50¢ pile. Hung and pressed, that blouse will bring me ten bucks. A tidy 2000% profit.

Some cheap chic fleas buy large lots of used clothing from major rag warehouses located around the country, primarily in El Paso, Los Angeles and New York. To penetrate this closed circuit you either need an 'in' or a substantial amount of bribe money in front. I scouted the warehouses in LA, and found that I needed at least $2000 to make an inroad. Since I had about $100 I had to forget it.

Warehouses in El Paso and other large cities may not require quite such a hefty ante, but most large-lot buyers figure on at least $500 to make their buying trips worthwhile. Warehouses sell by the pound (from $1/lb. down, depending on quantity), so you can load up your vehicle and haul it all to the market—ideally to a market dense with cheap chic fleas like me who buy selectively on a smaller scale. Amateurs who know will also take the time to sort through the heaps and buy what they want. Large-lot buying is a lucrative way to go if you've got enough investment capital, the right connections, and a reliable hauling truck.

I've never done it this way. My business works by a very selective buying of individual pieces from the various sources in fleadom: the market itself, garage sales, rummage sales, private deals, thrift shops, and whatever helpful friends want to hand me when they're cleaning house. This way I keep my shop restocked with new acquisitions but don't have to put out large capital outlays. Many of us work this way.

But all cheap chic dealers, large-lot or small-scale, need to acquire the expertise to buy goods with the greatest profit potential. This know-how breaks down into two basic components: fabric and style. Let's look at each of these in depth.

FABRIC

To compete with the rest of us it's essential that you know your fabrics. Labels help, but many times labels have vanished or been removed. You should be able to discriminate between silk and polyester with your eyes closed. With your eyes open, there's no excuse for bypassing a gabardine leisure shirt just because it's mixed in with kids' clothes and K-Mart specials.

Most cheap chic customers share my appreciation of fine natural fabrics, vintage and contemporary, and shop at the flea market to find them. My selection of quality fashions, and ability to "talk shop" with discriminating customers, has always been a boon to sales.

In the following survey, I've covered some of the most popular fine fabrics. Some are found exclusively in "vintage" clothing (vintage means primarily before 1950, although 50s fashions and these days even 60s fashions are considered of historical value); others are still used in contemporary designs. If you're just learning about fabric, it's a good idea to make yourself a swatch book with samples cut from damaged garments or linings and hems. That way you can train your fingers as you search, comparing textures with your samples.

Fabrics are classified in two different ways. The first breakdown refers to the source of the fabric fiber itself; the second to the weave of the fabric, which may be composed of a variety of fibers. Let's look first at the basic natural fiber families.

Silk

The soft, lustrous fiber obtained as a filament from the cocoon of the silkworm.

Silk has for centuries been the aristocrat of fine fabrics. Marco Polo was no fool. Silks are cool in summer, warm in winter (especially in layers), remarkably durable and delicious to wear. Raw silks are nubbier in texture; refined silks are diaphanous and—what else?—silky. Oriental silks, such as those used in kimonos, are always to be prized. You'll find old silks and new silks; all of them, providing they're in good condition, are musts for your stock of fine used clothing.

Although many manufacturers label silks with a "dry clean only" warning, most silks lend themselves well to handwashing in a gentle detergent. The only exceptions are silk crepes and velvets, which should be dry cleaned. So if you're debating whether to buy a soiled silk garment, and the item in question is cheap enough, it's worth the risk. Many stains are removable by handwashing without running up big cleaner's bills. Squeeze—don't wring—the garment gently after rinsing, then roll in a towel to absorb most of the moisture. Iron when still slightly damp on a low setting.

Cotton

A fiber derived from the soft, downy fibers of the cotton plant.

Good old 100% cotton is hard to beat for wearability, durability, and breatheability. Unlike most synthetics (especially polyester) which begin to pill after only a few washings, cotton wears and wears. Cotton is widely available in both vintage and contemporary fashions, and predominates in imports from the far east and south of the border. Quality ranges from cheap Indian gauzes that look pretty but wear poorly to close weaves that can last a generation.

Cotton can be machine washed but only in cold water. It is super-susceptible to shrinkage and hot water can turn a size ten into a size five. Machine dry it only on low. Iron when slightly damp, or with a steam iron at high setting.

Rayon

A natural synthetic, regenerated from cellulose, cotton linters, or chips of hemlock, spruce or pine.

Rayons have a silky sheen and cling and swirl provocatively. They are, however, super-susceptible to wrinkling, and must be ironed to show their glory. This is no wash-and-wear fabric, but it's well worth the extra care. Rayon Hawaiian shirts are a perennial cheap chic favorite; look also for rayon scarves, blouses, dresses, skirts, lingerie and men's shirts of the vintage variety. Rayon is still used in contemporary fashion, and some of the new rayon/polyester blends are surprisingly supple and easier to care for.

Vintage rayons don't need to be dry-cleaned, but it's a good idea to handwash them. Machine washing weakens and frays the fabric. Iron when still slightly damp or with a steam iron on medium setting.

Linen

A fabric woven from fibers of the flax plant.

Linen is a classical warm weather fabric. Men's linen sportcoats and suits are traditional, and linen is also used for women's sportswear, dresses and jackets. Like rayon, linen requires frequent ironing, for it crumples easily. This is also one of its charms; the crumpled linen jacket of the southern aristocrat has its own elan.

Vintage linens can be handwashed, though dry-cleaning works better for bulkier garments like jackets. Iron when still slightly damp, or with a steam iron on high setting. Linen/cotton blends require less care; there are also some linen/synthetic blends available that are more or less wash-and-wear.

Wool

A fabric woven from fibers derived from the fleece of sheep.

Wool is the classical cold weather fabric, sometimes scratchy but always warm. As a fine fiber, it is used in jackets, suits, overcoats and women's sportswear; as a coarser fiber in sweaters and knitted wear.

Woolen garments should be dry-cleaned to prevent shrinkage, although sweaters can be handwashed in Woolite, laid flat and blocked to size while drying. Wool far outlasts its modern acrylic cousins, which have a tendency to pill after only a few wearings. Wool/acrylic blends are easier to care for, while retaining most of the durability of wool.

Now let's look at fabrics classified by the nature of their weave, rather than by their fiber components.

Crepe

A thin, light fabric of silk, cotton or other fiber, with a finely crinkled or ridged surface.

The characteristic crinkle of crepe is the same crinkle we're familiar with in the rolls of crepe paper that often festoon festivities.

Silk crepe is the finest of all and is found mostly in vintage evening wear circa 1920-1950. Cotton crepe was generally used in daytime wear of the same period. Crepe is light and clingy, and easier to care for than some of its vintage cousins. You never have to iron it; ironing crepe, in fact, ruins it completely because it presses out the crinkles which are its essence.

Crepes must be dry cleaned, period. Even handwashing destroys the texture of the fabric, and crepe is super-susceptible to shrinkage as well. Crepe is rarely used in modern fashions, and although there may be synthetic crepes available I have never come across any.

Satin

A smooth, glossy fabric of rayon, silk, acetate or other fiber in which the filling threads are interlaced with the warp at widely separated intervals to produce the effect of an unbroken surface.

Smooth says it, glossy as the surface of a high mountain lake on a windless morning. Silk satins are the finest of all and are found mostly in vintage evening wear, lingerie, scarves and men's dress shirts. Rayon satins are almost as fine as their more aristocratic cousin. Modern synthetic satins of acetate and the like have the sheen of satin but none of the suppleness of the vintage variety. Synthetic satins rarely move with your body; they are apt to be stiff.

Silk and rayon satins can be handwashed in the same way as most variations of their fabric families. Synthetic satins don't wash well, and should be dry cleaned to avoid stiffening into armor. All satins should only be ironed on the reverse side of the fabric, either when slightly damp (if vintage) or with a steam iron on low setting.

Taffeta

A medium-weight fabric of rayon, silk, acetate or other fiber, usually smooth, crisp, lustrous and plain-woven, with a fine crosswise rib effect.

What is most characteristic of taffeta is its reflective quality, the way it catches the light and seems to shimmer. This is especially true of taffetas that interweave two or three colors of thread to produce an iridescent effect.

Taffeta has been used in many periods of history, but in twentieth century fashion it nearly disappeared after the Edwardian era until it resurfaced in the 1950s. During the 50s it was widely used as a dress-up fabric in skirts and date dresses for the teen set. Silk and rayon taffeta is usually found only in turn-of-the-century styles; by the time 1950 rolled around, acetate replaced its forbearers.

Taffeta can be fun to wear for its iridescence, but it is less supple than many other dress-up fabrics. Like sequined evening gowns, it is more fun to look at than to touch.

Taffeta should be dry cleaned and ironed with a steam iron at a medium setting.

Tweed

A coarse woolen cloth, usually handspun and handwoven in Scotland. The fabric is woven in a twill weave, in which filling threads are woven over one, then under two, warp threads to produce a characteristic diagonal pattern.

Tweed is the classic fabric of the country gentleman and gentlewoman. While numerous machine-made reproductions abound, fine tweed is still produced by hand primarily in Scotland, and Harris Tweed remains the mark of the country aristocrat. Tweeds are handsome, rugged, and used almost exclusively in suits, jackets and sportswear for men and women.

Tweed garments should be dry cleaned like other woolens. With proper care they will last a lifetime.

Gabardine

A firm woven fabric of wool, cotton or spun rayon, with a twill weave.

Tweeds are coarse; gabardines are fine. Wool gabardines don't scratch the way many woolen fabrics do. Some gabardines combine wool with rayon or cotton to increase the fineness of texture. As far as I know, there is no such thing as synthetic gabardine.

Gabardine is found in vintage sportswear, jackets and men's shirts. Particularly to be prized are old gabardine western shirts, which keep cowboys warmer in winter than their cotton counterparts.

Gabardine should be dry cleaned, and ironed only with a steam iron at a medium/high setting. A hot dry iron will make the matte finish of the fabric acquire an unwanted sheen.

Velvet

A fabric of silk, rayon, acetate or other fiber, sometimes having a cotton backing, with a thick, soft pile formed of the loops of the warp.

Luxurious and supple, velvet is both elegant and sexy. Quality ranges widely, from the premium silk velvets found in slinky 30s evening dresses to synthetic "velveteens" that retain little of velvet's essence but the nap. The higher quality the velvet, the more supple to the touch. If it feels like velvet but moves like corduroy it's probably velveteen or some recent offshoot.

Look for velvet gowns, jackets, hats, bags, skirts and robes. Men's velvet jackets have a special elan, and can transform the wearer into a 19th century dandy. A velvet evening gown makes a lady feel like a Lady.

Fine vintage velvets must be dry cleaned; synthetic velvets and velveteens can usually be washed. All velvets should be ironed only on the reverse side of the fabric, with a steam iron on low/medium setting. Steaming them works well too.

Voile

A fabric of silk, rayon, cotton, or other fiber, with an open, canvas-like weave.

The word *voile* comes from the French *veile*, which means veil. The name is well chosen to describe this fabric which is ethereal, diaphanous, and light as a feather.

Vintage voile is found primarily in afternoon tea dresses and evening wear. A voile tea dress is what you'd expect to see a stylish lady of 1931 wearing with a big straw picture hat while she plays croquet on an impeccably manicured lawn. Voile is an incredibly romantic fabric and wearing it makes you feel as if you just stepped out of the pages of *The Great Gatsby*.

Voile can usually be handwashed, particularly if it's made of silk and not susceptible to shrinkage like cotton. Wash it gently, roll it in a towel to absorb excess moisture, and iron while still slightly damp. If the fabric is really old and quite fragile you may want to dry clean it instead.

There are a number of synthetic voiles available which require less delicate care. But none of the synthetics can match the sheer floatiness of vintage voile.

Synthetics

Synthetics include nylon (the grandma of synthetics), acetate, acrylic, polyester, and the whole range of new fabrics that appear so rapidly these days it's hard to keep track of their names—let alone analyze their various characteristics.

My own prejudice against synthetics comes from the fact that fabrics composed of natural fibers tend to be more durable, more delightful to the touch and more responsive to the natural movements of the body: they allow the pores to breathe. Since most synthetics lack this quality wearing them in effect encases your body in a lightweight set of armor.

There is no question, however, that most synthetic fabrics are easier to care for and give you the convenience of wash-and-wear. While they don't last nearly as long as natural fabrics, many people in our throwaway culture don't find this a drawback.

Some of the latest synthetics, particularly those used in dancewear like Lycra and Qiana, do have a lot going for them; as a dancer I appreciate both the sexy swirls and instant drip-dry these fabrics offer. They are also great for traveling as they don't require ironing to look picture-perfect. I do include these fabrics in my boutique, and they are always good sellers that show off a body in style.

I'm particularly prejudiced against polyester (usually substituted for cotton) and acrylic (usually substituted for wool). My primary objection to these particular synthetics is their tendency to pill, which I mentioned earlier. After only a few wearings and washings, you're stuck with these nasty little pills of fabric all over the place. Which turns your fifty-dollar outfit into something that looks like last week's news.

A good compromise seems to be emerging in fabrics which blend the natural with the synthetic, particularly those which have a ratio of only 20-30% synthetic to 70-80% natural fiber. The best of these blends combine the qualities of natural fibers with the ease of care offered by synthetics. My favorite dancing skirt is a blend of rayon and (gasp!) polyester. I must admit I'm happy not to have to cart my travel iron along with me everywhere to keep this skirt looking fresh and pressed. If it were 100% rayon, it would require ironing each time I unpacked it from my suitcase.

STYLE

Once you know fabrics, cheap chic buying becomes a question of taste and style. What I buy may be old, but I always keep my eye out for new fashion trends. I flip through the pages of *Vogue* whenever I'm at a news-stand, and I pay careful attention to what style-conscious teens have decided is *in*, for their impact on the fashion world is even greater than *Vogue's*. This awareness helps me anticipate trends and capitalize on them. Keep up to date, just as you would if your boutique were a shop.

But also be careful not to overshoot your mark. In Manhattan, I currently keep myself stocked in classic styles of the 1950s and 1960s (which are not, I might add, my favorite periods of fashion); the same tight black sheath dresses and gold lamé mini-skirts the New Wave constituency gobbles up might be totally inappropriate for a mid-western market. There's a definite time lag before east coast fashions infiltrate the rest of the country, sometimes as much as two years. In fact, the time lag is such that by the time this book is in print the very New Wave styles

I mention here will probably be hot sellers in Milwaukee and I'll be busy plugging into the latest whims of New Yorkers. So it goes.

In any case, this up-to-the-minute trendiness is only one component of the well-stocked flea boutique. For your business to thrive, you must also appeal to a broader market. The bulk of my stock is comprised of contemporary, as opposed to trendy, fashions; these are both vintage styles that have resurfaced on a broad scale (like dirndl skirts and colorful cotton sundresses) and current reproductions that reflect their ancestry. Both are available to the discriminating buyer in fleadom.

There are also classic perennial favorites, timeless in their appeal. Well-cut jackets are always in demand, as are good wool and cashmere sweaters, silk scarves, and furs that have survived the years intact. There are a number of standard cheap chic items that persist as best sellers no matter what else is happening in the fashion world. These include rayon Hawaiian shirts (harder to find as the years go by, but always hot items); silk and rayon lingerie from the 30s and 40s; leather motorcycle jackets in particular and good leather jackets in general; embroidered jackets from the Korean War era; silk, rayon and cotton Japanese kimonos and Chinese robes and jackets; vintage and contemporary Western shirts; silk blouses and shirts of any era; classic men's hats like fedoras, Panamas and peaked caps; vintage vests, both casual and formal; good leather belts of all description.

Your stock should also include practical, durable clothing such as cotton T-shirts, tank tops and turtlenecks; rugged outdoor wear like chamois shirts, military survival clothes and just about anything manufactured by L.L. Bean, Pendleton and like. That way you'll have something for the sportster as well as the hipster.

Always buy as much good men's clothing as possible. It's harder to come by, and your male customers will not only appreciate you're remembering them—they'll also be willing to pay more than the ladies, who have a larger selection to choose from. Vests, jackets, shirts, ties, hats, suspenders. All great sellers, and unisexually applicable as well.

True antique period pieces, such as Victorian lace blouses and 1920s beaded flapper dresses, should be in excellent condition and eminently wearable. Keep the price tags on these items high; they don't come your way that often and earn their keep as "stars" which people can admire while making more modest purchases. It's always advisable to have a few "stars" in your stock, super-primo items that class up your act and draw people over to your display. I'm happy to spend $15 on a lovely embroidered silk kimono (when I'm not lucky enough to get it for a dollar). Eventually, someone will buy it for $50, and meanwhile everyone can oo and ah and probably stick around to buy one of the $5 blouses I got for a quarter.

What not to buy? Anything in bad repair, damaged or torn to the point it's not worth your (or you customer's) energy to repair. Every flaw is an opportunity for the buyer to knock down your price. I like having my merchandise clean, pressed, and in mint or almost-mint condition. Avoid odd sizes, especially those wonderful old crepes in size 44, or those 1920s pumps that would maybe fit a large midget. Buy for average sizes, with some allowance for biggies and smallies on either end.

Beware of buying too much clothing that is strictly of the costume variety. True, fleadom offers people a magical array of the funny and the fantastic, and this is one of its charms. But remember that although many people will be delighted with the 1950s taffeta "first prom" dress, how

many of them would actually *wear* it? (Now in New York, where people like to scream their individuality, they probably *would* wear it. But Manhattan is the exception, not the rule). Do include some strictly costume-y clothing of historical interest to make them smile, but don't inundate your stock with it. You want cash for your efforts, not just appreciative grins.

The golden rule is to buy as if you were buying for your own wardrobe (or your lover's wardrobe). I've seen a number of would-be buyers flounder because they bought for what they *thought* the flea market clientele wanted rather than using their own good fashion sense. All of them had incredible wardrobes, culled primarily from fleadom, but what they bought for potential customers was almost entirely tacky and trashy. Now the best of tacky is a style in itself, and I love to occasionally dress to be classically tacky, but tackiness reflected in the totality of your stock is going to bring you a whole lot of laughs and not much bread. People want clothes they can wear in their daily lives.

On the question of pants. For some vendors, this is a specialty in itself. But for the broader flea boutique, pants pose some problems. That's because people have no place to try them on, unless you devise an ingenious portable dressing room (which I did for awhile, but gave up as not worth the effort). Blouses, jackets, skirts, even dresses can be tried on over whatever the customer is wearing to give some idea of fit. Pants can't. So I usually include only pants of the less tailored variety, like drawstring pants, because that eliminates the problem of the try-on. If you do include tailored pants, or jeans, it's essential that you accurately measure waist and length and mark them accordingly. No one wants to buy a pair of pants on spec unless they're super cheap. They want to know if they're going to fit.

You'll also want to gear your stock to the current season. The flea market is impulse-buy territory; people are not apt to plan ahead for the coming winter in the middle of July. So keep your heavy sweaters stashed for September when people are thinking fall rather than hauling them in and out during a heat wave. Ditto for lightweight summer clothing. When there's a winter chill in the air it's time to pack up your sundresses and save them for next spring, when they'll bring you more profit. The only exceptions to this general rule are fine furs and good leather jackets, which people will buy as future investments, but even these will command higher price tags in the proper season.

The Display section in *The Professional Flea* discussed how to display your wares to best advantage, and how to keep your stock in tip-top shape. But the core of your operation is always your buying, and I've given away all the "trade secrets" I know about successful buying here. The rest is up to you. As a martial artist, I always welcome worthy opponents, and the same is true in my flea market business. If I have helped to make you into a serious competitor, I'm delighted.

──────────── Joel ────────────

Joel Kaufmann's Canal Street market in the Soho district of Manhattan helped launch me into the big city. Once again, my flea biz brought in bucks while I got my other acts together.

Now in its ninth year of operation, Joel's market has become a hive of activity for local fleas. Bordering on Chinatown, where street vendors hawk their wares at rock bottom prices, Canal Street, with its surreal hodgepodge of wholesale plastics, plumbing and electrical supplies, is the perfect setting for a flea market. It draws a cosmopolitan spectrum of buyers: recent immigrants from all nations, stylish young punks, oh-so-chic Soho habitues, and just plain folk.

I interviewed Joel sitting atop a shiny new Buick on Greene St. The owner of the vehicle graciously permitted our encampment while he shopped, with the sole stipulation that we keep the beer bottles off his paint job. Joel responded with his characteristic charm, complimenting the Buick man on the classy comfort of our roosting spot.

Witty, wise, and cynically human, Joel is the ingredient that makes his market work.

> *I spend the whole day out here, and this place is really my little barony. It's interesting running a little barony. If I don't like you, you find out soon enough, because I start forgetting about your space, I start doing things like that. And it's kind of enough to push you out of here. A couple times people have said, hey, this is not really democratic, and I said, you know—you're right. This has nothing to do with democracy. This is a feudal society.*
>
> *One reason this market is so good is that before anyone starts to sell here, they're pretty well prepped up. It's like I give them LaMaze before they come out and have childbirth here. That saves me a lot of misery: there's no misunderstandings, no confusion. And a lot of vendors act as my surrogates. They help people out, they take new people under their wing—which is normally something I would do.*
>
> *There are vendors who have been with us for six, seven years. Obviously, there's a pecking order; sometimes they lord it over*

people. But in some ways, they deserve it, having struggled this hard. This place wasn't always a pleasure to sell at. We didn't make any money those first couple years.

This market works now because we've been here nine years, and people have become habituated to it. There's a whole tradition behind it, which really has nothing to do with Soho; it has everything to do with Canal Street. We can actually claim, I think justifiably, that we built Canal St. on weekends. When we first opened on Sundays, there were only two or three stores that stayed open. Now on Saturdays and Sundays, Canal St. is mobbed.

This is the only real junk market in the city, and it's easily one of the best markets I've ever seen in my life. We have so much interesting stuff, there's such a variety. It's spectacular. I've seen a lot of what I consider good markets: big daddies. They're bigger— we're easily not the biggest by any stretch of the imagination. But that is exactly one of our strengths. On a good day here, we draw about 12,000 buyers. Divide that by fifty dealers and it gets pretty.

People constantly try to figure out how to do this. They see a full flea market, and they do some quick computations and think, jesus christ, this guy's making a fortune! Then they go off and try it themselves—and end up with 1.2 dealers. They think the flea business is easy; that all you have to do is be there and people come. Well, running a flea market is infinitely more work than doing a booth.

I do everything from paper work to cleaning up, and for every day I'm out here, I'd say there's at least 1.5 days of paperwork. Come the weekend, and I'm here by 5:30 or 6 AM. Believe me, if you don't think I sleep well—not so much Saturdays, Saturdays I'm wound up—but Sunday night! Wow! Does one get blotto!

For the size of business this is, and the dollar value of its sales, for one person to run it is kinda insane. I mean totally insane. There should be two people running this operation, and if everyone weren't so cooperative, it wouldn't work. There's a good understanding, a good relationship, a good level of cooperation here. Everyone understands the way it works.

This is a serious enterprise. It looks like a shambles, it looks kinda half-assed, but it really isn't. The amount of organization and labor that goes in, not only by me but by everybody else, is phenomenal. You have to get the stuff, you have to edit it, you have to schlepp it over here, you have to take the loss on something when you fuck up. And da-da, da-da, da-da. It's very labor intensive.

The sales tax card the state requires got rid of our basket cases. Either you make it, or you leave. People are really naked out here, and that can be unnerving. You are what you do out here, and just as good as you are or as crummy as you are, everybody's going to see you.

A lot of vendors here are people who have already made it in their fields; we've had a lot of stockbrokers and doctors who dropped out. Drop outs. They use the market as a transition, as a stopping point for awhile. They're making money and sort of contemplating their navals before doing something else.

I don't envision myself doing this forever. There's a period of time for which I'll do it—maybe another two, three years. Then there's other things to do.

Meanwhile, it's fun to watch people. I love that. As the summer progresses, it's even more enjoyable. I have fun. I love looking at people.

We've been all over the country—you name it. We do the Rose Bowl in California, we go everywhere.
You meet a lot of nice people in this line.
—George and Joyce, vendors
New Hope, PA Market

6

The Nomadic Flea

Amarillo, Texas. I screech to a halt in front of a Disabled Veterans store. It's hot and I'm tired, but there's nothing like finding a classic 30s Panama hat for a buck to perk up a wilting spirit. The leathery old man behind the counter points me to a few more shops down the road and soon I've crammed several bags full of super scores into the back of the van. By the time I hit the road again I'm revived and rarin' to go, ready for the highway.

Road fleaing is a great way to break up the miles. I've both bought and sold on the road, and this path takes me straight into the heart of America. I love it.

Buying on the road requires no more than your usual alertness, good maps, and a sturdy vehicle equipped to handle both back country roads and city traffic. When you can afford the time, stay off the superhighways entirely. You really see the country this way and are ready to leap out whenever opportunities present themselves along the roadside.

Watch for garage sales and local flea markets when you cruise through towns on the weekend. During the week, keep a sharp eye out for secondhand stores. When you stop in a town for gas or beer or food, ask the locals if there are any thrift shops around. Someone always seems to know. And do a quick scan of the phone book just to make sure you're not missing anything. I usually don't.

When you're pressed for time and traveling the freeways, you can still stop at selected exit towns along the way. I usually avoid congested areas unless I'm already familiar with the turf. City traffic snarls in unknown

territory can be a nightmare, especially during a summer heat wave. If you do go to shop in a large city you'll need a good local map with a street directory and a consultation with the local yellow pages and classifieds. Go for clusters; several shops located in the same general neighborhood. Ditto for garage sales, if you're passing through on a weekend.

I've found the most lucrative weekday stops to be in medium-sized towns in the 35,000 to 100,000 population range. Such towns are large enough to harbor at least a few thrift shops and small enough to maneuver through with ease. Smaller cities are also more likely to underprice their goods. The same Persian lamb coat that would cost you fifty bucks in Milwaukee may well be had for ten in Bristol, Tennessee. Even crossroads burgs may have at least one secondhand store, but you can't be sure. If you're eating up the miles stick to small cities near highway exits. You'll nearly always find a couple of shops to browse.

Becoming a true road flea—buying and selling your way across the country—requires more careful planning. You'll need to haul your display equipment, merchandise, and personal gear, and still have space for new acquisitions and traveling comfort. Serious road fleas should work out of a larger vehicle; a pick-up, camper, or van is usually sufficient, although some fleas travel in school busses and Winnebagos. With current gas prices you'll probably want to opt for a roomy but gas-efficient vehicle.

Whether you're traveling to a specific destination or simply doing a grande tour of fleadom, you'll need to plan your trip to coordinate with weekend sales. As a seller you may want to visit the same large cities you bypassed as a buyer because urban markets command higher prices than their more rural cousins.

To plan your route first check the directory and resource list at the end of the book. Though many of them are updated regularly, there are always new markets springing up and old ones are apt to change location. If you want to include a stop in a city not covered in any listings you'll have to do your own sleuthing. Secondhand shops usually know about the market so you could get in some buying on Friday while you do your research. You can also consult your waitress, gas station attendant, check-out clerk, and local classifieds and buy/sell papers. If there's a market you'll find it. Someone always knows.

Always arrive at your chosen destination on Friday. Even when you know the location of the market, local geography can be confusing. If the market isn't listed in a directory, you'll also need to find out about opening times, entry fees, and reservation policies. You can rarely arrive at a flea market at noon on Saturday and be assured of a space.

Once you've arrived at the market, bought your space, and settled in, follow your usual routine. First buy, then sell. If you're working with a partner who can set up shop while you buy, great. If not, lock up your vehicle and cruise the action for early morning bargains. The real customers rarely appear before noon anywhere so a later set-up will not cut into your sales and can multiply your stock.

When you're doing a two-day stint you'll need to plan for an overnight. Some markets allow vendors to camp on-site, but I've always found this rather dreary. A dormant flea market is usually no more than a parking lot, which isn't my idea of the great outdoors. I usually research local campsites and head for the woods.

When all else fails, there's always the KOA. You can do your laundry, take a hot shower, and recoup your energy for the Sunday market. If you're traveling first class you can even stay in a motel. Better yet, see how many visits to long-lost friends you can include in your itinerary. This boosts the spirit without breaking the pocketbook, and local friends will often be your most valuable sources of information.

The ranks of road fleas are swelling every day, and many retired folks have found their travels in fleadom keep them young and give them a sizeable enough income that they don't have to rely on pensions and retirement funds. There's been much ado in recent years about the plight of older people who feel useless and lost after they retire from the work force. This is certainly not a problem for the senior citizens of fleadom. Slim is pushing seventy and still hauls the bulk of his heavy oak furniture in and out of his trailer by himself. There's plenty more like him.

If you want to really get to know America, if you want to find out what this great big crazy country is all about, there's no better way to do it than becoming a nomadic flea. Every time I start to feel that America is just one gigantic McDonaldland full of mindless clones and petty bureaucrats I take to the road again. And every time I hit the open highway I'm amazed by the wonderful local character which enriches each region of our land, the warmth, the humor, and the solid practical wisdom of the Americans who populate the country-within-a-country I call fleadom.

Father Hill

Father Larry Hill was a parish priest in Santa Fe, New Mexico, where the Catholic tradition runs as deep as the Rio Grande gorge. When a heart condition forced him to restrict his activities he gave up his parish and began to work primarily with senior citizens. It was these 'old people' who led him to discover the flea market. On their meager budgets the flea market was obviously the best deal in town.

For the past two years Father Hill has conducted a weekly mass at Trader Jack's market. He was on vacation when I visited Santa Fe, so I was unable to interview him personally. But I did ask Trader Jack and Caggie how his flea market parish was faring, and Caggie had this to say:

> *Oh sure, he still comes out on Sundays to give mass. We had an Easter mass and nearly forty people showed up—and it was cold that day! I think it's a great idea, and they love it. These vendors are here early in the morning till late at night and they don't have time to go to mass. This way, a neighbor can watch their stuff while they go to mass.*
>
> *He started it because he said if the people can't come to him, he'd come to where the people are.*

I also wanted to let Father Hill speak to you in his own words, so I constructed the following passage from direct quotes given to Stephen Terrell for an article that appeared in the *Santa Fe Reporter* (September 17, 1981):

> *I admire these people out here, I admire how hard they work. They're out here every weekend trying to make a living. When can they go to church? They're so pooped when they get done, and a lot of them have to drive back to Espanola or the little villages up north. They are all good people, and I've gotten to know quite a few of them. I'm beginning to recognize faces every week.*
>
> *Reaganomics is going to drive a lot of people out here. People will go to stores and see what they want, and then come out here and buy it second-hand. I shop for the old people. These ladies can't*

afford to pay $35 for a new purse, but here you can pick one up for a quarter or a dime.

Jesus usually preached on the hillsides, out in the open. I'd like to think that this is the way the Lord would do it. He didn't need any fancy cathedrals. The church is coming back to reality, and this is reality here: poor people trying to make a living.

Service does not just consist of opening the door of a church. Who says religion shouldn't be fun? If you can't be happy in the face of the Lord, then forget it.

This is a serious enterprise. It looks like a shambles, it looks kind of half-assed, but it really isn't. The amount of organization and labor that go in is phenomenal.

You have to get the stuff, you have to edit it, you have to schlepp it over here. And da-da, da-da, da-da.

It's very labor intensive.

—Joel, owner
Canal Street Market, NYC

7

The Responsible Flea

It's a perfectly beautiful late fall afternoon in New York and I am busy berating myself for having missed what was the best flea market sales day for weeks. Isaac listens patiently while I make excuses to myself out loud.

"I didn't know the weather was going to be this good," I moan. "I mean, I listened to the weather report and I thought it was going to be lousy today. And I was tired, and all the way uptown, and I didn't feel like making the effort to come back last night. Especially since the weather report said cold and windy."

Isaac nods perfunctorily, and allows me to continue my monologue.

"And I even got up at seven this morning and looked out the window and it looked dreary and grey." He nods again. "So I figured I might as well crawl back into bed and sleep in for a change. How was I supposed to know the weather was going to turn sunny and clear? Damn! I needed the money this weekend too. God knows whether there will even be any more market days now that winter's coming!" I shut up for a minute.

"Well, you know what I think?" Isaac looks me straight in the eye. "I think you should take all this energy you're spending berating yourself and do something more productive with it."

"Like what?" I ask gloomily.

"Like—well, listen, you're a martial artist, aren't you?"

"Yeah, sure. But today I feel more like a fool than a fighter." I begin to pace the kitchen floor, spurred into action by his reference to the warrior in me. I begin to let my animal take charge.

Lightning fast, Isaac darts in low. As he rises to deliver a series of quick, light blows, I break through his rhythm and parry perfectly, feigning a kick to the groin. He steps back with a grin, graciously acknowledging the point I scored.

"Hey, you're getting pretty good, Isaac. That was real nice, the way you took ground with that low dart. It came out of nowhere."

"Thanks. I'm getting there. I think it has to do with that funny alertness you keep telling me a warrior needs. Don't you think that fleas need the same kind of alertness?"

"Yeah, I do. So what are you getting at?"

"Only what you already know. That the center of the warrior's job is cultivating the self-discipline she needs to be ready for anything."

"Of course." My eyes are clear now, my inner radar alert and active—despite the loss of a flea market day.

"So maybe you should write a chapter about self-discipline for the flea. I mean it's obvious."

"You're right. I never thought about it that way before."

"So stop bitching and start writing." Giving me a final grin Isaac walks into the studio and picks up his airbrush.

I take a couple of good deep breaths, allowing the air to fill me up from the base of my spine to the top of my head. Then I sit down at the typewriter:

Fleadom is an open market based on the free exchange of goods, and most fleas choose to participate in it precisely because of the freedom it affords them. When you're a flea, you're always your own boss: you can choose what you want to sell and when and where you want to sell it. The freedom of individuals to control their own resources is what makes the flea market economy at least as American as Mom's apple pie.

Freedom—as opposed to license—always carries with it the burden of responsibility. Throughout this book, we've discussed responsible freedom in terms of the right and proper business exchange. The importance of treating customers and buying sources with honesty and respect led us to the obvious conclusion that good karma fleas have more fun and more friends. They also build better businesses; businesses that endure in time.

But there is one final aspect of responsibility: the dialogue which is strictly between you and yourself. This is where the self-discipline comes in.

If you want to enter fleadom as a serious professional, rather than occasional hobbyist, you'll need to cultivate the self-discipline to rouse yourself into action at the god-awful hour of 5 AM so you have time to change the right front tire that went flat last night and still make it to the market in time for the early morning bargain buys. You'll sometimes have to brave the elements when you'd rather stay in bed; to sacrifice your druthers and high-tail it to the market even if you'd rather enjoy a leisurely Sunday brunch.

This kind of self-discipline has nothing to do with stoicism or the protestant work ethic. It's based purely on the nitty gritty facts of life: when you don't make it to the market you don't take in any money. And if the flea market is your major income source, or if your operating money is down to zilch, you simply can't afford to play hookie. This is basic survival economics.

I'm no stoic. When I'm fat and sleek I will indeed stay home rather than pull the rain tarps in and out on one of those on again/off again days. But there have been many times—and I'm sure there will be more—when I simply couldn't afford to miss a single market day, whatever the weather or my druthers.

During these lean and mean times I have usually been the model of the responsible flea. But as the anecdote that opens this chapter reveals, I am by no means immune to those inner voices which try to drown out the words of my hard-nosed business self. Whenever I give in to the pleasure-loving members of my inner board of directors during a time of true financial need I only end up berating myself for my folly. I don't even get to enjoy my holiday.

Now I *knew* that particular weekend what I had always known: you can never, never trust the weather report. You can also never be certain that a perfect morning won't make an about-face and turn into a hailstorm, or that a dreary dawn won't transform into a perfect blue sky.

There are going to be times when the flea market isn't fun at all. Days of slow sales that make you sing the bad day blues are but one of the events that make the life of the flea seem like a whole lot of hard work and not much fun. There are no real freebies in life and fleadom is no exception. As delightful as a good haul at a rummage sale or taking in the bucks on a boom day may be, there is, of course, another side of the coin.

Remember that flea markets are weekend operations. This means you may have to sacrifice some of the night life the rest of the world is enjoying on Friday and Saturday nights, unless you have the kind of

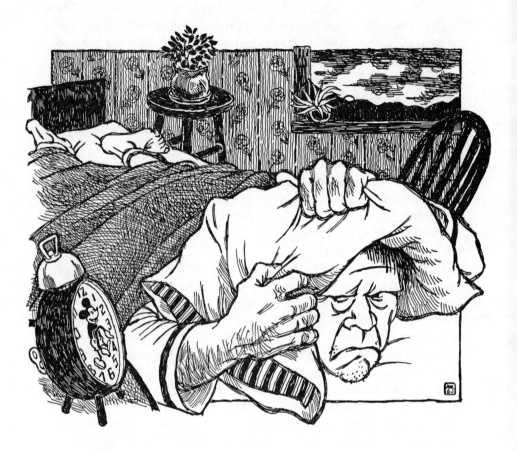

metabolism that leaves you refreshed after three or four hours of sleep. You may also have to wake up to the harsh intrusion of an alarm clock. Market days are long and sometimes grueling, even when the money is rolling in. As Joel puts it, "Wow! Does one get blotto!" And it's no fun at all if you're nursing a bitchy hangover.

You can allow yourself the luxury of skipping sales days when you're ahead of the game financially, but there's no room for luxury when it comes to buying. Used merchandise dealers must be continually vigilant buyers; they can't just call up the wholesaler and ask for a new shipment of stock. Unless you continue to buy you'll wind up with nothing to sell.

Like the account exec who *must* attend the sales conference in Des Moines even if she'd rather catch the opening of the latest Balanchine ballet, you *must* attend the rummage sale or garage sale or auction you know is vital to your specialty. Unless you are actually bedridden, *make* that important sale—even if it's twenty miles away and starts at 8 AM and you tied one on last night. You cannot afford to miss it. You can bet your boots your competitors will be there, creaming off the best of the bargains.

So you get the picture. To make it work you've got to be willing to work at it. Self-discipline will make you a better business person. It will also hone you into the lean and mean warrior you need to become to survive the economic battleground.

If you embark on your adventure into fleadom with no illusions about the realities of the road you've chosen you'll find it to be rich in rewards, tangible and intangible. Amazing treasures will come your way and you'll be part of a wonderful ebb and flow of humanity, sharing the magic of stories swapped among fleas, unexpected reunions with old friends and the making of new friendships.

If you travel this road with a combination of good old common sense and a sense of wonder that leaves you open to whatever comes your way you'll be the kind of flea who can add a hearty 'Amen!' to Jerry Junk's words:

"I always have, always will, get a kick out of doing this. Sitting out here, being with people, and making a buck. Making honest bucks."

Amen!

APPENDIX I
Resources: Directories & Publications

The publications noted here are primarily oriented to specialty collectors and dealers. They cover events such as auctions, farm sales and antique shows which exist outside the flea market circuit per se. Most include mini-directories of flea markets, which are useful for the particular region covered by the publication.

As more and more antiquers recognize the legitimacy of flea markets, papers formerly devoted to collectibles buffs are now expanding their flea market coverage. The Antique Gazette, for instance, recently added a special flea market supplement to each issue. It's gratifying to see the gap that once existed between antiquers and fleas merging into a cooperative coexistence, profitable to all.

It's also nice to see fleadom creating its own journalistic resource network.

DIRECTORIES AND PUBLICATIONS

Antique Gazette, 929 Davidson Dr., Nashville, TN 37205, (615) 352-0941. Monthly, $1.00/issue, $9.00/12 issue subscription.

Comprehensive trade paper featuring articles, book reviews, and excellent classifieds to buy/sell/trade just about every collectible specialty. East coast listings and ads for antique shows, shops, auctions and special events. New flea market supplement includes listings and ads for east coast markets.

The Jersey Devil, P.O. Box 202, Lambertville, NJ 08530, (609) 397-2400. Monthly, 60¢/issue, $6.00/12 issue subscription.

Trade news and feature articles, including updates on AAMP (Alliance of American Market Places) activities. East coast listings and ads for flea markets, antique shows and auctions.

Joel Slaters Antiques and Auction News, Box B, Marietta, PA 17547, (717) 426-1956. Fortnightly, 50¢/issue, $12.00/24 issue subscription.

East coast listings and ads for flea markets, antique shows and auctions. Short feature articles. Excellent, comprehensive coverage of auctions, estate and farm sales.

National Journal, P.O. Box 3121 Wescoeville, PA 18106, (215) 432-1090. Sample issue $1.00, $9.00/12 issue subscription.

Monthly collectors' newspaper (now in magazine format) with features on antique collectibles, and particular emphasis on glass, pottery and American dinnerware. Calendar of upcoming events of antique shows and collectors' conventions covers all states and Canada. Includes monthly book reviews and Art Deco Swap Spot.

SwapMeet USA, Box 200, Grover City, CA 93433. Semi-annual, $6.00/ 2 issue subscription.

Each issue includes a comprehensive annotated directory of flea markets in the US and in Canada (over 2,500 listings), along with indepth articles on specific flea markets and successful selling tips. They also publish an annual entitled Fairs USA, which sells for $12.00, and can be obtained from the same address.

Y-Not Antique and Flea Market Directory, P.O. Box 8561, Ft. Lauderdale, FL 33310, (305) 739-5961. Monthly, $1.00/issue, $9.00/12 issue subscription.

Southeast listings of flea markets, auctions and antique shows, with heavy emphasis on Florida. Some national listings from other regions. Most listings include information as well as location. Short articles of relevant interest to fleas.

BOOKS

The books reviewed here are informative, well-written, and full of additional information and resource lists. They cover areas not included, or given only a passing glance, in this book.

I'm glad to pass on others' expertise, and suggest you pursue your research into fleadom by ordering any of these books which spark your particular enthusiasms from the publishers.

Wallace-Homestead Flea Market Price Guide (Third Edition), by Robert W. Miller, paperback, 252pp., extensive photographs, $7.95, 1981, Wallace-Homestead Book Co., 1912 Grand Ave., Des Moines, IO 50305. (Solicits updates from collector/dealers who send stamped, self-addressed envelopes).

Best of the breed in the wacky world of perennial flea collectibles and current hot items. Well-organized, lavishly illustrated with photographs of flea esoterica, Miller covers everything from the blue-chip stocks, like sterling ("if it's marked 'sterling' grab it!"); to old camp (hand-carved Bing Crosby/Bob Hope bottle stoppers); new kitsch (Air Force Academy "football programs, brochures, service stripes, insignia—all sought after"), and the usual carnival glass, brass beds, campaign buttons and porcelain dolls that are the bread and butter of the collectibles market.

Miller notes what stars are rising ("Like Buck Rogers in the 30's, one day Star Wars items will bring high prices"); holding their own ("Plumbing accessories—everything *including* the kitchen sink is collectible"); faltering ("Beam Bottles: This was a 'hot' item ten years ago. It's cooled off but the 'faithful still collect'"); and stone cold dead ("Pet Rock: This object was a craze a few years ago. There's even a Pet Rock cemetary").

Any flea who aspires to join the wonderful world of profit from little, looney, sometimes lovely old and new collectibles, should start their education with this book. Prices fluctuate, but Miller is thorough in his evaluations, solicits reader input, and gives good estimates of resale value on established items, general guidelines on less common items, and says he really doesn't know when he really doesn't know. Fun to read, and a good book to put on the bathroom shelf for quick browsing and helpful humor.

Flea Market Handbook, by Robert G. Miner, paperback, 150pp., with photos, $7.95, 1981, Main St. Books, Mechanicsburg, PA 17055. (Order direct from publisher.) Dealer discounts available.

A useful book for Northeast antique buffs with expertise in, and preferably existing collections of, early Americana. Though he dabbles in various collectibles when opportunity knocks on the door of profit, Miner's forte is furniture, and he is an enthusiastic restorer as well as dealer of the antique pieces he sells.

Miner caught the flea bug selling off the less valuable valuables from his own collection at the market. He developed an amazingly prudent 10-year plan to culminate in a profitable small business which would sustain him in style after his retirement a decade later. He's a fanatical record-keeper, and deals in a large enough cash flow that he must untangle the IRS red tape like a shopkeeper.

I'm a lowbrow dimes-into-dollars flea with an aversion to triplicate forms. Ten-year plans and ledger books are not for me. But if you prefer a more conservative approach to fleadom, and have the bucks and know-how to back you up, Miner can teach you the ropes of his trade.

Farmers' Markets of America: A Renaissance, by Robert Sommer, paperback, 94pp., with photos and illustrations, $6.95, 1980, Capra Press, P.O. Box 2068, Santa Barbara, CA 93120.

A well-designed, handsome book full of neo-populist sentiments, including comprehensive charts of veggies and fruits with seasonal cycles, a survey of typical and unusual farmers' markets around the country, and even a fruit and veggie gourmet recipe section.

Sommer loves growing things and shares my enthusiasm about the individual bootstrapping that flea markets and farmers' markets engender. This is a good guide both for the shopper/consumer of homegrown produce and the small grower who wants to learn how to begin and sustain an ongoing business not subject to the insanities of the Dept. of Agriculture's programs, policies and prejudices favoring large corporate farming.

Many flea markets evolved from farmers' markets, and produce growers also sell at diversified flea markets today. Farmers' markets are an important component of fleadom, and Sommer's book is a good introduction to the American pioneer spirit that thrives in communities of small growers across the land.

Collecting Today for Tomorrow, by David Alan Herzog, paperback, 122pp., with photos, $4.95, 1980, Arco Publishing Inc., 219 Park Ave. S., NY, NY 10003.

A great book for collectors and dealers of one of fleadom's zaniest sub-specialties: radio (and early TV) advertising premiums of yesteryear. With the sharp eye of a pop sociologist, Herzog describes the evolution of our media-saturated culture, poking gentle fun at the ghost of an American past he obviously adores.

Tom Mix started it all in the 30's, and was "nothing short of compulsive when it came to offering premiums." The success of Tom Mix secret decoders, magic lights, spinning siren rings and other exotica bearing his 'straight-shooter' trademark led such upstarts as Sergeant Preston, Hopalong Cassidy, the Green Hornet and the legendary Lone Ranger to get in on the action. Herzog notes that "the mark of a true intellectual is to be able to listen to the finale of Rossini's 'William Tell Overture' without thinking of the Lone Ranger," and his understanding of the center of American popular culture is as acute as his expertise about the collectibles he prizes.

The book includes a comprehensive price list of items in both good and mint condition, and his final chapter discusses investments in the future, analyzing which current media kitsch is most likely to soar to collectible status in years to come. Herzog's info gives budding advertising-premium fleas all they need to know to become experts in the field.

The Underground Marketplace: A Guide to New England and the Middle Atlantic States, by Harriet and Jonathan Webster, paperback, 173pp., $6.95, 1981, Universe Books, 381 Park Ave. S., NY, NY 10016.

Webster and Webster have written a witty, functional guide that includes such often-overlooked secondhand sources as post office and police auctions, customs service auctions, government surplus auctions, real estate sales and mail order auctions.

This book is directed more to buyer/collectors than flea market dealers, and even includes highbrow art auctions at such venerable houses as Parke-Bernet. But the Websters know the nuts and bolts of the biz as well as the creme de la creme, and they offer good pragmatic advice for shoestring fleas as well. Especially valuable is their extensive information on how to find out about government and private auctions, and who to write to about getting on the appropriate mailing lists.

Full of pithy one-liners like "to understand the tension of an auction is to look squarely into the soul of money," the Websters' book is textured with anecdotes and is fun to read. I happily forgive their occasional lapses into East coast snobbishness for their lively use of language and their know-how about important sources of bargain-priced merchandise that can help launch fleas into a profitable business.

APPENDIX 2

Flea Markets in the United States and Canada

This list appears courtesy of SwapMeet USA. It is updated semi-annually. To subscribe send $6.00 to SwapMeet USA, Box 200, Grover City, CA 93433. (They also publish an annual entitled FAIRS USA, $12.00).

UNITED STATES

ALABAMA

ADAMSVILLE - Frontier Swap Meet, Docena Rd. (Ensley-Adamsville Cut-Off) Open Every Sat. & Sun, 8 am till dusk. 21 to 35 sellers, $2 per day. Up to 1000 attendance. Bill Barrett, 3713 Midway Road, Adamsville, Ala. 35005. (205) 674-9886.

ATTALLA - Mountain Top Flea Market, on Hwy. 278 West of Gadsden. Open every Sunday. Sellers fee: $2, $4 and $7. 1000 dealers. 30,000 avg. att. Melton Terrell, Rt. 1, Box 317D, Attalla, Al. 35954. Phone (205)589-2706.

BIRMINGHAM - Frontier Swap Meet, Docena Rd. Open every Sat. & Sun., 8 am to dusk. 20 to 35 sellers, $3 & $5 per day. Up to 1000 att. Bill Barrett, Rt. 15, Box 146, Docena Rd., Birmingham, Al. 35224. Phone (205) 786-2117.

BIRMINGHAM - Quality Antique Flea Market, at the State Fairgrounds. 1981 dates are: Oct. 17-18 & 24-25, Nov. 6-7 & 21-22, Dec. 5-6 & 19-20, call for 1982 dates. 250 dealers, $20 per weekend: 10,000 avg. att. Larry or Betty Emery, 1617 McDowell Rd., Jackson, Miss. 39204. Phone (601) 939-8596.

COLLINSVILLE - Collinsville Trade Day, located 6 miles from Collinsville on U.S. 11. Open Sat. and first Monday at 5:30 am.

GADSDEN - 431 Trade Day, 5 miles from Glenco, on Hwy 431. Open every Sat. and Sun. 7 am to 7pm. Up to 75 dealers, $2.50 per space. 2000 avg. attendance. Mona Hyatt, Rt. 9, Glenco, Ata. Ph: (205) 538-5238.

GUNTERSVILLE - The All American Trade Day, on Hwy. 431. Open every Sat. & Sun.. Indoor & Outdoor $3 per day. Karen Rusk, P. O. Box 46, Guntersville, Al. 35976. Phone (205) 878-4921.

JASPER - Hwy. 78 Trade Day. Open every Wed. 5 am to 4 pm. 40 sellers, $1 per space. 2000 avg. attendance. V.C. May, operator.

KILLEN - The Jockey Lot, on Hwy. 72, 8 miles east of Florence. Open every Sat., 8 am to 5 pm and Sun., 1 to 5 pm. Sellers fee: $6 inside, $3 outside. P. O. Box 88, Loretto, Tn. 38469. Phone (205) 757-1722 or (615) 853-6006.

LACON - Lacon Trade Day, 2 miles south of Flakville.

MARLOW - Country Trade Day, at Sellars 4-way Grocery, corner of Co. Rd. 32 & 9. Phone 965-2223.

MILLBROOK - "Just Ou'ta Montgomery" Bonanza Farmers & Flea Market, on I-65 N.S.E. Service Rd. Open every Sat. & Sun. 200 outside spaces, $3 per space, 20 spaces under shed, $5 per space. Phone (205) 285-5144. Mr. Chris Norris, P. O. Box 278, Millbrook, Al. 36054.

ROBERTSDALY - First weekend Trade Daze, 59 south. 1st weekend of month. Phone (205) 947-5932.

SCOTTSBORO - First Monday Trade Day, downtown (around courthouse square). Open First Monday of each Month and Sunday before. 80 dealers, $5 per space, $100 annual permit. Guaranteed same space each mo. 10 to 20,000 avg. att. Scottsboro Police Dept., 916 S. Broad St., Scottsboro, Al. 35768. Phone (205) 574-3333.

TRINITY - Midway Trade Day, on Hwy 24 between Decatur & Moulton. Open every Fri., Sat. and Sun. 60 sellers, $1 to $1.59 per space. 300 to 500 attendance. Flora Alred, Rt. 1, Trinity, Al. 35673. Ph: (205) 974-8057.

WETUMPKA - Trading Post & Auction, on Hwy. 14 West, 1¼ miles west of bridge. Open daily, 8 am to 5 pm. 5 to 45 sellers, 2000 avg weekend att. $5 per day sellers fee. Overnight space with electric (extra). Auction on Fri. night at 7:30 pm sharp. Trading Post, P. O. Drawer 528, Millbrook, Al. 36054. Phone (205) 567-7228.

WOODSTOCK - On U.S. 11. Strickland Memorial Civic Center. Open last Sat. of month. 15 to 50 sellers, $1 per space. 25¢ admission. Thomas Burns, P. O. Box 97, Woodstock, Ala. 35188. Ph: (205) 938-2049.

ARIZONA

APACHE JUNCTION - Apache Park 'n Swap, Apache Trail, (602) 273-1258, mailing address. 3801 E. Washington St., Phoenix, Arizona. 85034. Outdoor facilities, open Fri., Sat. and Sun. 400 dealers and 7500 attendance. 50¢ entrance, dealer's fee, Fri. $3.00, Sat. $3.00 and Sun. $4.00. Food concessions.

BULLHEAD CITY - Claypool's 900 Main St. Open every Sunday, 8 am to 3 pm. October thru May. Free sellers set-up and admission. 1 to 2000 attendance. Claypool's 725 Broadway, Needles, CA 92363. Ph: (714) 326-2109. Antiques, collectibles, jewelry, misc. items and a bake sale.

CASA GRANDE - Tri-Valley Swap Meet, 1300 E. Main St. Open daily, including evenings. Outdoors, 50-100 dealers, $3 per space. Attendance, 300 to 1000 daily. Doug Ballard, 1200 E. Main, Casa Grande, AZ 85222. Ph: (602) 836-5771.

HAVASU CITY - Flea Market, on the corner of Smoketree & McCullough St. Open Sept. thru May. 100 spaces. Claypool & Co., 725 Broadway, Needles, CA 92363. Ph: (714) 326-2109. Attn. Bill Bowers.

FLAGSTAFF - Big Tree Swap Meet - Flea Market. 6500 North Hwy. 89, Take Exit 201 off 1-40. Fri., Sat., Sun. April through November. Overnight camping available. Avg. dealers 50-75. 50¢ parking fee. Avg. att. 5,000. Mgr: N. J. Mathis and R. Willis, P. O. Box 2816, Flagstaff, Arizona, 86003. Ph. (602) 526-2583. Restrictions: No heisi findings, beads, Indian jewelry, food.

NOGALES - Campo Swap Meet, 150 Baffert Dr. 70-80. Dealers fee: $5.50. Att: free. Mgr: Rodrigo Castro, 259 Chula Vista Lane, Nogales, Arizona 85621. Ph: (602) 281-1621. Reservations required.

PARKER - Claypool's Shopping Center. Open 1st and 3rd Saturdays in month. October thru May. 8 am to 3 pm. Free set-up and admission. 10 to 20 sellers. 1 to 2,000 attendance. Claypool's, 725 Broadway, Needles, CA 92363. Ph: (724) 326-2109. Antiques, collectibles, jewelry, misc. items and a bake sale.

PHOENIX - Park 'n Swap. 3801 E. Washington St. Open every Fri. 7 am to 1 pm, Sat. 5:30 am to 4 pm and Sun. 5:30 am to 4 pm. 1900 sellers, Fee: $5 on Sat., $7 on Sun., $2 for tables. 25,000 to 40,000 avg. att. Bill Ehlis-Gen. Manager, 3801 E. Washington, Phoenix, Az. 85034. Phone (602) 273-1258.

PHOENIX - Swap-O-Rama, 3636 S. 48th St. Open every Wed., Sat. & Sun. Over 300 sellers, fee: $2 to $3. 5000 avg. att. Charlie Brown, mgr. Phone (602) 968-8609.

QUARTSITE - Quartsite Annual Gem & Odd Item Show, in the City of Quartsite. Annual, Feb. 1st thru 5th. Hundreds of sellers, fee: $25 to $75. 200,000 avg. attendance.

QUARTZSITE - Quartzsite Trailor Park. I.10 and U.S. 95. Open Fri., Sat., Sun. Outdoors. Dealers fee: $2 day, $5 weekend. Avg. Att: 500-5000. Dale Hopkins, P. O. Box 296, Quartzsite, Arizona 85346. Ph. (602) 927-6641. Res. Suggested.

SALOME - Salome West & La Rana Dorada Galeria, Milepost 55, Hwy. 60, 35 miles east of Quartzsite. Open daily, Sept. 1 through May 30. Outdoors. Dealers fee: $3. Free admission. Garland I. & George S. Eastlick, P.O. Box 693, Salome, Arizona 85348. Phone (602) 859-3484.

TUCSON - Tanque Verde Swap Meet, Tanque Verde and Grant Rd. Open year round, Wed., Fri., Sat. and Sun. all day until midnight. 800 sellers, $4 per day, $5 at night. 4 to 5,000 attendance, free admission. Richard Chapin, 602-A S. Pantano Rd., Tucson, Arz. Ph: (602) 885-2838.

TUCSON - Tucson Park 'n Swap, 36th and S. 4th Ave. Ph: (602) 623-4012. Mailing address, 3801 E. Washington St., Phoenix, Arizona, 85034. Outdoor facilities, Satudays and Sundays. 150 to 200 dealers. 5500 attendance. Dealer's fee, Sat. & Sun., $4 & $5. Advance reservations, food concessions.

YUMA - Yuma Park 'n Swap, 4000-4th Ave. Ph: (602) 726-4655. Mailing address, 3801 E. Washington St. Phoenix, Az. 85034. Outdoors. Open Sat. & Sun., winter weekends. 250 sellers, $4 per space. 7500 attendance.

WILLCOX - Farmers Market, Flea Market. Open Sat. only.

ARKANSAS

ALEXANDER - Stailey's Flea Market, Hwy 5. Open every Sun. Fee $3 per space. Free admission. Outdoors. Opal Stailey, Rt. 4, Box 94, Alexander, Ark. 72002. Ph: (501) 847-3726.

FORT SMITH - Flea Market & Antique Show, at the Muncipal Auditorium, 55 S. 7th St. 1981 dates are: Nov. 14, 15. 1982 dates are: Feb. 20, 21, May 15, 16, Aug. 14, 15 and Nov. 13, 14. open Sat 8 am to 6 pm, Sun. 8 am to 5 pm. 250 dealers, $10 per table. 2000 avg. att. For info, 2113 Dodson Ave., Fort Smith, Ark. 72901. Phone (501) 783-3658.

FORT SMITH - Fort Smith Flea Market and Auction House, 3500 Jenny Lind at S. Fresno. Open every weekend. 3000 Avg. att. Phone (501) 735-5520.

FORT SMITH - Zero Flea Market, at 2423 S. Zero St. Open every Sat. & Sun. 50 dealers, fee $4 per space. 2000 avg. att. Jaunita Reynolds, 4120 N. 32nd St., Fort Smith, Ark. 72904. Phone (501) 783-8058.

FORT SMITH - Fuzzs Flea Market, 3806 Midland Blvd. Open every Fri., Sat. & Sun. 30 to 35 sellers, $3 per day or $20 per month. Overnight parking. For info, 3806 Midland Blvd., Fort Smith, Ark. 72904. Phone (501) 782-6510.

HOT SPRINGS - Snow Springs Flea Mkt. Hwy. 7 North. Open Fri. & Sat. in summer and Sat. & Sun. in winter. Avg. 75 dealers. Dealers fee: $3.50 open & $4.50 sheds & tables. Free admission. Tables supplied. Avg. att: 2000 - 3000. John D. Woodall, P.O. Box 1032, Hot Springs, Ark. 71901. (501) 632-7530. Res. sug.

dance, free admission. Ben Bentley, P. O. Box 130 Applegate, CA 95703. Ph: (916) 878-2360. Antiques, collectibles, furniture & junque.

APTOS - Village Fair, 417 Trout Gulch Rd. Open Thur., Fri., Sat., & Sun., 10 am to 5 pm. Indoors. Attendance 500 - 2,000. Elma Toney, Ph: (408) 688-9883. All types merch.

ARCADIA - Edwards Swap Meet, Edwards Drive-In Theatre, 4469 Live Oak Rd. Open every Sat. & Sun. Ph: (213) 447-8179.

ARLINGTON - Swap Meet, Van Buren Drive-In Theatre. 3035 Van Buren Blvd., Arlington, CA 92503. Open every Sat. and Sun. 7 am to 3 pm. Ph: (714) 688-2360.

AROMAS - Stagecoach Territory (Big Red Barn), 1000 Hwy. 101. Open Sat. & Sun. 7-4:30, flea market. Shops in barn 7 days a week 10-5. Indoors and outdoors. Dealers fee $7 Sat. and $10 Sun. Attendance fee $1. Avg. weekend attendance: 10,000. Tables supplied. Managers: Al and Fran Ellingwood, 1000 Hwy. 101, Aromas, CA 95004. Phone (408) 422-1271 or 724-7766. Reservations suggested.

AUBURN - Auburn Flea Market, 1273 High Street, Auburn, Ca. Open Sat. & Sun. 8-4. Indoors. Dealers fee $9. Free attendance. Avg. att.: 3,000. Tables supplied. Managers: Bob France and Carl Johnson, 997 Lincoln Way, Auburn, CA 95603.

AZUSA - Swap Meet, Foothill Drive-In Theater, 675 E. Foothill Blvd., Azusa, CA 91702. Open every Sun. 6:30 am to 3 pm. Ph: (213) 334-0263.

BAKERSFIELD - Swap-O-Rama, 4501 Wible Rd. Open Fri. 10 am to 10 pm. Sat. & Sun. 7 am to 6 pm. Fee is free on Fri. $2 on Sat., $4 on Sun. Tom Ballard, 4501 Wible Rd. Bakersfield, CA 93307. Ph: (805) 831-9342. All types of merchandise.

BAKERSFIELD - Bakersfield Flea Market held at the Kern Co. Fairgrounds. 1982 dates are April 18 and October 24. Open 9 a.m. to 3 p.m. Sellers fee $12-25. R. G. Canning Ent. Inc., P. O. Box 400, Maywood, CA 90270. Phone (213) 588-5005.

BAKERSFIELD - South Union Swap Meet & Flea Market. 2546 So. Union. Open 6 am. - 6 pm. Sat & Sun. Outdoors. Avg. dealers: 300. Tables supplied. Mgr. Floyd. Owner: Walt Rowe, 2546 So. Union, Bakersfield, CA 93307. Phone (805) 831-6267. Overnight camping Wed. to Sun. at dark. res. sug.

LITTLE ROCK - Giant Flea Market, 8610 New Benten Hwy. Open every Sat. & Sun. 82 Dealers, $22.50 per weekend, 11 x 11 w/tables. 3400 avg. att. Hall Purses, Mgr. Phone (501) 565-9915.

LITTLE ROCK - Quality Antique Flea Market, at the State Fairgrounds. 1981 dates are: Oct. 17, 18, Nov. 7, 8 and Dec. 12, 13. Call for 1982 Dates. 150 dealers $20 per weekend. 5000 avg. att. Larry or Betty Amery, 1617 McDowell Rd., Jackson, Miss. 39204. Phone (601) 939-8596.

POTTSVILLE - Pottsville Flea & Farmers Market, on Hwy. 64. Open every Fri., Sat. & Sun. Indoor & outdoors. $3 per day sellers fee. For info P. O. Box 57, Pottsville, Ark. 72858. Phone (501) 968-3235.

SEARCY - Garage Sales Warehouse. Open daily, up to 200 sellers. Melvin Thacker, Rt. 2, Box 143A, Judsonia, Ark. 72081. Phone (501) 268-7989.

SEARCY - King Flu Flea Market, East Race St. Room for 200 sellers, John Glenn, 1503 Tulip Ave., Searcy. Ark. 27143. Ph: (501) 268-7993.

CALIFORNIA

ALAMEDA - Penny Mart, Island Auto Movie Theatre, 791 Thaw Way, Alameda, CA 94501. Open every Sat. and Sun. Ph: (415) 522-7205.

APPLEGATE - Applegate Flea Market, Applegate Rd. at the Civic Center. Open 2nd Sat. and Sun. of the month. 20 dealers, indoors & outdoors. Sellers fee $3 outside, $5 inside. 500 avg. atten-

CALEXICO - Santo Tomas Swap Meet, Hwy 98 & Pruett Rd. Open Wed. thru Sunday. Sellers, $4 per day. C.P. Martinez, 961 Lee Ave., Calexico, CA 92231. Ph: (714) 357-9536.

CASTRO VALLEY - A C Flea Market, corner of Foothill Blvd & Castro Valley Blvd. Open Sat. & Sun 7 am to 5:30 pm. 300 to 475 dealers indoors and outdoors. Fee $5. 8,000 to 10,000 att. Tom Laber, 20820 Oak St. Castro Valley, CA 94546.

CERES - Ceres Drive-In Theatre Flea Market, Hwy. 99 & East Whitmore Ave., 3 mi south of Modesto. Open Sundays 6 am to 3:30 pm. 200 dealers outdoors. Fee $5. 8,000 to 10,000 att. Mgr. George Enck, P. O. Box 35, Ceres CA. Ph: (209) 537-0832 or 537-3323. All types of merch.

CHOWCHILLA - Chowchilla Swap Meet, 24134 Rt. 16. Open every Thurs., 6:30 am to 3 pm. Paul Dorman. Ph: (209) 896-1882.

CHICO - Lemple's Swap Meet & Flea Market, 2144 Park Ave. Open every Sat. and Sun. 50 sellers, $3.50 to $5.00 per space. Ph: (916) 343-1932.

CHICO - Starlite Drive-In, Park Ave. Exit from Hwy. 99. Open 9-5, Sat. & Sun. Outdoor. Fee: $3 for a space 1 day, $5 for 1 space 2 days, $5 for 2 spaces 2 days.

CHULA VISTA - Flea World Swap Meet of San Diego. 1638 Industrial Blvd. (Main Street exit from Interstate 5, one block east to Industrial). Mail address 785 Anita Street, Chula Vista CA 92011. Owner-Managers: Flo and David Barrett. Ph: (714) 423-9615. Tuesday 8 am to 1 pm. Sellers $2. Buyers free. Saturday 7 am to 7 pm. Sellers $3 buyers 25¢. Sunday 7 am to 4 pm. Sellers $4 buyers 25¢. Facilities: 50 permanent buildings (all occupied and a waiting list) plus open spaces available. Snack bar 7 am to 4 pm. Free parking. PA announcements for vendors free.

CLEARLAKE PARK - Drive-In Flea Market, on Olempia Dr. Open on weekends and holidays. 25 sellers. $4.25 per space. 500 to 1000 att. Write: Flea Market. Star Rt. 1054 B, Clearlake Park, CA 95424.

COLTON - Maclin "Colton Auction", 1902 West Valley Blvd. Open 5:30 am. Thurs.-Sat. Space fee $11, Att. 5,000 - 15,000. Avg. sellers 250. Brad Larsen 7407 Riverside Dr. Ontario, CA 918761. Ph: (714) 984-5131.

CONCORD - Solano Drive-In, Solano Way & Hwy. 4. Open Sat. & Sun. 7 am to 4 pm. 150-200 dealers. Fee $4. Nancy Dauly, 601 Tunnel Ave., San Francisco, CA 94134. Ph: (415) 467-4849. All types of merch.

COSTA MESA - Orange County Fairgrounds Swap Meet, 88 Fair Dr. Open every Sat. & Sun. 1000 sellers, 40,000 att. Dealers fee:$10 per day. $1 per car adm. Mailing address: 1501 Westcliff Dr., Suite 330, Newport Beach, CA 92660. Phone (714) 546-2522.

CRESCENT CITY - Pack Rat Flea Market, Hwy. 101, Del Norte County Fairgrounds, Crescent City Ca. Open once a month. 45-50 dealers indoors. Dealers fee: $6 per table or $4 per space. Sat. $13 and Sun. $6. Manager: Erlene Vega, P. O. Box 425, Smith River, CA 95567-0425. Phone (707) 487-0845. Reservations suggested.

EL CAJON - Aero Drive-In Swap Meet, 1470 E. Broadway. Open Sat. & Sun. 7 am to 5 pm. 400 dealers. Fee $3 on Sat, $5 on Sun. 8,000 to 10,000 attendance. Art Ashcraft, 1470 E. Broadway, El Cajon, CA 92021. Ph: (714) 444-8800. All new merchandise, dealers must have city license. All types of merchandise.

EL MONTE - Starlite Drive-in and Swap Meet, 2559 Chico Ave. Open Sat. & Sun. Outdoors. Dealers fee: $5 Sat. and $10 Sun. Att. Fee: 50¢ Sat. & 75¢ Sun. Manager: Mark Nelson, 2559 Chico Ave., So. El Monte, CA 91733. Phone (213) 448-2810. Reservations suggested.

ELK GROVE - Old Town Elk Grove Flea Market, 9676 Railroad St. 95624. Open Sat. & Sun. Fee $6. Reservations. Avg. dealers 400, avg. att. 2,000. Jube Mullins - Grizzly Womack, 9676 Railroad St. Elk Grove, CA 95624. Ph: (916) 685-9168.

ESCONDIDO - Escondido Drive-in and Swap Meet, 635 West Mission Ave. Open Fri., Sat. & Sun. Indoors and outdoors. Dealers fee: Fri. $2, Sat. $4. Att. fee: Sat. 35¢ and Sun. 50¢. Joe Crowder, owner, 635 West Mission Ave., Escondido, CA 92025. Phone (714) 745-3100.

EUREKA - Redwood Flea Market, 3750 Harns. Open June 4th, July 16th, Aug. 20th, Sept. 10th, Otc. 1st and 22nd, Nov. 12th and Dec. 3rd and 17th. Over 120 dealers, $5 per space. 1500 avg. att., 25¢ adm. Rolla Krebs, 15 W. Clark, Eureka, CA 95501. Phone (707)442-2667.

FOLSOM - Sutter St. Merchants Assoc. Inc. 10th annual Peddler's Fair, Sutter St. Mall 985-4323, mailing adress, P. O. Box 515, Folsom, CA 95630. Outdoor facilities, Sept. 26, rain date Oct. 3. 200 dealers, 30,000 attendance. Dealer's fee $15 per space. Antiques and collectables.

FOLSOM - 3rd annual glass, china and pottery show. Sutter Street Mall. Hwy 50 east or west to Folsom turn off. May 9th, 1982. App. 100 dealers. Outdoors. Dealers fee: $35. Avg. att.: 4,000. Sutter Street Merchants Assn. Inc., P. O. Box 515, Folsom, CA 95630. Phone (916) 935-2386. Reservations required.

FOLSOM - 16th Annual Peddlers Faire, Sutter Street Mall, Hwy. 50 east or west to Folsom turn off. September 19th, 1982 Rain Date is September 26. Dealers: 300 outdoors. Dealers fee: $45. Att: 35,000. Sutter Street Merchants Assn., Inc. P. O. Box 515, Folsom, CA 95630. Phone (916) 985-9938. Reservations required.

FOLSOM - 16th Annual Flea Market, Sutter Street Mall, Hwy. 50 east or west to Folsom turn off. April 18, 1982 Rain Date April 25. Dealers: 300 outdoors. Dealers fee: $45. Free attendance. Avg. att.: 35,000. Sutter Street Merchants Assn. Inc., P. O. Box 515, Folsom, CA 95630. Phone (916) 985-9938. Reservations required.

FREMONT - Niles Flea Market, Hwy. 580. Opened last Sun. in Aug. 500 dealers outdoors. Open 4 am to 4 pm. 80,000. Avg. Att. Betty Hanna, P. O. Box 2672, Fremont, CA 94536, Ph: (415) 797-2708.

FRESNO - Woodward Park Antique Flea Mkt. Woodward Park 4 Drive-in Theater, 7150 N. Abby Fourth Sunday of each month. Adm. $1.25. Sellers $12.50. Reserved section available. Thaxters Antique Enterprises. Ph: (209) 222-6807. 3115 N. Van Ness Blvd., Fresno, CA 93704. No new or swap meet merch.

FRESNO - Cherry Auction Swap Meet, 4640 S. Cherry Ave., Fresno, Ca. Hwy. 99 to Jensen Ave. off ramp, west 1 block to Cherry Ave. (see our sign there on corner of Cherry & Jensen). Open Tue., Sat., & Sun. from 6:30 to ? Mgr. M. Frank Meyer, 2640 S. Cherry, Fresno, CA 93706. 24 hour info (209) 266-9856.

FRESNO - Sunnyside Drive-in and Swap Meet, 5550 E. Olive St., near Fresno airport. Open Sat. & Sun. Outdoors. Dealers fee: Sat $3 and Sun. $9. Att.. fee: Sat 35¢ and Sun. 50¢. Joe Wills, 5550 E. Olive St., Fresno, CA 93727. Phone (209) 251-1363. Reservations suggested.

GALT - Galt Flea Market, 1050 "C" St. Open every Wed., 7 a.m. to 3 p.m. Sellers fee: $6 per table, each add'l table $2. Gladys Farmer, 826 Southdale Ct., Galt, CA 95632. Ph: (209) 745-2437.

GARDENA - Vermont Drive-in swap meet, 17737 S. Vermont, Gardena, Ca. Open Sat. & Sun. Outdoors. Dealers fee: Sat $9, Sun. $10. George Vranau 17737 S. Vermont, Gardena, CA 90247. Phone (213) 324-2896. Reservations suggested.

GARDENA - Roadium Swap Meet, 2500 W. Roadium Beach Blvd. Open daily except Mon, 7 am to 3 pm. Attendance 10,000 to 12,000 per week. Ph: (312) 321-3920 daytime, 327-3646 night. All types of merchandise.

GOLETA - Santa Barbara Swap Meet, 907 S. Kellogg, Goleta CA 93017. Ph: (085) 964-9050. Outdoor facilities, every Sun. 7-4. Located at Santa Barbara Twin Drive-In Theatre.

HANFORD - Hanford Auction & Sale, 8967 Lacy Blvd. Open on Mondays.

JOHNSTONVILLE - Johnstonville Flea Market, Star Rt. 3, Box 46. Take US 395 80 N of Reno. 3 miles south of Susanville. Open Sat. & Sun. 7-? weather permitting. Outdoors. Dealers fee: $3. Charles Slavinski, Star Rt. 3, Box 46, Susanville, CA 96130. Phone (916) 257-2004.

KING CITY - King City Rotary Club Twelfth Annual Flea Market, Salinas Valley Fairgrounds. Sunday, April 5, 8 a.m. to 5 p.m. Booths $10 first space, $7.50 for each additional space. Check in allowed 4 p.m. evening before sale. Trailer space available. Table rentals: $3. Reservations: send name, address, number of spaces, inside or outside, with check or money order to above address. Inquiries: Wes Bengard, Bengard Insurance Agency, 301 Broadway, King City, CA 93930. Phone (408) 385-5438.

LAKE ELSINORE - Peddler's Village USA, corner Hwys 71 & 74, Ph: (714) 674-9974, mailing address Rex Read, 18180 Collier Ave., Lake Elsinore, CA 92330. Outdoor facilities, Sat. & Sun. 7-5. 200 dealers, 6000 attendance. Dealer's fee $3 per day. Ample parking.

LA VERNE - Mt. Baldy Swap Meet. 3515 White Ave. Open every Sun., 7 am to 2 pm. 110 sellers, $1.50 per space. Over 500 att., 25¢ per carfull. Ph: (714) 593-2110.

LANCASTER - Lancaster Flea Market, 155 East Avenue I. Open 9-5. Indoors and outdoors. Dealers fee: $12.50/$17.50. Att. fee: 50¢. Betty Smith, 44943 10th Street West, Lancaster, CA 93534. Phone (805) 948-4518. Reservations suggested.

LANCASTER - Lancaster Chamber of Commerce Flea Market, at the Antelope Valley Fairgrounds. Held Semi-annually on the 3rd Sunday of May and the 1st Sunday of Oct. Over 900 sellers. $7.50 to $12.50 sellers fee. 20,000 avg. att. Lancaster C of C, 44943 N. 10th West Lancaster, CA 93534. Ph: (805) 948-4518.

LA PUENTE - La Puente Auction Sales & Swap Meet, 15058 Valley Blvd. Open Thurs. thru Sunday, 7 am to 11 pm. 100 sellers, $3 per space. 1500 avg. att. Furniture Auction: Wed. 10 am and Fri 7 pm. Ph: (213) 968-4990.

LEUCADIA - Happy Peddlers. 1680 Highway 101, Leucadia, CA 92024 (Highway 101) between Grand and La Costa Ave. General Managers John Gutkosky and Jean Fass. Flea Market Manager, Muriel Stephens. Ph: Saturday and Sunday (714) 729-0530. Saturday sellers 8 am to 6 pm, $4. Sunday sellers 8 am to 6 pm. $6.50. Buyers both days no charge, 8:30 am to 5 pm. Free parking. (Sellers Sat. & Sun $10) Permanent booths and spaces; plus open space available without reservation. PA announcements for vendors free. Produce and canned goods sold by management.

LODI - Lodi District Chamber of Commerce Flea Market, 413 E. Lockeford St. Open first Sunday in May and the first Sunday in October. 8-4. Dealers: 500, indoors and outdoors. Dealers fee: Indoors $20; outdoors $12 and $15. Attendance fee 50¢ and parking $1.50. Avg. att: 10,000. Kathy McCarren, P. O. Box 386, Lodi, CA 95241. Phone (209) 334-4773. No food or beverages to be sold. Reservations required.

LONG BEACH - Charlies Unlimited, 1030 Long Beach Blvd., Long Beach. 9-7, seven days a week. Indoor. Dealers fee: $20 month and commission. Att: free. Avg. daily att: 600. Mgr: Butch Marquand, 1030 Long Beach Blvd., Long Beach, CA 90801. Ph: (213) 437-3098.

LOS ANGELES - LaMirada Swap Meet, 13963 Alondra Blvd. Santa Fe Springs, CA 90670. Open Wed. 5:30 a.m. - 3 p.m. Sat. 6 a.m. - 3 p.m., Sun. 5 a.m. - 3 p.m. Outdoors. Dealers fee: $4 Wed., $10 Sat., $14 Sun. Att. fee: 25¢ Wed, 50¢ Sat. & Sun. Avg. att. 15,000 - 20,000. Steve Wojciechowski, Phone (213) 921-9996. Restrictions: guns, ammunition, motorized vehicles, some food.

MALIBU - Malibu Chamber of Commerce Flea Market, at the Colony Mkt. Parking lot. Annual. 4th Sunday of October. 200 dealers. d$15 per space. Avg. att. 20,000. Malibu C. of C., 22653 Pacific Coast Hwy., Malibu, CA 90265. Ph: (213) 456-9025.

MARIN CITY - Marin City Flea Market, Sausalito Exit of Fwy 101. Open Sat. & Sun., dawn to dusk. Ph: (415) 332-5547.

MARYSVILLE - Swap Meet, 1468 Simpson Lane. Open Sundays. 100 dealers outdoors. Fee $5 w/tables, $6 covered booth. Ph: (916) 743-8713. ALL TYPES.

MERCED - Country Boy Flea Market, 3140 Beachwood Dr. Open Sat. & Sun., 8 am to 6 pm. 10 dealers indoor. Fee $15 to $35 for weekend.

MORGAN HILL - Morgan Hill Flea Market, 140 East Main. Open Sat. & Sun. 7:30 a.m. to 7 p.m. Dealers: 125 outdoors. Dealers fee $7 single & $9 double. Tables supplied. James Ahlin, 140 E. Main, Morgan Hill, CA 95037. Phone (408) 779-3809

MOSS LANDING - Pirates Cove Flea Market, Sand Holt Rd. Moss Landing, Ph: 633-2052, mailing address. P. O. Box 999 Castroville, CA 95012. Indoor and outdoor facilities, Thurs-Mon 11-5. Dealer's fee monthly.

MOSS LANDING - Flea Market, on Hwy 1 across from Moss Landing School. Open Sat. and Sun.

NATIONAL CITY - National City Swap Meet 3200 D Ave., National City CA 92050. Manager: Jim Wallace. Phone Fri., Sat. & Sun. (714) 477-2203. Sat. & Sun. sellers 7 am to 5:30 pm, $4 per stall each day. Buyers 25¢. Some parking 25¢, some free. Charge for leaving merchandise overnight: $1 Fri.; 50¢ Sat. Tables and racks may be left all week if stall rend paid in advance for next weekend. Over 600 stalls available. Reservations advisable for best spaces. Farmers Market sells produce and vegetables. Snack Bar open 7:30 am until 4 pm on Sat. & Sun.

NEEDLES · Claypool's Broadway and E. St. Open 2nd and 4th Sat. of month, 8 am to 3 pm, Oct. thru May. Free sellers set-up and admission. 10 to 20 dealers. 1 to 2,000 attendance. Claypool's, 725 Broadway, Needles, CA 92363. Ph: (714) 326-2109. Antiques, collectibles, jewelry, misc. items and a bake sale.

NEW BERRY SPRINGS · Trader John's swap meet, 45050 Fairview Rd. 15 min. east of Barstow on Hwy. 40. Open Wed. eve. 3 p.m. to 9 p.m., Sat. & Sun. 7:30 a.m. to 3:30 p.m. Dealers: 200 indoors and outdoors. Dealers fee: $3 day. Att. free. Avg. att. 2,200. John Tabor, 45050 Fairview, New Berry Springs, CA 92365. Phone (714) 257-3668. Reservations suggested.

NIPOMO · Buyers Mart & Swap Meet, 245 N. Frontage Rd. Open Fri., Sat., Sun. 6 a.m. to 4 p.m. Over 300 sellers. To 8,000 attendance. Spaces $1.50 on Fri., $3.50 on Sat., $5.00 on Sun. Buildings $75 mo. 14 × 20 ft. Ph: (805) 929-3878.

OAKDALE · Oakdale Flea Market & Antique City. 1907 E. F St. (Hwy 108 and 120). Open every Sat and Sun. 7 am to 6 pm. Outdoors. 30 sellers. $3.50 per day. 2000 attendance, free admission. Arthur Holzman. Ph: (209) 847-2741.

OAKHURST · Mountain Peddler's Flea Market. Hwy 41. For information: Eastern Madera Co. Chamber of Commerce, P.O. Box 369, Oakhurst, CA 93644.

OCEANSIDE · Oceanside Valley Drive In Swap Meet. 3480 Mission Ave., (2 miles east of Interstate 5 on Mission Ave.) Mail address: 635 West Mission Ave. Escondido, CA 92025. Ph: Sun. and Mon. (714) 757-5286, othe days (714) 745-3100. Owner Joe C. Crowder. Open Sat., Sun. and Mon. Sellers: Sat. 6:30 am to 4pm $4; Sun. 6:30 am to 4 pm $5.50; Mon. 6:30 am to 4 . pm $3.

ONTARIO · Maclin "Chino Auction", 7407 Riverside Dr. Open Sun. & Tues. Space fee $11, outdoor. Avg. sellers 250. Avg. att. 5,000-15,000. Brad Larsen 7407 Riverside Dr., Ontario, CA 91761. Ph: (714) 984-5131.

ORANGE · Orange Drive-in and swap meet, 291 N. State College; open Sat. & Sun. Outdoors. Dealers fee: Sat. $9 and Sun. $10. Att. fee 50¢. robert Nebel, 291 N. State College, Orange, CA 92668. Phone (714) 634-4259. Reservations suggested.

PALMDALE · 4 Corner's Swap Meet, Hwy. 138 & Pear Blossom Hwy. Open every Sat.

PALM SPRINGS · Sunair Drive-In Theatre. 68050 Hwy 111. Open Mon. & Tues. year round 4 pm to 11 pm and Oct. thru May on Sun. 8 a.m to 3 pm. 250 sellers. Fee-Sun. $4, Tues. $5. 3000 attendance. 50¢ per car or 25¢ per person admission. Wilson Arvahi. Mgr. Ph: (714) 328-1404.

PARAMOUNT · Paramount Swap Meet, 14711 S. Paramount. Avg. att: 8500-9000. Glenn Payne, Norm Masters, Darren Kurkowski, 14711 S. Paramount, CA 90723. Phone (213) 633-6641. Reservations suggested.

PASADENA · Pasadena City College Flea Market, corner of Colorado & Hill, first Sun. of Month (except January). Free admission. 360 dealers. Outdoor. Attendance 15,000. Dean Alvar Kauti, 1570 E. Colorado Blvd., Pasadena, CA 91106. Phone (213) 578-7385. Res. sug.

PASADENA · Rose Bowl Flea Market & Swap Meet. Rosemont Ave. & Arroyo Blv.(Pasadena Rose Bowl). Open 2nd Sun. of each month. 9 a.m. to 3 p.m. Over 2,000 dealers outdoors. Fee: $40 in advance. Reservations a must. Over 50,000 attendance. $2.50 admission. R. G. Canning Enterprises, P. O. Box 400 Dept. 44, Maywood, CA 90270. Phone (213) 588-4411. Everything under the sun.

PASO ROBLES · Swap Meet, at the San Luis Obispo Fairgrounds. Call for dates. Open 9 am to 5 pm. About 200 sellers, $7.50 for the weekend. 3000 to 5000 avg. attendance, 25¢ adm. Ph: (805) 238-3565.

PETALUMA · Flea Market. Cleveland and Bodega Hwy. Open Sat. and Sun., 6 am to 6 pm. Dealers fee $3 per space, 2 to 4,000 att. free admission. Roy Watt, 851 Cleveland Ave., Petaluma, CA 94952. Ph: (707) 763-2371.

POMONA · Mission Drive In Swap Meet. 10798 Ramona, Pomona, CA 91766. Open Sat. & Sun. 6-2. Indoors and outdoors. Dealers fee: $4 Sat. & $6 Sun. 50¢ admission fee. Tables supplied indoors. Ronald Bacon. Phone (714) 628-7943, 628-0019. Restrictions: No firearms, ammunition, tobacco, beverages, candy or food. Res. sug.

PORTERVILLE · Sierra Swap Meet,. 17950 Orange Belt Dr. (Old Hwy 65). Open Fri., Sat. & Sun. Phone 784-8762.

REDDING · Epperson Brothers Auction & Flea Market. 5091 Fig Tree Lane. Open Sat. 7 a.m. - 5 p.m. Sun. 6 a.m. - 5 p.m. Avg. Dealers: 300. Outdoors. Dealers Fee: $3 on Sat., $5 on Sun. Tables supplied. Avg. att: 4,000 - 6,000. Owner, Jack Epperson, 96002. Phone (916) 365-7242 or 365-3159. Restrictions: no prepared food (concessions avail.)

RICHMOND · Hilltop Drive-In. Hwy 80 Open every Sun. 7 am to 4 pm. 150 dealers. Fee $4. 3000 attendance. Nancy Douly. 601 Tunnel Ave. San Francisco, CA 94134: Ph: (415) 467-4849. All types of merchandise.

RIDGECREST · Ridgecrest Swap Meet. Ridgecrest Fairgrounds at Rt. 178 East. Open every other Sunday. 25 dealers and growing. $5 dealers fee - 25¢ attendance. Avg. att: 500. Mgr. Rae Leonard, 1320 Brady, Ridgecrest, CA 93555. Phone (714) 375-9163. Contact manager regarding Spring Festival, May 21-25. Also Desert Inn Power Fair, last week of Sept. first week Oct.

RIVERBANK · Riverbank Flea Market & Auction Yard. 2419 Patterson Rd. Open Fri. Sat. Sun. and Holidays. 53 sellers. $2.50 per space. Stephen Thorington, 2401 ˙ Patterson Rd., Riverbank, CA 95367. Ph: 869-3263.

RIVERSIDE · Van Buren Drive In Theater. 3035 Van Buren Blvd. Open Sat and Sun. 7 am to 1 pm. 200 to 300 sellers, fee $2 on Sat, $4 on Sun. Outdoors. 50¢ admission per car. Fred Williams Ph: (714) 688-2360.

ROSEVILLE · Denio's Roseville Farmers Market and Auction Inc., 98 Atkinson St. Open every Sat. & Sun. 300 dealers. Avg. att: over 20,000. Pat Vaughn, P. O. Box 999, Roseville, CA 95661. Phone (916) 782-2704.

SACRAMENTO · Auction City and Flea Market. 8521 Folsom Blvd. Open Tue. thru Fri. for reservations. Sale days are Sat. & Sun. 7 a.m. to 6 p.m. Avg. dealers: 450. Avg. att: 5,000. Indoors and outdoors. Dealers fee: $9.90 for first table, $4.40 for second table. Free admission. Tables supplied. Harold Hennessey, 8521 Folsom Blvd., Sacramento, CA 95826. Phone (916) 383-0880-0950. No firearms, no dogs, no camping out. Res. sug.

SACRAMENTO · Rancho Gas Station Flea Mkt. 12529 Folsom Blvd. Open Thur. Fri. Sat. Sun. Fee: $5. Avg. At. 1,500. William F. Higgins, 12529 Folsom Blvd. Rancho Cordova, CA 95670. Ph: (916) 985-2905.

SALINAS · Salinas Skyview Flea Market, 925 N. Sanborn Rd. Open Sat. & Sun. 7 a.m. - 3 p.m. Fee $4. Outdoor. 60-100 sellers. Att: 1,000 - 2,000. Art Jackson, 925 N. Sanborn Rd., Salinas, CA 93905. Phone (408) 758-6792. No guns, ammunition, tapes or live animals.

SANTEE · Santee Drive-In, 10990 Woodside (from Interstate 8 East, take Highway 67 to Woodside, turn left). Open Sundays from 7 am to 3 pm. Sellers: $2; buyers: 25¢ each, or 50¢ per car. Free drewings held. Managers: Mel Strum & Ben Ohre. 200 open spaces. Phone (714) 753-3882.

SAN BERNARDINO · Swap-n-save, 689 South E St., Dealers 500 outdoors. Every Sun. 6-2 p.m. $5 minimum dealers fee and attendance fee 25¢. Tom Scharf, 26211 Mirada St., Highland, CA 92346. Phone (714) 888-9076. No food, beverage, or illegal merchandise. Reservations suggested.

SAN BERNARDINO · Mt. Vernon Drive-in & Swap Meet, 632 Mt. Vernon. Open Sat. & Sun. Outdoors. Dealers fee: $3. Attendance fee 25¢. Robert Means, 632 Mt. Vernon, San Bernardino, CA 92410. Phone (714) 884-0405. Rev. sug.

SAN DIEGO · Spring Valley Swap Meet, 6377 Quarry Rd. Open Sat. & Sun. 7am-4pm. Over 1000 dealers outdoors. Dealers fee: $7 Sat. and $8 Sun. Att fee 50¢ parking free. Mailing address 6377 Quary Rd., Spring Valley, CA 92077. Phone (714) 463-1194. No firearms, animals or food.

SAN DIEGO · Midway Swap Meet, 3901 Midway Drive. Open Sat. & Sun. Outdoor. Avg. Dealers 200. Avg. Att. 3,000. Monte Kobey, P. O. Box 81492. San Diego, CA 92138. Ph: (714) 226-0650.

SAN FERNANDO · San Fernando Swap Meet, 585 Glenoaks Blvd. Take San Diego Freeway (405) to Simi Freeway (118) to Glenoaks Blvd., turn left. Held Sat., Sun., and Tues. from 6:30 am. sellers. Spaces $4 to 11. Atten. 6000. Mr. Harold Solie, P. O. Box 4955, Panorama City, CA 91412. Ph: (213) 361-9956.

SAN FRANCISCO · 601 Tunnel Ave. Open Sat, & Sun. 7 am to 5 pm. 150-200 dealers indoors and outdoors. Fee $4. 2000-7000 attendance. Nancy Doule, 601 Tunnel Ave., San Francisco, CA 94134. Ph: (415) 467-4849. All types of merchandise.

SAN JOSE · The Flea Market Inc., 12000 Berryessa Rd., Hwy 101 via 13th St. offramp, south on frontage road to Berryessa, then east. Open every Sat. and Sun. 7:30 to 5 pm. 1800 to 2000 sellers. 20,000 to 35,000 avg. att. Ph: (408) 289-1550.

SAN JOSE · Capital Flea Mkt, 3630 Hill Cap Ave. San Jose, CA 95136. At the Capital Drive-In. Open every Sat. & Sun., 6 am to 4:30 pm. Space $8 per day. Phone (408) 225-5800.

SAN JUAN BAUTISTA · Rocks Flea Market, Hwy. 101 between Gilroy & Salinas. Open every Tue., Sat. & Sun. 150 Sellers, $3.50 on Sat; $4.50 on Sun. 5 to 7000 att. Charlie Root, P. O. Box 479, San Juan Bautista, CA 95045. Phone (408) 722-3266.

SAN JUAN BAUTISTA · San Juan Bautista Annual Flea Market, P. O. Box 442, San Juan Bautista, CA 95045. Outdoor facilities; always held 1st Sun of Aug. 250 dealers, 20-30,000 att. Dealer's fee $25 per space.

SAN JUAN BAUTISTA · Rocks Flea Market, Hwy. 101 between Gilroy & Silinas. Open every Tues, Sat & Sun. 150 sellers, $3.50 on Sat; $4.50 on Sun. 5 to 7000 att. Charlie Root, P.O. Box 479, San Juan Bautista, CA 95045. Ph: (408) 722-3266.

SAN LUIS OBISPO - Sunset Drive In Swap Meet, 255 Elks Lane & Hwy 101. Open Sun. 8 am to 3 pm. 130 dealers. Fee $2. 1000 att. Adm. 50¢ per car. Mgr. Mark Gran, 255 Elks Lane, San Luis Obispo, CA 93401. Ph: (805) 544-8418. All types of merchandise.

SANTA ANA - Harbor Blvd. Drive-in and Swap Meet, 3700 McFadden Avenue. Take Harbor exit off of Garden Grove Freeway - So. Open Sat. & Sun. Outdoors. Dealers fee: Sat. $9 and Sun. $10. Att. fee 50¢. Bob Fisher, 3700 McFadden Ave., Santa Ana, CA 92704. Phone (714) 531-1272. Res. sug.

SANTA ANA - Santa Ana Bowl Swap Meet. Open Sat. & Sun. 7am to 4pm. Space price Sat. $5 and Sun. $7. Free admission. Northern Western Enterprises, 2082 S. E. Bristol, Suite 10, Santa Ana, CA 92707. Phone (714) 957-0131.

SANTA CLARA - Santa Clara Flea Market, 5500 Lafayette St., Santa Clara, CA 95050. Ph: (408) 247-9600. Indoor and outdoor facilities, Sat. and Sun. 200 dealers, dealers fee $4 per day. Parking fee 25¢ Sat. 50¢ Sun. Fresh produce, carnival rides. Nancy Douly, 601 Tunnel Ave., San Francisco, CA 93134. Ph: (415) 467-4849.

SANTA CRUZ - Skyview Flea Market, 2240 Soquel Dr. Ph: (408) 426-5842, mailing address 101 Alamo Ave., Santa Cruz, CA 95060. Outdoor facilities, Sat and Sun. 6:30 am to 4:30 pm. 350 dealers, attendance fee 25¢ Sat., 50¢ Sun., dealer's fee $2.50 Sat., $4.50 Sun. Ample parking, breakfast bar.

SANTA MARIA - Santa Maria Hwy Drive-In Theater, 3085 Santa Maria Way. Open every Sun., 6 am to 3 pm. $3 sellers fee. 50¢ adm. (car load). Ph: (805) 937-3515.

SAUGUS - Saugus Swap Meet, 22500 Soledad Cyn. Rd. Open Sun. Avg. 750 dealers, Att. 15,000. Fee $10 and up. Outdoor. Marshall Wilkings, P.O. Box S, Saugus, CA 91350. Ph: (805) 259-3886.

SEBASTOPAL - Midgleys Country Flea Market, 2200 Gravenstein Hwy. So. Open Sat. & Sun. Dealers: 600 outdoors. Dealers fee: $5. Free attendance. Avg. att: 8000. Ms. Rosalie Wade, 2200 Gravenstein Hwy. So., Sebastopol, CA 94572. Phone (707) 823-7874. No animals, hand guns, home made food, candy or drinks.

SIMI - Simi Drive In Theatre Swap Meet, 361 Tierra Rejada Rd. Open every Sun. 7 am to 4 pm, 4 pm to 11 pm on Tues. 400 to 500 dealers. $8 per day sellers fee. 75¢ per car load. 2 to 3000 att. John Blazac. Ph: (805) 526-6048.

STOCKTON - Stockton Flea Market, 2542 S. El Dorado. Open Sat. and Sun., 8 am to 6 pm. 150 sellers. $16.50 and up for the two days. 7 to 8000 att. Free adm. Harvey Peters or Roy Harwell, P.O. Box 492, French Camp, CA 95231. Ph: (209) 465-9933.

SUNNYVALE - Antique Trade Faire, El Camino and Bernardo Avenue. 40 miles south of San Francisco. Open first Sunday of every month, rain or shine 10-5. Dealers: 80-100, outdoors. Dealers fee: $15. Avg. att: 2000. Betty Rowland, 835 Mary Ave., Sunnyvale, CA 94087. Phone (408) 736-7222. Res. req.

TORRANCE - Alpine Village Swap Meet, 833 W. Torrance Blvd. Open Saturdays 8 am - 4 pm and Tue. 2 pm - 10 pm. 200 dealers outdoors. Free admission. The Swap Meet Corporation, 833 W. Torrance Blvd., Torrance, CA 90502. Phone (213) 323-2964. No food, pets, pornography or paraphanalia. Res. sug.

TULARE - Southern Flea Mart, 23090 Road 152. Open Sun. Space fee $4 - $4.50 - $6.50. Outdoor. John Southern, 680 Ventura, 93274. Phone (209) 688-8014 or 686-9948. No guns, or food catering trucks.

TURLOCK - Livestock Auction & Flea Mkt. Tue. 5 a.m. till ? Mgr. Jack Linn, P. O. Box 524, Turlock, CA 95380. Phone (209) 634-4326.

TWENTY-NINE PALMS - Starlight Drive-In's Swap Meet, Gorgonio Drive. Open Sat. & Sun. 6 am to ? . Space fee: $3, two for $5. Outdoors. Dealers 20-30. Att: 200-500. Ray Kinsman, 6937 Elm Ave. 29 Palms, CA 92277. Ph: (714) 367-7893.

UKIAH - Ukiah Flea Market, 3301 North State St. Open Sat. & Sun. year round. Avg. dealers: 50. Covered outdoors. Dealers fee: $4/table. Avg. att: 1,000. Ken Rosen, 765 N. State St. Ukiah, CA 95482. Phone (707) 462-4104. Restrictions: Hand guns, food.

UKIAH - Indoor Flea Market, 1061 Cunningham (off Talmage). Open Sat. & Sun. Indoors. Dealers fee: $5 per day per table. Att: 500-1,000. Att. fee: none. Mgr. Boyd Ferguson, 1061 Cunningham, Ukiah, CA 95482. Ph: (707) 468-9977.

VALLEJO - Napa-Vallejo Flea Market & Auction. 303 Kelly Rd., Vallejo, Ca. Open Sun. 6 a.m.-6 p.m. Indoors and outdoors. Dealers fee starts at $8 including table. Avg. att: 10,000. Nelson Harding, 303 Kelly Rd., Vallejo, CA 94590. Phone (707) 226-8862. Res. sug.

VALLEJO - Flea Market - Super Swap, 900 Fairgrounds Drive. Intersection Highways 80 & 37. Open Sat. & Sun. Indoors and outdoors. Avg. dealers 100. Avg. att. 4,000. Fee $5 day or $8 weekend. Reservations. James E. Kenny, P.O. Box 9, Vallejo, CA 94590. Ph: (707) 553-8080.

VAN NUYS - California Open Air Mart, 5943 Sepulveda Blvd., Open Sat. & Sun 8-3. Dealers: 150 indoors and outdoors. Dealers fee: $25 day. Admission: $1 per person, under 12 free. Mgr: Lowell A. Dorfman, 5943 Sepulveda Blvd., Van Nuys, CA 91401. Ph: (213) 785-0296. Restrictions: no used merchandise, except licensed antique dealers. Res. sug.

VENTURA - Ventura Flea Market, at the Fairgrounds. 1982 dates are Feb. 7, Mar. 28, May 23, Aug. 1, Oct. 31, Dec. 5. 10,000 avg. att. $12 to $25 per space. R. G. Canning Ent. Inc. P. O. Box 400, Maywood, CA 90270. Phone (213) 588-2727.

VENTURA - 101 Drive-in & Swap Meet, 4826 Telephone Rd. Open Sat. & Sun. Outdoors. Dealers fee: Sat. $3, Sun. $9. Attendance fee Sat. 35¢, Sun. 50¢. Brad Paulson, 4826 Telephone Rd., Ventura, CA 93003. Phone (805) 644-5061. Res. sug.

VERNALIS - The Orchard Flea Mkt. 2553 E. Hwy 132. On Hwy. 132 between Tracy and Modesto. Open every Sat. & Sun. Outdoors. Dealers fee $5. Free attendance. Mgr. Paulette, P. O. Box 705, Vernalis, CA 95385. Phone (209) 835-8972. No food, gun, candy or produce.

VISALIA - Visalia Sales Yard, 29660 Rd. 152. 2 miles east of Visalia on Hwy. 198. Open Thur. & Sun. 250 dealers. Outdoors. Dealers fee: $4 per 10'. Free admission. Avg. Att. 1,000. Paul Furnas, 29660 Rd. 152, Visalia, CA 93291. Phone (209) 734-9092. Restrictions: no prepared food, drinks, etc.

WATSONVILLE - Our Swap Market, highway 152 "Santa Cruz County Fairgrounds". Open Sat. & Sun. Indoor if raining & outdoors if sunny. Sellers, 300. Bill Reed, 260 Rodriguez St., Watsonville, CA 95076. Ph: (408) 724-3801. Overnight parking.

WATSONVILLE - The Depot Flea Market, 545 Salinas Rd. Open Fri. thru Mon, 10 am to 4 pm. 7 to 10 sellers. 1 to 4000 att., free admission. Jack Reeves, 1525 Old Valencia School Rd., Aptos, CA. Ph: (408) 722-7544.

WHITTIER - Sundown Swap Meet, 12322 Washington, Blvd. Open Fri. Sat. Sun. 400 sellers, avg. att. 5,000. Outdoor. Fee: $4 and $4.50. William J. Bianchi, 12322 Washington Blvd. Whittier, CA. Ph: (213) 696-7560. Res.

COLORADO

COLORADO SPRINGS - City Flea Market, Kiowa at Bijou. Open 1st weekend of each month. 120 dealers. $13 fee for weekend. 2,500 avg. att. 50¢ admission. 1804 S. Nevada # Colorado Springs, CO 80906. Ph: (303) 475-7324.

COLORADO SPRINGS - Flea Market Inc., 3701, N. Nevada. Open Sat. & Sun. 7 am till 4 pm. Outdoor Fee: $5. Dealers: 400. Att* 5,000 and up. Ginger Haggard, P.O. Box 7834, Colorado Springs, CO 80933. Ph: (303) 475-9439. Res.

COMMERCE CITY - Mile High Flea Market, 5200 E. 64th Ave. Open every Sat. & Sun. 6 am to 5 pm. Have over 1000 spaces. Phone (303) 289-4656.

DENVER - Evans Flea Market, at the Evans Drive-In, 2705 W. Evans. Open every Sat. & Sun., 6 am to 6 pm. $2 sellers fee.

DENVER - Denver Antique Market, 2727 W. 27th Ave. Open Sat. & Sun., 10 am - 6 pm. Indoor. $25 for 8×10 lockable booth. Antiques and collectables only. Reservation req. Avg. att. 500. Sellers, 65. Andy & Sally Burnett, 11306 E. 7th Ave. Aurora, CO 80010, Ph: (303) 364-9469, 455-9175 or 455-9948.

DENVER - Bonanza Flea Market, 5695 N. Federal Blvd. Open year round. Sat. and Sun. Summer 6 am to 5 pm, winter 8 am to 4 pm. 600 dealers. $8 per space. 6 to 9000 att. Ph: (303) 455-5891 or 433-4743.

DENVER - Mile High Flea Market, Inc. 5200 East 64th AVe. Commerce City, Open Sat. & Sun. 7 am to 5 pm. Fee: $5. Outdoors. Att: 4,000. Andrew L. Hermes, 5200 East 64th, Commerce City, CO 80022.

ESTES PARK - Barter Mart Flea Market, 2652 Big Thompson Cnyn. Open May 1st thru Oct. 1st, every Sat. and Sun., 9 am to 6 pm. Outdoors. Fee: $3. 500 avg. att. Jan Wear, 2652 Big Thompson Canyon, Drake, CO 80515. Ph: (303) 586-5444. Antiques, gifts, jewelry and junk.

FT. COLLINS - Ft. Collins Bazaar & Farmers Market, 2345 E. Mulberry. Open May 1st thru Nov. 1st, on the weekends. 50 to 75 sellers, $6 per day, $10 weekend. 2000 avg. att. John Ferrie, P. O. Box 1562, Ft. Collins, Co. 80522. Phone (303) 221-1225.

LONGMONT - Longmont Furniture and Misc. Auction, 10 S. Main St. Open every Saturday. 35 dealers, $2 per table, 500 avg. att., free adm. Howard L. Munsell, Box 1044, Longmont, CO 80501. Ph: (303) 776-2116.

PUEBLO - West 11th St. Flea Market, 2106 W. 11th St. Open Sat. & Sun., 8 am to 5 pm. $2 per space. 45 to 50 sellers. 2 to 4000 att. Free adm. Nick Gonzales, Ph: (303) 542-2516.

FLEA MARKET AMERICA

CONNECTICUT

BERLIN · Berlin Antique & Flea Market, Webster Square Plaza Shopping Center. Open Sat. & Sun. 10 am to 6 pm 10 by 10 space $12 per weekend.

CANTON - The Cob-Web, Jct. Rt's 44-202-179, West of Hartford. Open Sun. - May thru Sept. 50 dealers, outdoors. Dealers fee: $10. Free admission. Dolly Rudder, P.O. Box 354, Canton, CT. 06019. Phone (203) 693-2658 and 693-0141. Res. sug.

ENFIELD - D & D Auction Galleries, 35 Pearl St., via Rts. 5 or 91. Open year round, Sun. from 9 am to 5 pm. 30 - 40 dealers indoors. Contact manager for cost and availability. Richard Fortin, 12 Dale St., Windsor Locks, CT 06096. Ph: (203) 623-3229. Antiques & Collectibles.

FARMINGTON - The Attic, Rt. 6 via Rts. 1-84, 10, 177; across from Farmington Drive-In. Open June thru Sept. Sun. 11 am to 6 pm. Indoors and outdoors. Fee $5, reservation requested. Lillian Cartwright, The Attic, Rt. 6, Farmington, CT 06032. Ph: (203) 677-7287. All types of merchandise.

GOSHEN - Torington Kiwanis Flea Market and Antiques. Goshen Fairgrounds. Ph: 489-8716, mailing address 31 James St. Torington, CN 06790. Indoor and outdoor facilities. 45 dealers. 1200 attendance. Attendance fee 50¢, dealers fee $10. Ample parking and food concessions.

MANCHESTER - Trader World. 1-86 eastbound at exit 94. Open April or May thru Oct. or Nov. depending on weather. Sundays from 7:30 am to 5 pm. 15-25 dealers outdoors. Fee $5. Frank and Sandy Halm, 444 Tolland Tpk, Manchester, CT 06040. Ph: (203) 646-9378. Clothing, antiques, odds and ends.

MILFORD - Milford Swap 'N' Shop. Cherry St. & Post Rd. Open every Sun & all holidays. 600 sellers. $7.50 per space. Attendance $1 per car 50¢ walk in. R. Van Buren. Ph: (203) 878-5600.

NAUGATUCK - Peddler's Market, 1106 New Haven Rd; Rt. 8 to Rt. 63, across from Beacon Valley Golf Range. Open Sundays fromthe middle of May to the middle of November, 9 am to 5 pm. 20-30 dealers outdoors. Fee $6. Alice S. Slade, 1106 New Haven Rd., Naugatuck, CT 06770. Ph: (203) 729-7397. Antiques, crafts, produce, flowers, baked goods, miscellaneous.

NEWINGTON - Gem Antique Flea Market, 2985 Berlin Tpke. Open every Sat. & Sun.

NIANTIC - The Barn Shoppes, 41 W. Main St.; Conn Tpk, exit 72, then 2 mi. east on Rt. 156. Open year round, Sat. and Sun., 10 am to 6 pm. 10-12 dealers & craftsmen at work indoors. Fee $7 wknd, reservations needed. Maureen F. Wirth, 26 Nichols, Waterford, CT 06385. Ph: (203) 442-5968. Antiques, collectibles, crafts, leather, gift items.

NORWICH - The Great Norwich Flea Market, 790 W. Thames St., Conn. Tpk exit 79a to Rt. 32. Open Sept. to the beginning of June, Sun. from 9 am to 5 pm. 40-70 dealers indoors and outdoors. Fee $10, less for longer term. Tables $1 each. One weeks notice required. Alan Delfiner, 50 Carrol Ave., Norwich, CT 06360. Ph: (203) 889-7408. All types of merchandise.

OLD SAYBROOK - Moore's Trading Post, Mill Rock Rd.; off Rts. 9 and I-95. Open year round Sat. and Sun. 9 am to dusk, except July, Aug. and Sept. to 10 pm. 20 permanent shops indoors, 200 spaces outdoors. Fee $5 wknd. Dean A. Moore, Mill Rock Rd., Old Saybrook, CT 06475. Ph: (203) 388-9047. Antiques, paintings, furniture & misc.

SOUTHINGTON · Southington Outdoor Flea Market, Queen St., Rt. 10; off I-84 exit 32. Open May thru Nov., Sat., Sun., and Holidays, from 8 am to dusk. Outdoors. 20 to 35 dealers, $5 per day. Clair Nison, P.O. Box 369, Southington, CT 06489. Ph: (203) 628-4873 after 4 pm.

TORRINGTON · The Market Place, 1530 E. Main St. Open mid-May to mid-Nov., Sat. and Sun. from 9 am to dusk. Outdoors. 50-60 dealers. $7.50 per day. Rosemary M. Rosette, c/o Moscarrillo's Florist, 1443 E. Main St. Torrington, CT 06790. Ph: (203) 482-4498 or 489-8338.

WALLINGFORD · Redwood County Flea Market & Country Store, So. Hartford Turnpike. Phone (203) 269-5947, mailing address: Roberta Dubar, 4 East St., Wallingford, CN 06492. Outdoor facilities, Fri. 11-dusk, Sat. Parking, restaurant, County Store.

DISTRICT OF COLUMBIA

GEORGETOWN - Antique Fair and Flea Market, Wisconsin Ave. & Que St. N.W. Open every Sunday 9 am to 6 pm, March thru Nov. Ph: (202) 333-0289.

WASHINGTON - Barracks Row Flea Market, 745 8th St. S.E. Open Sat 9 am to 5 pm; Sunday 10 am to 5 pm. Ph: (202) 543-1023 or 543-9688.

DELAWARE

DELMAR - Lee's Flea Market, on U.S. 13, 7 miles N. of Salisbury. Accomodates 300 sellers, $5 for 20 x 20 space. Open every Sat. & Sun.

DOVER - Spence's Flea Market 550 S. New St. Open every Tuesday & Friday 8 am to ??. Ph: (302) 734-3441.

LAUREL - Shore's Largest Flea Market, on the southeast corner of U.S. 13 Dual Hwy. & 9 E. Open all year Sat., Sun. & holidays, except Thanksgiving & Christmas. Indoor & Outdoors.. 40 sellers, $4 per space. 2000 avg. att. Geo. & Helen Purnell, Phone (302) 875-2478.

NEW CASTLE - New Castle Antiques Mall, 7th and Delaware St. Open every Sat. May 3rd to Sept. 27th, 11 am to 6 pm. Bob or Betty Cherico. Ph: (302) 328-9385 weekday, 32-2065 weekends.

NEW CASTLE - New Castle Outdoor Flea Market, Hares' Corner at Rt. 40 & 273. Open on Fri., Sat. & Sun. 8 am to 4 pm. Dealer info: phone (302) 328-4101.

REHOBOTH BEACH - Golden Door Shows Flea Market, Rehoboth Ave. Sat., Sun. & holidays. Phone (302) 875-5084.

FLORIDA

APOPKA - Three Star Flea Mkt. Open Sat. & Sun. dawn to dusk. 50 sellers. Indoors and outdoors. Fee: $5. 2,000 to 3,000 att. Mary C. Shepherd (owner), Rt. 1 Box 380 C. Apopka, Fla. 32703. Ph: (305) 293-2722.

ARCADIA - Arcadia Drive-In Flea Market, located on Hwy. 17 N. Open Sun., 8 am to 5 pm. 15 to 25 dealers. Phone (813) 494-2321.

ARCADIA - Economy Flea Market, downtown U.S. Hwy 17 South. Open every Sat. and Sun.

AUBURNDALE - Flea Market, Drive-In Theatre, on Hwy 92 & 559. Open every Sun.

BIG PINE KEY - Flea Market, at the St. Peters Catholic Church. Open every Sat., 6 am to ? Rosa Hoffman, P.O. Box 876, Summerland, Fla. 33042.

BARTOW - Outdoor Flea Market, Hwy 17 South, at the Drive-In Theatre. Open every Sun., 6 am to 2 pm.

BAYARD - Bayard Flea Market & Antiques. 12561 Phillips, Hwy U.S. 1 South. Open every Sat. and Sun.

BOULOUGNE - Traders Village Flea Market & Auction, U.S. 1 & 301. Open daily, 9 am to 6 pm. Auction on Sat. at 8 pm. Sellers fee: $4 to $6 per space per day. Gene Tierce. Ph: (904) 536-9951.

BRADENTON - Roma Flea Market, 5715 Hwy 301 South of Oneco. Open every Sat. and Sun., 8 am to 5 pm. Tom Lewis, Mgr.

BROOKSVILLE - Colburn's Flea Market, 1211 U.S. 98 North. Open Sat. & Sun. Avg. att. 3,000 plus. Reservations preferred. Col. Denver D. Colburn, 1211 U.S. 98 North. Brooksville, Fl. 33512. Ph: (904) 796-2908.

BROOKSVILLE - Spring Hill, Airport Mart. 11555 Spring Hill Blvd. Open Fri., Sat. & Sun. 9-4. Indoor and outdoor., $30 mo. 8 x 12 Lockup space. $1 outdoors. Avg. dealers: 136. Avg. Att. 1,000. Louis F. Mlecka, P. O. Box 908, Brooksville, Fla. 33512. Phone(904) 796-2424. Auctions Fri. & Sat. 7:30 pm. Res. Req. inside.

CLEARWATER - Big Swapper (Gulf to Bay Drive-In). 25 N. Belcher Rd. Open Sun. 8 am to 3 pm. Dealers fee: $2. Outdoor. Avg. dealers 90. Avg. att: 1,200. Jim Payne, 25 N. Belcher Rd., Clearwater, Fla. 33515.

COCOA - Jumping Flea Market, U.S. North. Open every Sat. and Sun. Over 50 sellers.

COCOA - Village Flea Market, downtown area. Open daily, 8 am to 5 pm. 30 to 40 sellers, $3 per space. 1000 avg. attendance.

CREEL CITY - Creel City Flea Market. Open Sat. and Sun. 8 am to 5 pm. Ph: (813) 494-3673.

CROSS CITY - Norma's Mini Flea Market, on Hwy. 19 & 98. Open every Sat. 25 dealers, $2 to $3 per space. Norma Reynolds, P.O. Box 1372, Cross City, Fla. 32628.

DADE CITY - Joy-Lan Drive-in, U.S. Hwy. 301 N. Open 6 a.m.-4 p.m. Outdoors. Dealers fee: $2. Free attendance. Eddie Lee Whidden, P. O. Box 498, Dade City, Fla. 33525. Phone 567-5085. No guns or animals sold

DANIA - Swap Shop. Hwy Drive-In Theatre, on U.S. 1. Open every Sat. and Sun.

DAYTONA BEACH - Mason Ave. Flea Market. Open every Sat. and Sun., 8 am to 6 pm. About 70 sellers, indoor and outdoor. 1500 avg. att.

DAYTONA BEACH - Interstate Flea Market, I-95 at U.S. 92. Open Sat. & Sun., 8 am to 4:30 pm. Up to 500 spaces, $6 per space. Phone (904) 252-1999. Jim & Mert Kennedy, Mgr.

DELAND - Country Flea Market, 2700 North Blvd., Hwy 17. Open every Sat. and Sun. Joe Ralston. Ph: (904) 734-1962.

DELAND - 500 yds. east of I-4 on Fla. #44 at the Agriculture Center. Open every Wed. 7 am to ??, indoor and outdoor. Sellers fee: $4 and $3 for the day. Travers Burdetter. Ph: (309) 734-1612.

DELRAY BEACH - Thieves Flea Market, 2399 N. Federal Hwy. #1 North. Open every Sat. and Sun. 6 am to 2 pm.

DELRAY - Delray Drive In Swap Meet, U.S. 1 Delray Fla. Every Sat. and Sun. 6-2. Dealers fee$1 Sat, $3 Sun.

FORT LAUDERDALE - Thunderbird Swap Meet, 3121 W. Sunrise Blvd. Fort Lauderdale Fla. 33313. Outdoor facilities, Wed., Thur.. Fri., Sat. and Sun. 6-4. 1000 dealers, 15,000 attendance. Dealers fee Wed. $3, Thur-Fri. $2, Sat. $4, Sun. $5.50. Att. fee 25¢, parking 25¢ weekdays, $1 Sun. Food concessions.

FT. LAUDERDALE - Sunrise Flea Market, Sunrise Blvd. and 31st Ave. Open every Fri. and Sat., 10 am to 9 pm and Sun. 10 am to 7 pm. 96 sellers. Indoors. Ph: (305) 949-7959 or 931-4624 or 733-4617.

FT. LAUDERDALE - Oakland Park Flea Market. Oakland Park Blvd. at 31st Ave. Open every Fri. & Sat., 10 am to 9 pm. and Sun. 10 am to 7 pm. 100 sellers. Indoors. Ph: (305) 949-7959 or 931-4624 or 733-4617.

FORT MEYERS - Ortiz Ave. State Rt. 80-B. Open Sat. and Sun. 7 am to 5 pm. $4 selling fee. Barbara Collins, Rt. 1 Box 551 F. Fort Meyers, Fla. Ph: (813) 694-5019.

GIBSONTON - Palm Grove Flea Market, 12104 S. Hwy. 41. Open 7 days a week. Indoors & outside. $3.50 sellers fee. Phone (813) 677-6400.

HALLANDALE - Hallandale Flea Market, U.S. Highway 1 and Hallendale Beach Blvd. Open Sat. & Sun. 8 a.m. - 3 p.m. Indoors June to Nov. 1; outdoors Nov. to June 1. Dealers fee $7 Sat. & $10 Sun. Attendance fee: 25¢. Lenny Rose, P. O. Box 805, Hallandale, Fla. 33009. Phone (305) 454-0777.

HALLANDALE - Hallandale Flea Market & Swap Shop, at the Gulf Stream Park - Hallandale Beach Blvd. & U.S. #. Open Year Round. Sat. & Sun., 6 am to 3 pm. 1000 dealer spaces. Ph: (305) 454-0777.

HOLIDAY - Flea Market, on U.S. 19 in Holiday. Open every Fri, Sat. and Sun. R. Johnson, Mgr.

HOMOSASSA - Howards Flea Market, Rt. 2, Box 205, Homosassa, Fla. 32646. Open Sat. & Sun. Indoors and outdoors. Dealers fee: $4.50. Free attendance. 3 tables supplied per booth. Avg. att: 3000. John Raymond, Karen Howard, St. Rt. 2, Box 8626, Inverness, Fla. 32650. Phone (904) 628-4656. Res. sug.

HUDSON - Sunshine Flea Market. 2815 Sunset Blvd. Open Sat. and Sun. Office open daily except Mon. Indoor and outdoor. Avg. dealers 250. Avg. Att. 4,000 to 7,000. Res. Charles Stumm, 2815 Sunset Blvd. Hudson, Fla. 33568. Ph: (813) 863-1805.

JACKSONVILLE - Cribb's Flea Market, on San Juan St. Open every Sat. & Sun. 80 spaces, $4 per day sellers fee.

JACKSONVILLE - The Market Place, 6839 Ramona Blvd. Open Sat. & Sun., 8 am to 5 pm. Jacksonvilles largest flea market. Phone (904) 786-1153.

JACKSONVILLE - Thieves Flea Market, 2106 N. Edgewood. Open Tues. thru Sun. 9 am to 6 pm. W.O. Stricklan, Ph: (904) 786-9919.

JACKSONVILLE - Liberty Street Flea Market, 28th & Liberty St. Open Sat. and Sun. 8 am to 5:30 pm. 40 to 100 sellers, $3.50 outdoors, $4.50 indoors. Della Larson, 2130 Armsdale Rd., Jacksonville, Fla. 32218; Ph: (904) 751-4669.

JACKSONVILLE - Bargain House of Fleas, 6010 Blanding Blvd. Open every Sat. and Sun., 8:30 am to 6 pm. Matt Skenes, Mgr.

JACKSONVILLE - Uncommon Market, 10557 Atlantic Blvd. Open daily, 8 am till dark. 100 dealers, fee: $4 covered, $3 open air. Randy Martin, Ph: (904) 641-6666. (NEW MARKET)

KEY LARGO - Key Largo Flea Market, U.S. 1 and Mahogany Dr. Ph: (305) 451-9902, mailing address, Rt. 1, Box 145, Key Largo, Fla. 33037. Outdoor facilities, every Sun. year round. 50-60 dealers, 500-1000 attendance. Dealers fee $4. Ample parking, food concessions.

LAKE CITY - Lake City Flea Market, at the Columbia Co. Fairgrounds. Open every Sat. & Sun., except for fair dates, Sat. 8 am to 5 pm, Sun · 9 am to 5 pm. 50 sellers plus room for more . Sellers fee: $4.50 under shed, $3 outside. Phone (904) 752-1999 or 752-6709.

LAKELAND - Sunshine Flea Market, 3375 Hwy. 98 South, Bartow Rd. Open Fri., Sat. & Sun. Sellers fee: $3.12 per space, Fri. is free if pd. with Sat. & Sun. Phone (813) 665-9722 or 646-2062.

LAKELAND - Lakeland Farmer's Market, 2701 Swindell Road. Open Thur., Fri., Sat. & Sun. Indoors and outdoors. Free attendance. Ann Edwards, 2701 Swindell Road, Lakeland, Fla. 33805. Phone (813) 682-4809. No food concessions, animals, alcohol or ammunition sold. Res. sug.

LAKE OKEECHOBEE - Cypress Hut Flea Mkt. Open Sat. & Sun. from 6 am. 60-85 dealers. Gil Boggs, Mgr.

LAKE WORTH - Trail Drive-In Theatre Swap Meet, Lake Worth Rd. Lake Fla. every Sat and Sun. 6-2. 250 dealers, 4000 attendance.

LARGO - White Elephant Mkt. Place and Fleas. 1300 Starkey Rd. Open 6 days except Mon. from 10 am.

LAKE PANASOFKEE - Emert Flea Mkt. State Rd. 470 at 72nd Ave. (St. Lumber Yard) Fri., Sat., and Sun.

LAKE PARK - The Flea & Me, 914 Park Ave. Sat & sun.

LEESBURG - Vivians Flea Mkt., 2 miles north of Leesburg on Hwy 441 Fri., Sat. & Sun from 8 am. Arleen Hoag, Mgr.

LONGWOOD - Longwood Flea Market, 1 mi. north of 434 toward Sanford on 17-92. Open 7 days a week.

LYNN HAVEN - Peddler's Alley, 702 thru 716 Ohio Ave. Open 7 days.

LUTZ - Lutz County Flea Market, 2½ miles north of Lutz on Hwy 41, Fri. 12 to 5, Sat. & Sun. 7:30 am to 5. 100 dealers.

MAITLAND - (15 min. from Orlando). The Maitland Flea Market, Inc. 1941 U.S. highway 17-92. Open Sat. & Sun. 8-5. Avg. Dealers: 300. Avg. Att. 4,000. Fee: $3.50 day. Dale F. Tucker, owner, 1941 Highway 17-92, Maitland, Fla. 32751. Reservations, call Wed.-Fri. 9-5. Ph: (305) 339-2920.

MALABAR - On U.S. Rt. 1, Collectors Mall. Open every day except Wed. 10 am to 5 pm. 15 to 20 sellers. Virginia Matlock, Box 44, Palm Bay, Fla. 32905. Ph: (305) 724-0100.

MARGATE - Lake Shore Swap Shop, 1000 State. Ed & Margaret Fla 33317. Ph: 972-3248. Every Sun. 6-2. 150 dealers, 3000 attendance, dealer's fee $3.

MARIANNA - Bargain Barn & Flea Market, 1134 W. Lafayette St. Open on Mon., Tue., Fri. & Sat., 9 am to 5 pm. Phone (904) 526-4889.

MELBOURNE - North Brevard Flea Mkt. 4410 Harbor City Blvd. U.S. 1 North. Sat. & Sun. from 8 am.

MIAMI - Cocoanut Grove Flea Mkt. Dinner Key .Auditorium. Sun. 8 to 4.

MIAMI - Tropicaire Flea Market, Inc., 7751 SW 40 St. Open Sat. & Sun. Avg. dealers: 600. Outdoors. Dealers fee: $4 Sat. and $9 Sun. Att. fee: 25¢ Daily att: Sat. 5,000 and Sun. 15,000. James Miller, 7751 SW 40th St., Miami, Fla. 33155. Phone (305) 264-4535. Restrictions: Guns, autos, food, drug paraphernalia. Res. req.

MILTON - Bostic's Big Oak Flea Market, Hwy. 90 and West Spencer Field Road, Ten miles east of Pensacola. Open Fre., Sat. & Sun. Indoors and outdoors. Dealers fee: $3.50. Free attendance. Max Bostic, 140 Indiana Circle, Milton, Fla. 32520. Phone (904) 594-8985.

NORTH FT. MYERS - Big Swapper (Northside Drive-In). U.S. 41 Norht. Open Sat., Sun. 8 am - 3 pm. Fee: $2. Avg. Dealers 75, Avg. att. 1,500. Chuck Rose, P.O. Box 1629, Ft. Myers, Fla. 33902. Ph: (813) 995-2254.

NORTH MIAMI - 7th Ave. Flea Mkt. 13995 N.W. 7th Ave. Open Thurs., Fri., and Sat., 10 am to 9 pm. Sun. 10 am to 7 pm. 80 sellers indoors. Ph: (308) 949-7959 or 931-4624 or 733-4617.

NORTH MIAMI - N. Miami Flea Mkt. 14135 N. 7th Ave. Open Thur. Fri., Sat., 10 am to 9 pm. Sun. 10 am to 7 pm. 120 sellers indoors. Ph: (305) 949-7959 or 931-4624 or 733-4617.

NAPLES - Naples Flea Market, at the Trail Drive-In on U.S. 41 & Immokalee Rd. Open Sat. & Sun., 7 am to 4 pm. Outdoors. 50 to 70 dealers, fee: $5 on Sat., $6 on Sun. 3 to 6000 avg. att. Phone (813) 597-4187.

NORTH FORT PIERCE - Biz-e Flea Mkt., 3252 U.S. 1. Open every Sat. & Sun. 100 sellers. sellers fee: $6.25. Phone (305) 569-0147.

OCALA - Super Flea Mkt., 3840 N.W. Gainsville Rd. ½ mi No. on old 441. Wed. only.

OCALA - Jerry's Surplus Outlet Flea Mkt. Fri., Sat. & Sun. Hwy. 441 S.

OKEECHOBEE - Currys Flea Market on Hwy. 441 S. Open every Fri., Sat. & Sun. Outdoors. 45 dealers, $4 per space. Reservations are advised for the winter season. Phone (813) 763-5005.

OKEECHOBEE - Chobee Farmers Porduct & Flea Market, on Hwy. 78 W. Indoor & outdoors. Open Sap. & Sun., 60 sellers, $5 per space. Phone (813) 763-7009.

OLDSMAR - Oldsmar Flea Market, 180 North Race Track Rd., open year round, Fri., Sat. & Sun. 9 am to 5:30 pm. 90 sellers inside, 200 outside. Sellers fee $10 and up. Richard Ferkich, Phone (813) 855-5308 or 855-1324.

ORLANDO - Cypress World Flea Market, at 11000 South Orange Blossom Trail. Open every Sat. & Sun., 7 am till dark. 40 dealers, $2.50 per space. Phone (305) 857-2076.

ORLANDO - Chuck's Standard Flea Mkt. Corner of Mercy Rd. & Old Winter Garden Rd. Sat & Sun. 35 to 40 dealers.

ORLANDO - Eastland Indoor Mkt. Eastland Center 6120 E. Colonial, just east of 436 on Hwy. 50 next to Food World. Open 7 days 9 to 5.

ORLANDO - Big Mac's Flea Mkt. Pine Hills Drive-In, 5050 W. Colonial Dr. Sat. & Sun. 9 to 5.

ORLANDO - Big Swapper (Pine Hills Drive-In). Pine Hills. Open Sat. & Sun. 9 to 5. Avg. dealers 45. Avg. att. 200-300. Fee: $3. Big Mac, P.O. Box 15712, Orlando, Fla. 32808.

ORMOND BEACH - Big Swapper (Nova Drive-In). Open Sat. & Sun. 7 am - 5 pm. 125 Dealers. 2,000 attendance. Fee: $3. Wayne Bottorf, P.O. Box 1047, Ormond Beach, Fla., 32074. Ph: (904) 672-3014

PACE - Bostic's Big Oak Flea Market, W. Spencer Fiald and Hwy. 90. Open Sat. & Sun. Open air building, 15 inside booths and 40 outside tables. Phone (904) 994-7432.

PALMETTO - Country Fair, Inc., junction of Hwy. 301 & U.S. 41. Open every Wed., Sat. and Sun. 350 dealers, fee: $3 per day. 3500 avg. att. W.W. Cartwright, P.O. Box 609, Palmetto, Fla. 33561. Ph: (813) 722-5633.

PANAMA CITY - Rain or Shine Flea Market, at 2327 W. Orlando Rd. Open daily, Mon. thru Fri., 9 am to 5 pm., Sat. & Sun., 7:30 am to 5 pm. 50 to 75 dealers, $2.50 per day, $5 per week or $15 per month. Phone (904) 763-6489.

PENSACOLA - T & W Flea Market, at 2001 N. T St. Open daily. Phone (904) 433-4315.

PENSACOLA - Quayside Thieves Mkt. S. Palofax St. at Municipal Auditorium. Sat. & Sun. 9 to 5. 40 sellers. T. Cummings. Mgr.

PENSACOLA - Dixieland Flea Mkt., 1203 N. T St. Open Fri., Sat. & Sun. 8 am to 5 pm. Indoor and out. Ph: (904) 438-5753.

157

PENSACOLA - Shady Oaks Flea Market, 60th & Fairfield. Open 7 days a wk. Avg. sellers, 20. Demon Hinton, 1704 N 60th, Pensacola, FL 32506. Ph: (904) 456-9534.

PENSACOLA - Westside Flea Mkt. & Auction, 4610 Mobile Hwy. Open daily. Over 100 sellers on wknds. $3 per space with table Mon.-Fri. Ph: (904) 456-9811.

PINELLAS PARK - Wagonwheel Flea Market, 7801 Park Blvd. Open Sat. & Sun. 8-5. Avg. dealers: 1,300. Outdoors, 500; covered, 800. Outside $4.50 day and covered, $6.50 day. $1 a day per table supplied. 50¢ parking per car load. Att: 20,000 to 30,000. a weekend. Hardy Huntley, 7801 Park Blvd., Pinellas Park. Fla. 33565. (813) 544-5319. No guns, ammunition, fireworks or drug using materials. Res sug.

PINELLAS PARK - 49er Flea Market. 10525 49 St. No. ¼ mile north on 49th St. off U.S. 19 overpass. Open Sat. & Sun. 8-? Dealers:150. Outdoor. Att: 2500. Ned or John Burket, 10525 N. Clearwater, Fla. 33520. Phone (813) 576-3367.

PLANT CITY - Country Village. Corner of State Road 39 and Sam Allen Road. Open Wed., Sat. & Sun. 150-250 dealers, outdoors. Dealers fee: $3 and $4. Ferris Waller, Rt. 9 Corner Sam Allen Rd. & 39, Plant City, Fla. 33566. Res sug.

RIVERVIEW - Four Aces Flea Market, Open Fri. thru Tue., seller fee: weekday $3, weekend $4. Phone (813) 677-1231.

RIVERVIEW - Seven Star Auction & Flea Mkt. Hwy 301 So. on Alofia River. Open Wed., Sat. & Sun. 7:30 till dark. Mailing address: P.O. Box 1067, Riverview, Fla.

ST. AUGUSTINE - Ye Olde Flea Mkt., U.S. #1 North (north of old city gate, 1½ miles toward Jacksonville). Open Fri., Sat., .Sun. 30 dealers indoor and out. Seller fee $4-1 day, $7-2 days, $9.50-3 days, with tables. Avg. atten. 1000 per day. Wm. Touchton, Rt. 4, Box 13, St. Augustine, Fla. 32084. Ph: (904) 824-0933.

SANFORD - Sanford Village Super Flea Market, 1500 French Avenue, Sanford FLA. Open Wed., Fri., Sat. & Sun. 7:30 am - 5 pm. Avg. dealers: 200. Indoors and outdoors. Dealers fee: $5 to $10. Tables supplied. Avg. att: 2000-5000. J.W. "Red" Jones, P.O. Box 2196, Sanford, FLA. 32771. Phone (305) 323-5454. Res. sug.

SARASOTA - Trail Drive-in Flea Market, 6801 N. Tamiami Trail. Across from airport. Open Fri. & Sat., 8-4. Outdoors. Free admission. Tables supplied for $1 a day. Dealers fee: $2 Sat. & $3 Sun. Avg. att: 20,000. Harold Jordan, mgr. Ph: (813) 355-6329.

SEFFNER - Joe & Jackie's Flea Mkt. Uptown Seffner Hwy 574, 3 miles north of Brandon. Open 7 days.

STUART - B & A Flea Market & Mini Mall, 2201 S.E. Indian St. Open every Fri., Sat. & Sun. Indoor and outdoors. 47 inside shops, $60 to $250 per mo. 175 outside spaces, $3 to $6 per space. 5000 avg. att.

STUART - B & A Flea Market, 2885 South Federal Hwy. Open Sat. & Sun., rain or shine all year round. 200 dealers indoors and outdoors. Dealers fee $3 to $6. Free attendance. John Rossiter, 2201 S. E. Indian Street, G-1, Stuart, Fla. 33494. Phone (305) 283-7015. No food or produce.

TAMPA - AAA Flea Mkt., U.S. 41 So. Fri. & Sat. 9 to 5. Neal Hoopengarner, Mgr.

TAMPA - Big Swapper (Fun-Lan Drive-In). East Hillsboro & 22nd St. Open Sun. 8 am - 3 pm. Outdoor. Avg. dealers 25. Avg. Att. 300. No fee. Mike McKinney, P.O. Box 11188, Tampa, Fla. 33610. Ph: (813) 234-2311.

TAMPA - Top Value Flea Mkt., 8120 Anderson Rd. Open Sat. & Sun., 7:30 to 5 pm. Over 600 sellers. 15,000 attendance. Ph: (813) 884-7810. Howard Gardner, Mgr.

TAMPA - Early Attic Flea Mkt., 5005 W. Westshore. Mon thru Fri.

TAMPA - Hillsborough Drive-In Flea Mkt. Open Sat. & Sun.

TAMPA - Underground Tampa Flea Market, 6224 E. Columbus Drive. Open Fri., Sat. & Sun. Ms. Joyce Williams, Tampa, Fla. 33619. Phone (813) 626-0847. Res. sug.

TAMPA - The American Legion Flea Market, 929 E. 139th Ave. Open every Sat. & Sun. Indoor and outdoors.

TITUSVILLE - Frontenac Flea Market, on U.S. 1, between Titusville & Cocoa. Open every Fri., Sat. & Sun. Facilities for over 500 dealers. Phone (305) 631-0241.

TITUSVILLE - Swap Meet at the Drive-In, Hwy 50. Sat. & Sun., 6 am to 5 pm. Dale King, Mgr.

VENICE - Adventure Alley Flea Market. 509 Cypress. Open Sat. & Sun. 9-5. 20 dealers. Indoors. Charlie Hail, 509 Cypress, Venice, Fla. 33595. Ph: 484-3457.

VENICE - Venice Flea Mkt. Venice bypass 41. Wed. Sat. & Sun., 6 am to 5pm. Dale King, Mgr.

VERO BEACH - Highlands Country Style Flea Mkt. So. U.S. 1, across from the Midway Park. Open Sat. & Sun.

WALDO - Waldo Farmers and Flea Market, 1½ miles north of Waldo on U.S. Hwy 301. Ph: (904) 468-2255, mailing address P.O. Box 194, Waldo, Fla 32694. Fri noon till 10, Sat-Sun 7-6. Dealers, fee $3.50.

WEBSTER - Farmers Flea Market, on Rt. 471. Open on Mon. Sellers must have a city and county license. Ph: (904) 793-2021.

WEST PALM BEACH - Farmers Flea Market, 1200 S. Congress Ave. Open Thru., Fri. & Sat. 10 a.m. to 9 p.m. Sun. 12 noon to 6 p.m. Dealers: 250 outdoors. Dealers fee: $15.50 up (4 days). Free attendance. Jeannie R. Martin, 1200 S. Congress Ave., West Palm Beach, Fla. 33406. Phone (305) 965-1500. Rev. required.

ZEPHYRHILLS - Formerly Clark's Flea Market, 1111½ Hwy. 54 East. Open every Tue., Wed. & Thur., 6 am till ? 50 dealers, $4 per day. Fisher Ames, Operator. Phone (305) 782-4175.

ZOLFO SPRINGS - Flea Market, Hwy. 17. Open Sat. and Sun. 7 am to 6 pm. Kyle Sellar, 200 Ave. K. S.E. Ap. 341, Winter Haven, Fla 33880.

GEORGIA

ACWORTH - Delight's Antiques & Flea Market, 4375 Cobb Parkway. Open every Fri., starts at 10 am, Sat. & Sun., 8 am. Over 300 dealers, $1 to $4 space rental. Phone (404)974-5256. Delight Tumlin, 4361 Dallas Rd., Acworth, Ga. 30101.

ALBANY - America's Flea Market, 1030 Gordon Ave. Open every Fri., Sat. & Sun. Largest indoor flea mkt. in southwest Georgia. William Shockey, Mgr. Phone (912)435-6231.

ATLANTA - FOREST PARK - Flea Market at Forest Square, 4855 Jonesboro Rd. Open every Fri., Sat. & Sun. 175 dealers, indoors. 5000 avg. att. Joane Browne, P. O. Box 1382, Forest Park, Ga. 30051. Phone (404) 361-1221.

ATLANTA - Georgia Antique Fair & Flea Market. Lakewood Park Fairgrounds. Open second weekend of each month. Fee: $30. Res. Avg. dealers: 400. Avg. att. 5,000. ELCO Enterprises, Inc. P.O. Box 54048, Atlanta, Ga. 30308. Ph: (408) 872-1913.

ATLANTA - Atlanta Swap Meet & Flea Market, North 85 Drive-In Theatre. Open every Sunday. Sellers fee $6. Ken Cambell. Ph: (404) 993-0768 or 237-8079.

ATLANTA - Atlanta Flea Market, 2424 Piedmont Rd. N.E. Open every weekend, noon on Fri., Sat. and Sun. 320 sellers, $180 per mo. sellers fee, indoors, 25,000 avg. attendance. H. Jones, Ph: (404) 266-2495.

BRUNSWICK - Brunswick "Weathering Oaks" Flea Market & Campground, on Hwy. 17. Open on Sat. & Sun. $3 a day or $5 per weekend, campsites are $1. phone (912) 265-0529.

DUNWOODY - Dunwoody Flea Market, 2490 C, Mt. Vernon Rd. Open every Fri., Sat. & Sun. Phone (404) 394-5397 or 457-2330.

GAINESVILLE - Mule Camp Trade Days, on Hwy. 13 at Black Shear Place. Open 3rd weekend of the mo. Phone (404) 536-4863 or 536-8068.

KINGSTON - Ruby's Trade Day, at Hardin Bridge Rd. & Hwy 411. Open every Thur.

MARIETTA - Antique Fair & Flea Market, 119 Cobb Parkway, N. 41 Hwy. Open 1st weekend of month.

RIVERDALE - Auntie's Antique & Flea Market, 7471 Hwy. 85. Open every Sat. & Sun. Phone (404) 478-9084.

SAVANNAH - Coastal Empire Flea Market, held at the Montgomery St. Drive-In. Open every Fri., Sat. & Sun. 9 am to 5 pm. 50 to 75 dealers, $2 to $4 per space per day. 1500 avg. att.

DOUGLASVILLE - Red Barn Antique Village on Hwy. 78. Open year round, every Sat. and Sun. Outdoors, $3 per space. Bill Wilson Ph: (404) 942-3598.

SUMMERVILLE - Ye Old Trading Grounds, 1 mile N. on Hwy. 27. Open every Tues., Sat. and Sun. 150 dealers, $1 per space. 3 to 4000 avg. att. Ph: (404) 857-1433.

SUMMERVILLE - Peddlers Corner. Open on Tues. 30-50 sellers. $1 fee. Outdoors.

CALHOUN - New Town Flea Market, on New Town Rd. Open every Fri., Sat. & Sun. 50 sellers with room for 100's more. $1 per space. Earl Abernathy, Rt. 5, Calhoun, Ga. 30701. Phone (404) 625-9088.

HAWAII

HONOLULU - KAM Super Swap Meet, at the KAM Drive-In, 98850 Moanalua Rd. Open every Wed., Sat. & Sun. 8 am to 3 pm. Phone 488-5822.

ILLINOIS

ALSIP - Tri-State Swap-O-Rama Flea Market. 4350 West 129th St. Open Wed., Sat., & Sun. 7-4. Dealers: 800. Indoor and out. Att: 5,000 to 6,000. Swap Shop, Inc., 5630 N. Elston Ave., Chicago, Ill. 60646. Ph: (312) 774-3900. Res. sug.

AMBOY - Antique Show & Flea Market, 4-H Fairgrounds, Rt. 30. Open 3rd Sun. each month 9 am to 5 pm. 50¢ admission. Robert Mitchell. Ph: (815) 857-2253.

AURORA - Skylark Swap-O-Rama, Skylark Drive-In Theatre, west on Aurora Rd. 1 mile. Open Sundays April - Nov. 60 dealers outdoor. Fee$4, avg. atten. 1500 daily. Swap Shop, Inc., 5630 Elston, Chicago, IL 60646. Ph: (312) 774-3900.

BARRINGTON · Flea Market. Rt. 14 off Rt. 59 Langendorf Park. Open Sept. 8, 10 am to 4 pm. Sponsored by Barrington Jr. Women's Club. Mrs. A.W. Munson, 803 Dundee Ave., Barrington, IL 6000. Ph: (312) 381-4224.

CAHOKIA · Wild Goose Flea Market. 1028 Camp Jackson Rd. Indoor. 200 dealers. Ben Sobelman, 12031 Jerries Lane, Florissant, Mo. 63033. Ph: (314) 355-7464. Res. sug.

CHICAGO · Jew Town · Maxwell Mkt. 800 W. Maxwell St. Open Sun. $25 yr. license fee, Mayor of Chicago Lic. Dept. Space fee: $6 Sat. & $8 Sun. 50,000 att. and up. Mountana Charlies, Rt. 53, Romyo, Ill.

CHICAGO · Swap-O-Rama Flea Market, 6333 S. Cicero Ave. Open Nove. thru April Thur. 7 am to 4 pm. Indoors. Swap Shop. 8101 Milwaukee Ave. Niles. IL 60648. Ph: (313) 774-3900. Sellers fee $4

CHICAGO · Midway Swap-O-Rama, 6333 S. Cicero, Chicago. Open Fri. nite, Sat. & Sun. year round. 140 sellers indoor and out. Fee $8, avg. atten: 3000. Swap Shop, Inc. 5630 Elston, Chicago, IL 60646. Ph: (312) 774-3900.

CHICAGO · Paris Flea Market. Every Sun. 7-5. Sheridan Drive. 7801 S. Harlem Avenue. Phone (312) 233-2551.

CHICAGO · International Amphitheatre SwapOrama, 4300 S. Haisted. Open Sun. once a month. 500 indoor dealers. Dealers fee: $25. $1 attendance. Avg. att: 10,000. Swap Shop Inc. 5630 N. Elston, Chicago, Ill. 60646. Phone (312) 774-3900. No food. Res. required.

CHICAGO · Brighton Park SwapOrama, 3300 W. 47th Place at Kedzie. Open Sat. & Sun. year round. Avg. att. 4,000. Dealers: 210, indoors. Dealers fee: $10 Sat. / $12 Sun. Swap Shop Inc. 5630 N. Elston, Chicago, Ill. 60646. Phone (312) 774-3900. No food items.

DANVILLE · Flea Market, 2719 N. Vermilion, at the K-Mart Plaza. Open May thru Sept. Fri & Sat., 9 am to 5 pm. Ph: (217) 446-6339.

DANVILLE · Weekend Flea Market, Old Grant Schoolhouse. Sat. & Sun. 9-5. South on Ill. Rt. 1. Free admission. Ph: (217) 446-5094.

DES PLAINES · VFW Flea Market, 2067 Miner, Rt. 14. Open 3rd Sunday of each month 11 am to 5 pm. H. Dyeus. Ph: (312) 823-2511.

ELMHURST · 310 W. Butterfield Rd. Amer. Legion Hall. Open every 2nd Sunday of the month 11 am to 5 pm. H. Hycus. Ph: (312) 823-2511. Indoors.

GENEVA · Kane County Fairgrounds, Rts. 64 & Alt. 30. Open 1st Sun. of each month, 7 am to 5 pm. Indoors & outdoors. 250-600 dealers. $15 fee outdoors, $20 fee indoors. Mrs. J.E. Robinson, 307 Sandholm, Geneva IL 60134. Ph: (312) 232-6264.

GODFREY · Flea Market, Godfrey Community Center. Open 1st Sunday of every month. Vernon Massey, P.O. Box 752, Jacksonville, IL 62650. Ph: (217) 243-3722.

GRAYSLAKE · Lake County Fairgrounds. 40 miles north of Chicago, 3 miles west of I-94. Sun. 9-5. Over 80 sellers. Free parking. Space: $12.

GRAYSLAKE · Grayslake SwapOrama. Rt. 120 and 83. Open Every Sunday April - Nov. 150 dealers outdoors. Dealers fee $6. Attendance fee: 50¢. Avg. att: 2,000. Swap Shop Inc. 5630 N. Elston, Chicago, Ill. 60646. Phone (312) 774-3900.

GRAYSLAKE · Flea Market, Family Outdoor Theatre, Rt. 120, Grayslake, Ill 60030. Ph: (312) 223-8155. Outdoor facilities, every Sun. 8-4. Attendance fee 25¢ perr person.

HIGHLAND · Helvetian Flea Market, Madison County Fair Association Hall, Lindendale Park. Open 2nd Sun. of the month, 10 am to 5 pm. 125 dealers indoors. Fee $6 per table. Free att. D.R. Seifried, RR I-A Holiday Manor, Highland, IL 62249. Ph: (618) 654-2581.

MARION · Flea Market Plus. 9:30-5, Thurs., Fri., Sat. 29th and Home Avenue, Marion, Ill.

MAYWOOD · Maywood Swap-O-Rama, 8600 W. North Ave., Maywood, IL. Open Sundays year round, except during racing. 240 dealers indoor and out. $6 fee, avg. atten. 4000. Swap Shop, Inc., 5630 Elston, Chicago, IL 60646. Ph: (312) 774-3900.

MT. PROSPECT · "Lumberyard" Swap O Rama, 100 N. Northwest Hwy. Rt. 14 at Rt. 83. Open Sat. & Sun. Oct. to April. 100 sellers. Fee $10, avg. atten. 1500-2000. Swap Shop, Inc., 5630 Elston, Chicago, IL 60646. Ph: (312) 774-3900.

NORTHLAKE · Northlake Swap-O-Rama Flea Market. 401 Lake Street. Sun. 7-4. Dealers 75-100. Outdoor. Att: 800-1200. Swap Shop, Inc., 5630 N. Elston Ave., Chicago Ill. 60646. Ph: (312) 774-3900. Res. sug.

OREGON · Trading Fair - open 3rd Sunday each month from 8-5. Ogle County Fairgrounds. Rt. 2. 50¢ admission. For info call (815) 239-1188.

PALATINE · 53 SwapOrama. Rt. 12 at Hicks Rd. at "53", Drive-in Theatre. Open Sundays in April thru November. 100 dealers outdoors. Dealers fee: $6. 50¢ attendance fee. Avg. att: 1500. Swap Shop Inc., 5630 N. Elston, Chicago, Ill. 60646. Phone (312) 774-3900.

PEOTONE · Flea Market. Will County Fairgrounds 1 mi. east of 157. Open Sundays Robert Mitchell, Ph: (815) 857-2253.

PINCKEYVILLE · Southern Ill. People Place. 4th weekend every month. Shirley Woosley. Phone (618) 357-8110.

PRARIE VIEW · Country Boys Flea Market. Qpen Wed., Sat. & Sun. 193 Milwaukee Ave. Rt. 41, Prarie View, Ill. 60069. Phone (312) 541-1952.

ROCKFORD · Rockford Flea Market. Foresi Hills Lodge - Rt. 173. Open 8-4. Outdoors. Admission 50¢. Paul Arduini. Phone (815) 633-5328.

ROCKFORD · Greater Rocky Antique & Flea Market. Corner of 11th St. & Sandyhollow Rd. I-90 to Bypass 20, Hwy. 51 11th St. North exit. Open Sat. & Sun. year round. Dealers: 100-150. Indoors & outdoors. Dealers fee: outdoors $8 & indoors $19. Free admission. Avg. att: 3000-4000. Carol & Jerry Shorkey, 6350 Canyon Wood, Rockford, ILL. Ph: (815) 397-6683.

ROSEMONT · O'Hare Expo SwapOrama, 9721 W. Bryn Mawr at River Rd. Open 1st Sunday - monthly - year round. Dealers: 300 indoors. Dealers fee: $25. Attendance $1. Avg. att: 6,000. Swap Shop Inc., 5630 N. Elston, Chicago, Ill. 60646. Phone (312) 774-3900. Res. sug.

SPRINGFIELD · Springfield Drive-In Flea Market. 3135 Singer Ave. Open 10-4. Outdoor. Avg. dealers 250. Avg. att. 1,000. Fee: $1. Richard Goyne, 3135 Singer Ave., Springfield, Ill. 62703. Ph: (271) 528-4111.

ST. CHARLES · Kane County Flea Market, Inc. Randall Rd. between Rt. 64 & Rt. 38. Open 1st Sunday of each mo. & 2nd weekend in Aug. Space fee, $20 outside, $25 inside. Avg. att. 7,000 to 10,000. Mrs. J.L. Robinson, 307 Sandholm St., Geneva, 60134. Ph: (312) 232-6264.

TREMONT · Tremont Flea Market. Open every Sat. & Sun., May thru Sept. 700 seller spaces. Rt. 9 and Rt. 121. Phone (309) 925-5112.

VOLO · Volo Sales Flea Market and Antique Car Show, Rt. 120. ¼ mile west of Rt. 12. Ph: (815) 385-3896, mailing address, Rt. 1 Box 562a Round Lake IL 60073. Indoor and outdoor facilities, every Sat. and Sun. 8-5. 30 to 40 dealers, 8000 attendance. Attendance fee $1, dealer's fee $12 for weekend. Ample parking, near by campgrounds.

INDIANA

ANDERSON · Olympia Exposion Center. 1312 W. 29th St. Behind Sun Valley Speedway. Open Sat. & Sun. Indoor, and out. George or Brian Canaday, 1312 W. 29th St., Anderson, Ind., 46012. Ph: (317) 643-6305. Limited Overnite parking. Res. sug.

AUSTIN · Flea Market, So. Fourth St. Open every Sat. Ph: (812) 794-3313.

BARGERSVILLE · Bargersville Flea Market, Jct. of Hwy's 135 & 144. Open April thru Nov. 200 dealers, $7 per space. Bill Buechett, 570 Main, Whiteland, In. 46184. Phone (317) 535-4670 or 535-4730.

BLOOMINGTON · Y & W Drive-In Theatre, on Northe 37. Every Sunday 8 am to 4 pm. Phone (812) 339-6319.

BLOOMINGTON · Bloomington Flea Market & Antique Show, summer, held at the Monroe Co. Fairgrounds, monthly, indoors, 150 booths, winter, held at the National Guard Armory, monthly, indoors. G & G Promotions, 113 Gentry St. Bloomington, In. 47401. Phone (812) 333-1922 or 334-3354.

BROOKVILLE · Brookville Flea Market, on Rt. 52. Open every Wed. 7 am to 1 pm. 100 to 200 sellers, up to 1000 in att. Phone (317) 647-3574.

BROWNSTOWN · Jackson Co. Flea Market & Craft Show, at the Jackson Co. Fairgrounds. Open 3rd weekend in June, (Fri., Sat. & Sun.). 85 dealers, inside & out, $6 per space. About 1500 in att. Nancy Erp, 1133 Stadium Dr., Seymour, In 45274. Phone (812) 522-5264.

CANAAN · Flea Market, 12th Annual Canaan Fall Festival. Open Sept. 10, 11, 12. $5 per day or $7.50 weekend. Gary Handlon, Rt. 4, Madison, IN 47250. Ph: (812) 839-4112.

CARLISLE · Flea Market, open 2nd and 4th weekends of each month.

CEDAR LAKE · The Barn and Field Flea Market. 9600 W. 151 Parrish. Open Thurs. thru Sun. 300 dealers. 10,000 avg. att. Sat. & Sun. Overnite parking. D. Corey, P.O. Box 411, Cedar Lake, Ind., 46303. Ph: (219) 696-7368.

CEDAR LAKE · Jobes Flea Market, on Rt. 41. Open every Sat. & Sun.

CEDAR LAKE · Uncle John's Flea Market, 10 miles south of Rt. 30, on Rt. 41. Open every Fri. Sat. & Sun. Ph: (219) 969-7070.

CENTERVILLE · The Flea Marketeers, 103 W. Main St. Open 7 days a week, 9 am to 7:30 pm. Phone (317) 855-2231.

CENTERVILLE · Beechwood Pavillion Flea Market. PB 2, U.S. 40, west, Centerville IN 47330. Ph: 962-4159. Indoor and outdoor facilities. Sat. and Sun. 8-5. 10-15 dealers, 1-3000 attendance. Dealer's fee $2 outside $3 inside. Parking.

CENTERVILLE · Dan's Flea Market, R.R. #1, Box 230B. Open April thru Nov., Sat. & Sun. 7 am to 6 pm. 35 dealers, $5 per day fee. 2000 avg. att. Camping available, $1. Dan Winters. Phone (317) 935-5868 or 855-2648.

159

FLEA MARKET AMERICA

CLARKSVILLE - Trading Fair II, 520 Marriott Drive (off I-65). Sat. & Sun. 10-6. Ph: (812) 288-0600.

CLOVERDALE - Country Corner Flea Market, 2 miles west of Cloverdale on Hwy. 42. Open every Fri., Sat., Sun. & holidays. Indoors & out. Ted Howard, Phone (317) 795-4501 or 795-3528.

COLUMBIA CITY - Flea Market, Auction Center, E. Business Rt. 30 to Gateway Industrial Park. Open weekends. 9 am to 6 pm. 300 dealers. Free admission. ½

CONNERSVILLE - Flea Market, rear of 2207 Vermont. Open daily. C. Loyd, Mgr.

DECATUR - Community Center open 1st Sun. of every month, 8 am to 5 pm. Indoors. Fee $5 per space. Outdoor spaces available. Free admission. James Johnson, 110 So. 10th St., Decatur, IN. Ph: (219) 724-3538.

FORT WAYNE - Flea Market, Speedway Exchange Bldg. Open on Sat. & Sun. however call for dates. Ph: (219) 484-1239.

FT. WAYNE - Speedway Mall Flea Market, 217 Marciel Dr. Open every Fri., Sat. & Sun. Indoors & out. 150 dealers, 2000 avg. att. Phone (219) 484-1239.

FT. WAYNE - New Haven East 30 Drive-In Theatre. Open every Sun. 8 am to 4 pm. Phone (219) 749-8314.

FRANKLIN - Franklin Antique Show & Flea Market, Fairground St. Open Sept. thru May, every third weekend. 42 inside dealers. Huge crowds. Elmer Judkins, 122 Woodland Dr., New Whiteland, In. 46184. Phone (317) 535-5084.

FRIENDSHIP - Friendship Flea Market, Hwy. 62, 6 miles west of Dillsboro. Held 2 times a year, May & Aug. 200 to 500 dealers, outdoors. 2000 to 5000 avg. att. Tom Kerr, Phone (606) 341-1400 or 525-2569.

GRIFFITH - Swap-O-Rama Flea Market, Ridge Rd. Drive-In Theatre. Ridge Rd. & Cline Ave. Open every Sun. May thru Nov. 7 am to 4 pm. Fee $5. 25¢ admission. Swap Shop, 8101 Milwaukee Ave., Niles. IL 60648. Ph: (312) 774-3900.

HAMMOND - 41 Swap-O-Rama, 2500 N. Calumet Ave., 41 Drive-In Theatre. Open every Sun., April thru Nov. 150 dealers, outdoors, $6 per space. 50¢ adm., 2000 avg. att. Swap Shop Inc., 5630 N. Elston, Chicago, Il. 60646. Phone (312) 774-3900.

HOAGLAND - Monthly Flea Market, at the Hayloft. Open 4th Sun. of the month, 10 am to 5 pm. Phone (219) 745-4060 after 6 pm. Don & Betty Stroebel, Mgrs.

INDIANAPOLIS - Hi's House of Treasure. 6405 Mass Ave. Open every Sat. & Sun. 10 to 5.

INDIANAPOLIS - Big Red Flea Market. 11777 Lafayette Ave., Open Fri., Sat., Sun. Auction Sat. Nite. Indoors and out. Mason Promotions, Rt. 1 Whitstown, Ind., 46075. Ph: (317) 769-3266. Res. sug. Overnite camping.

INDIANAPOLIS - Traylor's Antique Flea Market, 7159 East 46th St. Open Sat. & Sun. 9 am - 5 pm. Indoors and outdoors. Fee: $5 outdoors. Dealers 50-100. Att: 1,500. Leo & Laura Traylor, owners, 4512 Callahan St., Wanamaker, IN. 46239. Ph: (317) 545-0339. Weekdays: (317) 862-5192. Res.

INDIANAPOLIS - Liberty Bell Flea Market, 8949 E. Washington St. Open Fri. 1-9, Sat. 10-9, Sun 11-7. Fees: Outside, $4 day, inside $20 weekend. 100 dealers. Kenneth Hall, 8949 E. Washington St., Indianapolis, Ind. 462-19. Ph: (317) 898-3180.

INDIANAPOLIS - Flea Market. 8949 E. Washington St. Open year round. Indoor. Fri 12 am to 9 pm, Sat. 10 am to 9 pm, Sun 11 am to 7 pm. Fee $3. Ph: (317-898-3180.

INDIANAPOLIS - Big Top Flea Market. 1002 E. 52nd St. Indianapolis, Indiana. Wed. - Sun. Ph: (317) 283-7500.

INDIANAPOLIS - Flea Market Magic, Eastgate Shopping Center. Fri. Sat. Sun. Ph: (317) 356-4892.

JACKSONBURG - Flea Market, Jacksonburg Rd. Open every Sat. 9 am to 5 pm. Sun 12 to 5 pm. Ph: (317) 489-4066.

JACKSONBURG - Flea Market, Jacksonburg Rd. Open every Sat. 9 am to 5 pm. Sun 12 to 5 pm. Ph: (317) 489-4066.

KINGSLAND - Flea Market, SR 1 and US 224. Open 2nd weekend of every month, 9 am to 6 pm. Indoors and out, tables furnished. Ph: (219) 597-7375.

KINGSLAND - D & D Country Flea Market, S.R. #1 & U.S. 224. Open every 2nd Sun. 9 to 4. Phone (219) 622-7777 or 587-7375.

LAKE STATION - Dunes Swap O Rama, Dunes Drive-In, 1227 Ripley St. Open Sundays from May to Nov. 50 dealers outdoor. $1 fee, avg. att. 1000. Swap Shop, Inc., 5630 Elston, Chicago, IL 60646. Ph: (312) 774-3900.

LAYFAYETTE - Flea Market, Anderson Auction Gallery, 20 Elston Rd. Open 4th Sat. & Sun of each month. Free admission. Ph: (317) 474-6114. New Market.

LEBANON - Old Cannon Works Flea Market. Open every Sat 11 am to 8 pm. and Sun 12 to 6 pm. Indoors. Jerry or Roxanne. Ph: (317) 482-3220 or 482-6180.

LOWELL - The Livery Stable Antique Mart. 3 mi. E. of Rt. 41, 5 mi W of I-65. Open every Sat. & Sun. 11 am to 5 pm. Ph: (219) 696-9395. Antiques and collectibles.

MARION - Marion Flea Market. Jct. St. Rd., 9 & 37 S. Every Sat. & Sun. Ph: (371) 674-5124.

MARTINSVILLE - The Collector's Fair, Hwy. 37 & Hwy. 252. Open April to November. Outdoors and indoors. Att. fee: free. Avg. att.: 800. Mgr. Joy Franklin, P.O. Box 1681, Martinsville, Indiana, 46151. Ph: (317) 342-6833 or 537-2524.

METAMORA - Traders Rondervous - Canal Days, on Hwy 32. Annual, held 1st weekend in Oct. Over 500 dealers, $15 and up for space. 35,000 avg. att. Phone (317) 647-6512.

MITCHELL - Ed's Gift Shop Flea Market and Crafts. State road 60 E. Open Sat. and Sun. April through Oct. also Memorial Day, July 4th, and Labor Day. 10 dealers, $2.50 per day. 500 to 1500 attendance, free admission. Ed Hirsch, RR1, Mitchell Indiana 47446. Ph: (812) 849-4815.

MITCHELL - Flea Market & Crafts, Hwy. 6o at Ed's Gift Shop. Open Sat., Sun. & Mon. holidays outdoors. Ph: (812) 849-4815.

MODOC - Half-way Flea Market, St. Rd. 36 and Carlos. Open Sun. Indoors and out. Fee $3 inside and $2 outside. Reservations Mrs. Charles M. Oxley, Rt. 1 Box M-16A, Modoc, IN 47358. Ph: (317) 853-5029.

MONTICELLO - Flea Market, Parking lot N.E. corner Illinois & Harrison, behind Post Office. Open Sat. Aug. 28, 8 am to 5 pm. Sponsored by the Women's Civic League. $5 fee. Mrs. Paul Haworth, 518 W. Jefferson, Monticello, IN 47960.

MUNCIE - Flea Market, 1928 E. Memorial Dr. Open every Sunday 9 am to 6 pm. Ph: (317) 288-1218. Antiques & collectibles.

MUNCIE - White River Flea Market, Sat. & Sun. 9-6. Ph: (317) 747-0253.

MUNCIE - Flea Market, Pan-Cake Inn, 26th & So. Madison Ave. Open Sat. & Sun. dawn to dusk. Fee $3. Under canopy shelter. Ph: (317) 284-7684.

MUNCIE - Greenwalt's Flea Market, at the Delaware Co. Fairgrounds. Monthly, call for dates. Keith Greenwalt, R.R. #9, Box 35, Muncie, In. Phone (317) 289-0194.

MUNCIE - Ski-Hi Drive-In Theatre, Jct. of Rd's 3 & 26. Open every Sun. 8 to 4. Phone (317) 284-6411.

MUNCIE - White River Flea Market, 2200 White River Blvd. Open every Sat. & Sun. 9 to 6. 100 to 175 dealers, $20 for 10 x 10 space for both days. 3 to 5000 in att. Indoors : out. Phone (317)747-0253.

NASHVILLE - Olde Time Flea Market, St. Rd. 46 E. Open every weekend, 9:30 to dusk. Entrance: Brown Co. Travel Trailers. Phone (812) 988-7930.

NEW HAVEN - Weekly Indoor Flea Market, at Bargain World, 3003 Ryan Road. Spaces $5 per day, free admission. Good quality used merchandise and antiques. Ph: (219) 482-4529.

NORTH LINTON - North Linton Flea Market. Open Sat. & Sun. Phone (812) 847-2870.

NORTH VERNON - Mister Bills Flea Market, Hwy. 50, 2 miles E. of N. Vernon. Open every Sat. & Sun. sellers fee: $3 single, $4 double. Phone (812) 346-5431 or 346-4504.

PERU - Flea Market, 3 mi. east on Hwy 24. Reservation Campground, open every Sunday 10 am to 5 pm, Fee $3 inside, $2 outside. Ph: (317) 473-4647.

RENSSELAER - Rensselaer Antique & Flea Market, located at Merrioll & McKinley. Open every Sun. indoors & out. Phone (219) 866-7493.

RICHMOND - Eastern Indiana Flea Market, at the Wayne Co. Fairgrounds. 1981 dates: Oct. 17-18, Nov. 21-22, Dec. 12-13, call for 1982 dates. John & Pat Ford, P. O. Box 68, Springport, In. 47386. Phone (317) 755-3565.

ROANOKE - Flea Market, Thunderbird Lodge. Open 3rd Sunday of the month, 10 am to 6pm.

SHIPSHEWANA - Shipshewana Auction & Flea Market on Rt. 5 south end of town. Held every Tue. & Wed. (seasonal). 2000 sellers, $5 & up per space. 5000 to 10,000 att. Auction Tue. 6 am & Wed. 7 am. Phone (219) 768-4129.

SOUTH BEND - Thieves Market, 2309 E. Edison at Ironwood. Open Sat. & Sun., 10 am to 6 pm. 45 permanent shops, plus outdoor market. $3 per day. Free admission. Ph: (219) 233-9820.

TERRE HAUTE - Flea Market, 3708 Wabash Ave. Open 2nd Sun. of every month. Sponsored by the Women of the Moose.

TERREHAUTE - 3rd Weekend Flea Market, 2304 Margaret Ave. Open every 3rd Sat. & Sun. of each month 10 am to ? Outdoors. 130 spaces, 16 x 24, $10 per day. Susan McCarthy, Mgr. Phone (812) 877-0837.

TRAFALGAR - Trafalgar Flea Market, St. Rd. 135 & 252. Open every Sat. & Sun. Indoors & out.Dealers wanted. Phone (317) 933-3402.

VEEDERSBURG - Steam Corner, R.R. 1, Box 18, runs 4 times a year, call for dates for 1982. 150 dealers, $7.50 per day. Indoors & out. Don & Ruth Staggs, RR1, Box 18, Veedersburg, In. 47987. Phone (317) 798-5710.

WILLIAMSBURG - Raye's Flea Market, Open daily.

ZANESVILLE - Flea Market, 17727 Indianapolis Rd., So. of Fr. Wayne on Hwy 3. Open every 2nd & 4th Sun. of the month. Ph: (219) 638-4765.

ZIONSVILLE - Big Red Flea Market, on U.S. 52, 11777 Lafayette Rd. Open daily year round. Indoors & out, dealers booth 12 x 12, $25 per week. 3000 avg. daily att. on weekends. Mason Prod., Rt. 1, Whitstown, In. 46075. Phone (317) 769-3266.

160

IOWA

DES MOINES - Iowa State Fairgrounds Flea Market, East 30th Street and University Avenue. Open monthly. Indoors. Dealers fee: $16 for 15' x 10' space. Free attendance. Tables supplied for $3 each. Evelyn Jennings, 2601 Capitol Avenue, Des Moines, Iowa 50317. Phone (515) 262-4282. No food or alcoholic beverages sold. Res. sug.

DESMOINES - Flea Market at Eastgate, 1528 Euclid, Des Moines, Iowa, 503176. Ph: (515) 266-2138. Indoor facilities, open Fri., Sat. and Sun. 50 dealers, 5000 att. Dealer's fee, $25-35. Ample parking, food concessions.

KEOKUK - Bryant Flea Market, 6 miles north on River Rd. Open 3rd Sun of the month, 9 am to 4 pm. Over 300 sellers, $6 per space. Free admission, 700 to 1200 att. Richard Bryant, Rt. 2, Sweet Acres, Keokuk, Iowa, 52632. Ph: (319) 463-7727.

MARSHALLTOWN - Central Iowa Flea Market. Central Iowa fairgrounds. 2nd and 4th Sun. 9-4. Indoor. 100 dealers, 500 att. Carole Storjohann, Central Iowa Fair Office, R.R. 2, Marshalltown, Iowa, 50158. Ph: (515) 753-3671. Res. req.

OTTUMWA - Collector's Fair, Colosseum basement. Held on Sept. 18-19th, and Nov. 13-14th, 1976. 50 to 60 sellers, $8 per space, both days. 50¢ admission, 2000 attendance. Dwight Jones, 602 Morris St., Ottumwa, Iowa 52501. Ph (515) 682-0071.

TOPEKA - Topeka Flea Market, 17th & Topeka Blvd. (Shawnee Co. Fairgrounds) Open 3rd Sun. each mo. (closed June, July, Aug., Sept.) Indoor. Fee: $6. 200 dealers. 5,000 att. Res. Leon A. Schartz, P.O. Box 1585, 67501.

KANSAS

HUTCHINSON - Hutchinson Flea Market, 20th & Main, Kansas State Fair. Open 1st Sun. each mo. (closed July, Aug., Sept.) Fee: $6. Indoor. Reservations. Dealers: 200. Att: 5,000. Leon A. Schartz, P.O. Box 1585. Hutchinson, Kansas, 67501. Ph: (316) 663-5626.

OPOLIS - Opolis Flea Market, Box 42, Opolis, Kansas. Junction 171 & 57. Open Sat. Sun., and holidays. Indoors and outdoors. Att: 250. Dealers: 8-10. Mgr. Norma Kukovich, Box 42, Opolis, Kansas, 66760. Ph: (316) 231-2543.

WICHITA - Wichita Flea Market, 85th St. North & I 135. Open 4th Sun. of each mo. (closed Dec., Jan., Feb.) Fee: $5. Dealers: 400. Att: 5,000. Leon A Schartz, P.O. Box 1585, 67501. Ph: (316) 663-5626. Res.

WITCHITA - Village Flea Market, 2301 S. Meridian. Open Fri., Sat. & Sun. 9-6, entire year. Dealers: 150 indoors and outdoors. Dealers fee: $16. Free attendance. Attendance: over 5000. Dale Cooper, 2301 S. Meridian, Witchita, Kansas 67213. Phone (316) 942-8263. Res sug.

KENTUCKY

BARDSTOWN - Annual Bardstown Antique Flea Market, Hwy 62 EAst, (502) 348-5003, mailing address, Bardstown, KY 40004. Indoor facilities. Annual April event. 104 dealers, attendance fee $1. Dealer's fee, 1 table $25, 3 table booth $55.

BARDSTOWN - White's Flea Market on US 62. Open Fri. Sat. & Sun indoors and outdoors. $4 set-up fee. Ph: (502) 348-9677.

BEREA - Robbie's Antique and Flea Market. Every weekend 8-6. 3 miles south on U.S. 25-Rt. 3.

BEREA - Todd's Flea Market, on Hwy. 21 West. Open daily. Phone (606) 986-9961.

BOONVILLE - Boonville Flea Market, on Rt. 3. Open on Wed., 25 to 50 dealers.

BOWLING GREEN - Flea Market, 1 mile north Green River Parkway Hwy 31. Ph: (615) 799-8184 or 2912. Mailing address, Fred & Ruth Hicks, Fairview, TN 37062. Outdoor facilities, $3 per weekend for 8 foot tables, space for can and table $5 per day.

BURLINGTON - Burlington Antique Flea Market, held at the fairgrounds. Monthly, 25 to 75 sellers. Paul Kohls. Phone (513)922-5265.

CAMP NELSON - Camp Nelson Flea Market. 20 mi. south of Lexington - off U.S. 27 on old U.S. 27 at the Ky. River. Open weekends and holidays April thru Nov. Outdoor. Dealers: 25-30. Att: 300. Fee: $3 day. Jean Goins, Camp Nelson Recreation area, Camp Nelson, Ky. 40444. Ph: (606) 885-9304.

COVINGTON - Flea Market, at the American Legion Hall, 203 Daytonia, 38 & Winston. Open every Sat., 6 to 20 dealers. Phone (606) 291-8834.

ELIZABETHTOWN - Etown Flea Market. U.S. 31 W. North J. In old Lincoln-Mercury Bldg. Open Fri., Sat. & Sun. Outdoor and indoors. Dealers: 300 Att: 5,000-10,000. Fee $3 outside. Phone (502) 737-7411.

GEORGETOWN - Georgetown Flea Market, located at I-75 and U.S. 62. Open every Fri., Sat. & Sun.

GEORGETOWN - Country world Flea Market, U.S. 460 East. Open Fri., Sat., Sun. Fee: Fri. free, Sat. $4.50, Sun. $6.50. Outdoors. Dealers 100-200. Att: 2,000 Sat. 6,000 Sun. Glenn Juett, 111 Montgomery Ave. Georgetown, Ky. 40324. Ph: (502) 863-0474 (office), 863-0289 (home).

GREENVILLE - Town & Country Flea Market, on U.S. 62. Open every Mon. & Tue. 75 to 85 sellers. Phone (502) 338-4920.

GLASGOW - Antique Flea Market, at the Glasgow Flea Mkt. Bldg. 31 E. South St. 50-100 dealers indoors and outdoors. Fee $4 outdoors, $6 indoors. Free admission. Effie Emmett Ph: (502) 678-4620.

HENDERSON - Outdoor Flea Market, 3199 Hwy 41 N. Open every Sun. (502) 826-4045.

INDEPENDENCE - North Kentucky Year Round Flea Market, at 5209 Madison Pike. Open every Fri., Sat. & Sun. Phone (606) 356-9602. Dick Young, 1602 Crossridge Ln., Louisville, Ky. 40222.

LEITCHFIELD - Bratcher's Flea Market, on U.S. 62 East. Open every Wed. & Thur., 6 am to 2 pm. 40 to 50 dealers. Phone (502) 259-3571. Gladys Bratcher.

LOUISVILLE - The Kentucky Flea Market, held at the Kentucky Fair & Expo Center. Phone (502) 451-1212. Dick Young, 1602 Crossridge Ln., Louisville, Ky. 40222.

LOUISVILLE - Clay St. Flea Market, 120 N. Clay St. Low, KY 40202, (502) 584-9942. Indoor facilities, daily 9:30 - 5. 17 dealers, dealer's fee monthly.

MONTICELLO - Kay's Fleaground, Kelley Lane Rd., Open year round on Fri., Sat. & Sun., 9 am to 6 pm.

MT. STERLING - Annual Flea Market, held in the Municipal parking lot downtown. Held in Oct. 100 to 300 sellers. Phone (606) 498-3785.

MT. STERLING - 120 South Queen St. Sat. & Sun. 9-6. Ph: (606) 498-4722 or 498-6937.

NICHOLISVILLE - Flea Market at the Windmill Restaurant, on U.S. 27. Open every Sat. & Sun. 40 to 50 sellers. Phone (606)498-4722.

PADUCAH - Paducah Flea Market, located on Ninth & Monroe. Every Sat. 9 a.m. - 6 p.m. & Sun. 12 noon - 6 p.m. Indoors & Out. Avg. 100 dealers. year round. Dealers Fee $3.50 12 x 15 space outside, $4.50 10 x 10 space inside. Overnight parking on lot. Free admission. Reservations advised. Phone (502) 442-9661 or 443-9665. 2nd year in business.

RICHMOND - Blue Grass Campground, 627 East, 6 miles N. of Richmond. Open April thru Oct., Fri., Sat. & Sun. sellers fee: $2 to $5. Phone (606) 623-0990.

RICHWOOD - New Burly Tobacco Warehouse. Open every Sat. & Sun., 8 am to 5 pm. 200 to 300 dealers. 2 to 4,000 avg. att. Phone (606) 371-5800.

SHELBYVILLE - Shellbyville Flea Market held at the Big Top Warehouse on U.S. 60 E. Open 1st full weekend of month from March thru Oct. Variable attendance. Average 35 - 50 dealers weekly. Free admission. Dealers fee: $15 per 3 days. Ample free parking. 2nd year in business. This mkt. held in tobacco warehouse. Rain or shine. Plenty of open room. Phone (502) 633-1244.

WALTON - Lakeside Flea Market & Auction, on U.S. 25. Open every Tue. 6 am to 2 pm. 30 to 50 dealers. 300 to 500 avg. att. Phone (606) 744-0504.

Winchester - Winchester Flea-Farmers Market, 5000 W. Lexington Rd. (US 60). Open Fri., Sat. & Sun. & Holidays year round. Fee $5-$15, avg. atten. 2000 to 5000. Jim Oliver, P.O. Box 15, Winchester, KY 40391. Ph: 744-5000.

LOUISIANA

BATON ROUGE - Deep South Flea Market, 5350 Florida Blvd. Open year round, Fri. 12 to 9 pm. Sat. 10 am to 8 pm, Sun 12 to 8 pm. 200 to 275 dealers, $10 per day. Indoors. 6 to 8000 att. Bill Vallery. Ph: (504) 923-0333 or 293-5078.

BELLE CHASSE - 201 Schlief Dr. Show. end of August, 3 - 5 dealers, $10 per speace. Indoors. V.B. Schlief. Ph: (504) 394-4274.

BREAUS BRIDGE - Pioneer Flea Market & Zoo. I-10 Exit 109. Six mi. east of Lafayette. Open Sat. & Sun. Indoors and outdoors. Fee: $2.50 and $5. Dealers: 20. Att: 200. Gerald Goudeau, 223 Lunc St. Lafayette La. 70506. Ph: 235-2752.

CROWLEY - Crowley - Crowley Flea Market, I-10 Exit 1111. Open 1st full weekend of month, 7:30 to 6 pm, 45 sellers, $15 for the weekend. Free admission 3 to 5000 attendance. Maxie Trahan, 511 S. Ave. I. Crowley, LA 70526. Ph: (318) 783-4303.

GILBERT - Five - S. Hwy. 15 North. Open Thur. - Sat. 9-5. Sun. 2-5. Avg. dealers: 12. Dealers fee: $5 per day. Attendance free. B. L. Smith, Rt. 1 Box 107C, Gilbert, La. 71336. Phone (318) 5527.

JENNINGS - Finders Keepers Flea Market, 425 N. Railroad, Ph: (318) 824-6275. Mailing address 814 Alice Jennings. LA 70546. Indoor and outdoor facilities. Every Sat. 8-6. Every Sun 12-6. 20 dealers, 2000 attendance. Dealer's fee $20. Unlimited parking. Food concessions.

KENNER - Mama & Papa Flea Market, 2502 Airline Hwy. Open year round. Tues 10 am to 5 pm. Fri 12 to 5 pm, Sat 10 am to 5 pm. Ph: (504) 721-2670.

LAFAYETTE - Pioneer Flea Market, on Hwy I-10, 6 miles E. of town. Open every Sat. & Sun., 9 am to 6 pm. 25 dealers, $5 fee. 500 avg. att. Camping on grounds. Phone (318) 235-2141.

LAFAYETTE - Cajun Country Flea Market, 123 Carmel Ave. Open every Fri., Sat., 10 to 7, & Sun. 12 to 6. 55 dealers. Sellers fee: $160 per mo. or $50 per weekend. 1500 avg. att. Phone (318) 232-3642.

LAFAYETTE - Gigi's Flea Market, just off 167 N. Open every 1st & 3rd weekend. Gigi Grill, Mgr. (318) 896-8456.

PINEVILLE - House of Elite's Mini Flea Market. 1411 Melrose St., Pineville, LA. Indoors and outdoors. Dealers fee: $8 day. Att. fee: none. Mgr. Johnnie Andrews, 1040 Lakeshore Dr. Pineville, LA 71360. Ph: (318) 448-1168.

MAINE

BRUNSWICK - Antique Flea Market, 341 Bath Rd. Open Oct. thru May, 9 am to 5 pm, Sat. and Sun. Indoors, 12 dealers, $6 per day 1 Eugene J. Lassier, Jr., 341 Bath Rd., Brunswick, ME 04011.

BRUNSWICK - Antique Mall, 341 Bath Rd. Open all year, 9 am to 5 pm, daily. 20 indoor shops. Eugene J. Lassier, Jr., 341 Bath Rd., Brunswick, ME 04011.

EAST HOLDEN - East Holden Flea Market, Rt., 1A, off I-95. Open from June to the end of Oct., 9 am to 6 pm, Sat. and Sun. Indoor and out. Indoor space is $5 per day, $9 for the weekend. Outdoor space is $4 per day. Dorothy & George Hogan, Box 68, East Holden, ME 04429. Ph: (207) 843-6472.

FREEPORT - Red Wheel Antiques, Rt. 1 & I95 at Yarmouth Rd. 15 miles north of Portland. Open Sat. & Sun. & holidays May to mid-October. Avg. dealers: 100, outdoors. Dealers fee: $6 Sat. & $7 Sun. Free attendance. One 8 ft. table supplied. ¾ Ed Collett, yarmouth Rd., Freeport, Maine 04032.

GORHAM - Gorham Flea Market, 114 Main St., intersection of 25 and 114, west of Portland. Open all year, 10 am to 5 pm, Sun. Indoor and Outdoor, avg. 15 sellers, $4 per day. Walter Libby, Mighty St., Gorham, ME 04038. Ph: (207) 839-3153. New & used merchandise.

NEWCASTLE - Sale-Ho, Rt. 1. Open May 15 to Oct., 8 am to 5 pm, Fri., Sat. and Sun. Indoor and outdoor, 21 to 24 dealers, $5 per day, under tent. Robert Foster, Rt. 1, Newcastle, ME 04553. Ph: (207) 529-5422. Antiques and collectibles.

NEWCASTLE - Foster's Flea Market & Antique Mall, U.S. Route 1. 50 miles north of Portland. Indoors and outdoors. Jay Lawrence, Box 96, Newcastle, Maine 04553. Phone (207) 563-8150 or 677-3373.

SACO - Cascade Flea Market. Corner Rt. 5. Cascade Road. Open Memorial Day until Oct. Outdoor. Dealers: 100. Att: 10,000. Al Riviezzo, 15 Saks Mobile Park. Rochester, N.H., 03867. Ph: (207) 282-1800 or 282-5778.

WELLS - Bow-Mar Hall Flea Market, Post Rd., 2 miles from I-95 exit 2. Open all year, 8 am to 5 pm, Sat. and Sun. Indoors and outdoors, 10 to 30 dealers. For information and current rates: Marlene & Robert Blair, Post Rd., Wells, ME 04090. Ph: (207) 646-7475. Used merchandise & handicrafts.

WOOLWICH - Montsweag Flea Mardet, Corner Tr. 1 & Mountain Road. Open Sat. & Sun. May thru Oct. Fri., Sat. & Sun. in July & Aug. Fee: $5 day. Outdoor. Dealers: 50. Att: 1,500. Norma Thompson, P. O. Box 252, Woolwich, Maine 04579. Phone (207) 443-2809. Res.

WOOLWICH - Nequasset Flea Market, Rt. 1, north of Brunswick. Open Memorial Day to October, 7 am to 5 pm, Sat. and Sun. Outdoors, 20 to 45 dealers. Reservations are required. C.L. Dunbar, Rt. 1, Woolwich, ME 04579. Ph: (207) 443-3547. Quality merchandise.

MARYLAND

BALTIMORE - North Point Village Shopping Center, 4035 North Point Blvd. Open year round, Sat. & Sun., 20 to 60 sellers, $3.50 on Sat, $5 on Sun. Fred La Sorte, Ph: (301) 477-8725.

BALTIMORE - North Point Drive-In Theatre Flea Market, North Point Blvd. Open every Sun., April thru Oct., 7 am to 4 pm. Sellers fee. $3 per space. Outdoors. 25¢ admission. Ph: (301) 477-5084.

BALTIMORE - Pulaski Hwy. Farmers Flea Market, above Middle River Rd. Open every Sat. and Sun. Sellers fee: $15 for the weekend. Indoors. Ph: (301) 789-1335 or 687-5505.

BALTIMORE - County-Pakton Flea Market. No admission. No parking fee for buyers. Sun. 7 am to 5 pm, rain or shine. 250 seller spaces available. Dealers: pre-assigned space 16' x 16' $20.00 prepaid. ($25.00 day of event). Pakton, MD 18 mi. N. Baltimore, 12 mi S. York, PA, Exit 33, off I-83. For info: Pakton Steal Markets, Bell man Promotions, P.O. Box 1113, Columbia, MD 21044. Ph: (301) 995-0118 or 679-2288.

BALTIMORE - County-Pakton Swap Meet. Buyers 50¢ admission, no parking fee. Seller 50¢ admission plus parking fee by sections: Front (gold) $3.00, Middle (brown) $2.00, Rear (white) $1.00. Sell or buy anything. Gates open 7 am to 5 pm Sundays. May 21, July 16, Sept. 10, Oct. 22, 1978. Pakton, MD 18 mi. N. Balto., MD. Info: Pakton Steal Market, Bellman Promotions, P.O. Box 1113, Columbian, MD 21044. Ph: (301) 995-0118 or (301) 679-2288.

BELAIR - Trading Post, 1800 Conowingo Rd. Open every Sat. & Sun.

BETHESDA - Farmer's Flea Mkt. 7155 Wisconsin Ave. Open April thru Oct. Outdoor. Fee: $16.50. Dealers: 50. Att: thousands. Jim Ban Fils, 35 Wisc., Circle. Wash. D.C. 20015. Ph: (301) 986-1593.

BOWIE - Free State Mall Flea Market, Rt. 450. Open every Sunday 10 am to 6 pm.

BURTONSVILLE - Barrys Antiques, 3411 Spancerville Rd., Rt. 198. Open every Sat. 10 am to 6 pm.;Sunday 11 am to 6 pm. Courtney Barry, P.O. Box 212, Burtonsville, MD 20730. Ph: (301) 0481 or 421-9871.

COLUMBIA - 8th Year. The New Columbia Flea Market, The Mall. April 23 thru Oct. 15. Every Sun., rain or shine. 10 am to 5 pm. Rt. 29 between Balto., MD and Washington, DC. Over 100 spaces in the covered parking area. Sellers fee, $20.00 per Sun., $100.00 for 6 weeks. For info: Bellman Promotions, P.O. Box 1113, Columbia, MD 21044. Ph: (301) 995-0118 or 679-2288.

FREDERICK - Rhodside, indoor/outdoor Flea Market. U.S. 15 & Biggs Ford Rd. 4 miles north of Frederick, Md. Open daily. See also "Collector's Cottage" on premises. Avg. dealers: 50. Dealers fee: $4 to $8. Free attendance. James L. Bryan, Rhodside Public Markets, Inc., U.S. 15 & Biggs Ford Rd., Frederick, Md. 21701. Phone (301) 898-7502. Res sug.

FREDERICK - Antique Center and Flea Market, Carrol & South St. Open year round, Fr., Sat., Sun. and holidays, 9 am to 6 pm. Free admission, 25 dealers. Ph: (301) 662-5388.

OCEAN CITY - The Golden Door Shows Flea Market. ConventionHall, 4001 Philadelphia. Open Easter Sat. to Mid-Oct. 10 am to 6 pm. Usually outdoors. Fee: $10. Dealers 30-50. Att: several thousand. Leroy F. Phillips, 214 E. Market St. Laurel, Delaware, 19956. Ph: (302) 875-5084.

PARKTON - Swap Meet. Buyers 50¢ admission, no parking fee. Seller 50¢ admission plus parking fee by sections: Front (gold) $3.00, Middle (brown) $2.00, Rear (white) $1.00. Sell or buy anything. Gates open 7 am to 5 pm. Sundays. May 21, July 16, Sept. 10, Oct. 22, 1978. Pakton, MD 18 mi. N. Balto., MD. Exit 33 off I-83. 12 mi S. York, PA Exit 33 off I-83. Info: Pakton Steal Market, Bellman Promotions, P.O. Box 1113, Columbia, MD 21044. Ph: (301) 995-0018 or 679-2288.

REGISTERSTOWN - 218 Main St. (rear). Open every Sun. Ph: (301) 883-3212.

RISING SUN - Hunter's Sale Barn, Inc. Take I-95 to exit 7. Take Rt. 275 to Rt. 276. Turn right, drive 2 miles. Open Mon. 3-10. Dealers: 60. Att: 1500. Indoors and out. Norman Hunter, Box 427, Rising Sun, Maryland. Ph: (301) 658-6506. Res. sug.

TRAPPE - Ferry Boat Antique Mart, take Rt. 301 to Rt. 50. Open every day, Mon. thru Thur, 10 am to 4 pm, Fri., Sat., and Sun. 10 am to 8 pm. Indoors and outdoors. Over 50 sellers. 2 to 4000 attendance. Ph: (301) 476-3001. Antiques, collectibles and crafts.

UNION BRIDGE - Flea Market, on Elger St. Open every Sat. & Sun., 10 am to 6 pm. Ph: (301) 775-2010.

WEST FRIENDSHIP - Flea Market, held at the Howard Co. Fairgrounds. Open every Sunday.

MASSACHUSETTS

AUBURN - Auburn Antique & Flea Market. 773 Southbridge St. Open Sun. 9-5. Dealers: 100. Fee indoors $10, outdoors $5. Harry P. Kotseas, 38 Loring St., Auburn, Mass. 01501. Ph: (617) 832-5458 or Sun. 832-2763. Res.

AUBURNDALE - Flea Market, 132 Charles St. Open every Sat. and Sun.

BEDFORD - The Great Road Indoor Antique and Flea Market, from Rt. 93 take 128 south, exit 44N, Rts. 4-225, follow to the Great Rd. Shopping Center. Open every Sun., 9 am to 5 pm. Admission 35¢. Ph: Paul, 275-2559 on Sun. or 322-4693 on weekends.

BRIMFIELD - Gordon Reid's Famous Antique Flea Market, Auction Acres U.S. Rt. 20. Open Wed. 4 pm until Sat. 5 pm. Outdoor, space fee $60. Avg. att. 10,000. Gordon Reid, 138 Kespert Ct., Swansea, Mass. 02777. Ph: (617) 379-0828.

BUZZARD BAY - Antique Mart, 61 Main Street. Rt. 6 and 28 across from Cape Cod Canal and R.R. Bridge. Thur. thru Sun., mid June to Christmas. Sat., Sun. & Mon., year round. 15-20 dealers indoors. Tables supplied. Free attendance. James B. Potts, Jr. 61 Main St., Buzzards Bay, Mass. 02532. Phone (617) 759-7556. No clothes or new items. Res. required.

CHARLTON - Bev's Flea Market, Rt. 20, Charlton, MA 01507, Ph: (617) 248-7031. Outdoor facilities, 75 dealers, dealer's fee $5. Open every Sat. and Sun. (except open 3 times a year Fri., Sat. & Sun. when Brinefield Gordon Reid's opens.)

CHESHIRE - Cheshire Barn Flea Market, Rt. 8, 5 miles north of Pittsfield on Rt. 8. Open Sun. May thru Oct. Indoor and out. Dealers 25-30. Fee: $12. Att: 1,000. Michael C. Hutchinson, Hutchinson Lane, Cheshire, Mass. 01225. Ph: (413) 743-3700.

FRAMINGHAM · Framingham Carousel Flea Market, Old Connecticut Path; 1 mi. from Mass. Turnpike Exit 13 and Rt. 9. Open late April thru late Oct., Sun. and announced holidays, 9 am to 5 pm. 40-100 dealers outdoors. Fee $7. Sidney Lebewohl, 116 Concord St., Framingham, MA 01701. Ph: (617) 872-4470 or 8426. All types of merchandise.

GRAFTON · Grafton Flea Market. Rt. 140 UptonGrafton Town Line. Open every Sun. and Mon. Holidays. Dealers: over 100. Indoors and outdoors. Dealers fee: $5 outside & $10. Adults 50¢ attendance. Tables available for rent. Att: over 3000. Harry Peters, Box 206, Grafton, Mass. 01519. Ph: (617) 839-2271.

GREENFIELD · Stoneleigh-Burnham Antique Flea Market, Rt. 5. Ph: (413) 774-2711, mailing address, Donald Mackey, Suffield Academy, Suffield, CT 06078. Indoor and outdoor facilities. July 3-4 and Sept 4-5. 150 dealers, 4000 att. Att. fee: 50¢, dealer's fee $25 inside, $15 outside. Ample parking. All dealers antique or collectibles.

GROVELAND · Groveland Flea Market, at Groveland Bridge, near Haverhill. Open year round, Sun. from 8 am to 5 pm. 27 indoor dealers, 15 outdoors. Fee $6 & $8. Marion Sloban, 18 Middle St., Merrimac, MA 01860. Ph: (617) 346-8054 or (Sat 2-5 pm) 372-5212. All types except clothes.

HUBBARDSTON · Rietta Flea Market, on Rt. 68. Open every Sun. & Hol. 70 dealers indoors, 200 outdoors; fee: $5 and up. 5 to 8000 avg. att. Ronald Levesque, P.O. Box 35, Hubbardston, Mass. 01452. Ph: (617) 632-0559.

LENOX · Caropreso, on Rt. 7 and 20. Open every Sat. and Sun., 10 am to 5 pm. Indoors and outdoors. 35 sellers, $15 indoors, $8 outdoors. Ph: (413) 442-2893.

LEOMINSTER · Red's Gift & Flea Shop. 710 N. Main St. Indoors, open 7 days a week. Jerry Brotheim, 710 N. Main St. Leominster, Mass., 01453. Ph: (617) 537-0181.

LYNN · Lynnway Antique & Flea Market. Rt. 1A, at Loew's Drive-In Theatre. Open April thru Oct., Sun. from 6 am to 5 pm. 150 sellers outdoors. Fee $5, reservations suggested. Costos Mavros, 159 Washington St., Lynn, MA 01902. Ph: (617) 595-5904. Antiques, arts & crafts.

MERRIMACK · Merrimack Antique & Flea Market, at Broad St. Open every Sunday, 8 am to 5 pm. 125 sellers, 75 outdoors.

METHUEN · Fanny's Flea Market, Methuen Mall, Pleasant Valley St. (Rt. 113). Open year round. Sun. from 10 am to 5 pm. 200 dealers· indoors. Fee $10 up. Chuck Romanow, 187 N. Woodstock Rd., RFD 1. Southbridge, MA 01550. Ph: (617) 765-9343. Antiques, crafts, desirable collectibles.

NEPONSET · Neponset Swap 'n' Shop, 775 Galivan Blvd. Open every Sun. and holidays. 350 dealers, $7 per space. 6000 avg. att., $1 per car, 50¢ walk in adm. M. Bornstein. Ph: (617) 282-3500.

NEW BEDFORD · Country Fair, Coggeshall St. off Rt. 195 Exit 22 or 23. Open year round, Sat., Sun., Mon. and holidays from 9 am to 5 pm. 150-300 dealers indoors. Fee $8 or $10. Ted Soares. County Fair, 85 Coggeshall St., New Bedford, MA 02746. Ph: (617) 994-4644. Antiques, arts & crafts, nostalgia.

NORTH ATTLEBORO · Witschi's Giant Flea Market, Rts. 1 and 295. Open Sundays from the first week of April thru Thanksgiving (depending on weather). 7 am to ? . 100-150 dealers spring and fall, less in summer. Fee $6. William and Sylvia Witschi. Ph: (617) 699-4712. Mostly antiques, rest general.

NORTHFIELD · Ken Miller's Flea Market, Warwick Ave. off I-91 Exit 28N. Open Sundays from mid-April to mid-Oct., 6 am to 5 pm. 20 indoor dealers. 100 outdoor. Fee $6. Ken Miller, Warwick Ave., Northfield, MA 01360. Ph: (413) 498-2749. All types of merchandise.

NORTON · Norton Flea Market Antique Sale, Inc. Rt. 140. Mansfield exit off I-95. Open 3rd Sunday in April thru last Sunday in Oct. Over 100 dealers. Outdoors. Dealers fee: $10. 50¢ attendance fee. Pino & Bernheimer, P. O. Box Al, Norton, Mass. 02766. Phone (617) 339-8554. No food, drinks or pets.

PLYMOUTH · Cape Cod Flea Market, Cordage Park, via Rts. 3 or 44. Open year round. Sun. and Mon. holidays from 10 am to 5 pm. 60 dealers indoors. Write for fee & reservation. Paul Reynolds. 374 Webster St., Marshfield, MA 02050. Ph: (617) 834-6709. Antiques, collectibles, crafts.

SALEM · Flea Market & Antique Marketplace, on Congress St. Bldg. #1. Open every Sat. and Sun., 10 am to 5 pm. Indoors. Ph: 774-6677 or 745-9393.

SWANSEA · Oceangrove Antique & Flea Market, 458 Oceangrove Ave., Swansea, MA 02777. Ph: (617) 678-9598. Sat. and Sun. 10 to 5. 20 dealers. 400 attendance, dealer's fee $20, attendance fee 25¢ Sun. Ample parking. Food concessions.

WELLFLEET · Wellfleet Drive-In Flea Market, Rt. 6, Cape Cod. Open every Sun. April thru Oct., 9 am to 5 pm. 150 dealers, $5 per space, outdoors. 1000 to 2000 avg. att. Eleanor Hazen, P.O. Box 811, Wellfleet, Mass 02667. Ph: (617) 349-2520.

WESTFORD · Westford Flea Market, Rt. 110, off I-495 Exit 20. Open April thru Oct., Sun. from 8 am to 5 pm. 20-70 dealers outdoors. Fee $5 w/tables in summer, $7.50 in winter. Roy Ellingworth, 17 Snow Drive, Westford, MA 01886. Ph: (617) 692-2854. All types of merchandise.

WEST FALMOUTH · Saconesset Homestead Flea Market. Rt. 28 A End Old Homestead Rd. Open Memorial Sunday, Oct. 7. Fee: $10-$12. Indoor and outdoor. Att: 1,000. Res. M. Dorothea Gifford, Box 366, W. Falmouth, Mass. 02574. Ph: (617) 548-5850.

WEST PEABODY · Macsonny's Flea Market, Russell Plaza Shopping Center, off Rts. 1, 114, & 128. Open year round. Sundays and occasional Monday holidays, 9 am to 6 pm. 250 dealers indoors. Fee $10 in winter, $7.50 in summer. Mrs. Mack Paul, 4 Long Street Rd., Peabody, MA 01960. Ph: (617) 535-9888, or 532-0606. Depression glass, trendy collectibles.

MICHIGAN

CEDAR SPRINGS · Northern Exchange, 12595 Northland Drive. Open May 23 and continuing every Tue. - Fri. - Sat. thru Sept. 29. Avg. dealers 100 outside. Dealers fee: $4. Free attendance. Avg. att: 4,000-5,000. Trudy Towns or Harold Fields, 12595 Northland Drive, Cedar Springs, Mich. 49319. Phone (616) 696)9645 or 696-0125.

CHARLOTTE · Weekend Flea Market, 202 Pearl St., at the old Dolson Car Factory. Open every Fri., Sat., & Sun., 10 am to 5 pm. Indoor and outdoors

COPE · Copemich Flea Market, on Rt. 115. Open every Sat. and Sun. outdoors.

DAVISON · Midway Flea Market, 205 Davison Rd. Open Weekends. Indoor and outdoor. Fee: $18 two days. Ken Lamson, 504 N. Dayton, Davison, Mich. 48423. Ph: (313) 653-8766. Res.

DETROIT · Big "D" Flea Market. Every weekend. Fri. 12-6. Sat. & Sun. 10-6. 2311 E. Vernon Hwy., between Chene & DuBois.

ELBA · Elba Flea Market, 4 miles E. of Davison, on old M-21. Open every Sat. & Sun. Indoor and out. 45 to 60 sellers, $5 outdoors, $7.50 indoors. John Bryning. 6195 Fulton St., Mayville, Mich. Ph: (517) 843-6104.

GAYLORD · The Purple Flea. Open every weekend. Just off W. M-32 on McVannel Road, 1 mile west of Gaylord. Call for info: (517) 732-5335 or 732-7005.

GRAND RAPIDS · Beltline Drive-In Flea Market. 1400 W. 28th St. Open May 3 until end of Sept. Dealers: 350. Att: 5,000. Jack Loeks, 1400 W. 28th St., Wyoming, Mich., 49509. Ph: 616-6302.

GRASS LAKE · Wholesale Dealers Auction. Open on Tues. and Wed. Ph: (517) 522-8160.

HOUGHTON LAKE · Flea Market half mile south of the I.G.A. Open every Sat. & Sun.

IONIA · Country Store Antique Flea Market, South M-66 at the city limits. Open Wed. thru Sun. business hours.

JACKSON · Spikes Flea Market & Auction, 2190 Brooklyn Rd. Open year round, Sat 9 am to 9 pm; Sun. 10 am to 5 pm. Auction Sat. 6 pm. Spike Jackson, Mgr. Ph: (517) 783-5550. General merchandise.

KALAMAZOO · Eastland Outdoor Market & Auction, corner of Sprinkle and Miller Rd. Open Thur. thru Sun., 9 am till dusk. Auctions on Sun. Ph: (616) 381-7084.

MUSKEGON · Farmer's Market. Open every Wed. until cold. about 200 sellers, $2.50 per space, 2 to 3000 attendance.

MUSKEGON HEIGHTS · Mona Civic Center, 3521 Hoyt St. Open yr. round from 6 am to 4 pm. Dealers: 400. Fee: $4. Indoors and outdoors. Att: thousands. Ralph Sharpe, 3521 Hoyt St., Muskegon Hts., Mich. 49444. Ph: (616) 733-4064.

NEW BALTIMORE — New Baltimore Flea Market, Green St. and County Line Rd. Open every Sat. & Sun. 8 am to 6 pm.

NORTH OF MONTAGUE - Hump T Dump, 9510 Old U.S. 31. Open Tue. - Sat. 10:30 - 6:30. Sun. 12:30 - 6:30. Closed Monday. Outdoors. Dealers fee: $5. Sharon Briggs, Rt. 2, Box 131, Montague, Mich. 49437. Ph: (616) 894-8753.

PAW PAW - Reits Flea Market, RR #1 Red Arrow Highway. Open May thru Oct. Fri., Sat., Sun. & holidays. Fee: $3.50 outside, $7.50 inside. Thousands att. William & Cathy Reits, RR #1 Box 222. Paw Paw, Mich., 49079. Ph: (616) 657-3428. Campground facilities.

PONTIAC - Country Fair Antique Flea Market, 2045 Dixie Hwy. Open every Fri. 4 pm to 9 pm., Sat. and Sun. 9 am to 6 pm. Indoors. Ph: (313) 338-7880.

ROYAL OAK - Royal Oak Flea Market, 316 E. Eleven Mile Rd. Open every Sunday (except Easter), 9 am to 5 pm. 90 dealers, $7 to $15 per space. 8000 to 12,000 avg. att. Indoors. Steve Sendek, 316 E. Eleven Mile Rd., Royal Oak, Mich. 48067. Ph: (313) 548-8822.

SAGINAW - Saginaw Flea Market, held at the Fairgrounds. Open every Thursday, April thru Oct.

SAUGATUCK - Saugatuck Flea Market, 64th St. and Blue Star Hwy. Open every Sat. & Sun. 10 am to 5 pm. Feb. thru Nov. Ph: (616) 857-2726. Furniture, collectibles, dep. glass and jewelry.

SAUGATUCK - Saugatuck · Saugatuck Flea Market. 64th St. & Blue Star Hwy. Open Sat. & Sun. 10 am to 5 pm. Feb. thru Nov. Ph: (616) 857-2726. Furn., collec., depression glass, jewelry.

SIKESTON - Tradewinds Trading Post, 823 W. Malone. Open Thurs., Fri., Sat. 80 sellers indoor, unlimited outdoor. $4 fee, tables available at extra charge. Avg. atten. 2000 daily. Dan Byrd, 823 Malone, Sikeston, MO 63801. Ph: (314) 491-3965.

SOUTHFIELD - Open Air Flea Market Bel-Air Drive-In Theatre. Open Sundays. 200 dealers, avg. att. 10,000. $10 space fee. Fred Pellerito, 300 Town Center, Suite 1780, Southfield, MI 48075. Ph: 358-1680.

SOUTH HAVEN - North Star Flea Market, Blue Star Hwy. & North Shore.Dr. Open every Sat. & Sun. May to Sept. Dealers fee $3. Ruth Shochet, P. O. Box 24, Rt. 2, South Haven 49090. Ph: (616) 637-3680 or 637-2649. New Market.

TAYLOR - Bargain Bazaar Flea Market. Eureka Rd. at I-75. Wed.-Sun. 8-10. Mgr. Bill. Home Ph: (313) 562-3740. Bus. Ph: (313) 287-2340.

THREE OAKS - Featherbone Flea Market, downtown, at the Square. Open every Sat. and Sun. 15 to 20 sellers, $3 per space and up. William Larsen, P.O. Box 355, Sawyer, Mich. Ph: (616) 756-7320 or 426-3015.

TRUFANT - Trufant Auction & Flea Market, 303 North C Street. Open April thru Sept. Dealers 250-300. Outdoors. Fee: $3. Maurice Petersen, Rt. 1 Box 201, Trufant, MI 49347. Ph: (616) 984-2168.

WAREN - Country Fair Flea Market. 20900 Dequindre. Open every weekend. Fri. 4-9; Sat. & Sun. 10-6. Free parking and free admission. Dealer reservations taken daily 9-5. Phone (313) 757-3740.

WESTLAND - Merri-Trail Flea Market. 8244 Merriman Rd. Open Fri., Sat., & Sun. Indoors. 100 dealers, 500-1000 att. Edward Betel, 8240 Merriman, Westland, Mich. 48185. Ph: (313) 421-1311. Res. Req.

YPSILANTI - Giant Flea Market, 4 mi. east of Ann Arbor. Take I-94 to Huron St. exit, north to Michigan St., right 2 blocks. Open Fri. 6 pm to 10 pm, Sat. & Sun. 10 am to 6 pm. Ph: (313) 971-7676 days; (313) 487-5890 weekends. Antiques, collectibles, arts & crafts, misc.

MINNESOTA

ALEXANDRIA - Great Northern Flea Market. National Guard Armory on Main Street. Aug. 23 & 24. Sat. & Sun. 10-4. 25 dealers indoor. 1500 att. Sarsaparilla Prod., 1536 27th Ave., S. Apt. 301, Fargo, N.D., 58103. Ph: (701) 235-6080. Res. req.

BATTLE LAKE - Rainbow Bait Flea Market, Hwy. 78 No. 20 mi. off Int. 94 east of Fergus Falls 17 mi. Open Memorial Day weekend to Labor Day weekend, Sat. & Sun. Outdoor. Fee: $5 day. Lori Edlund, Box 302, Battle Lake, Minn. 56515. Ph: (218) 864-5569.

BLOOMINGTON - Flea Market, Mann-France Drive-In Theater, France Ave. & Hwy 494. Open Sundays 7 am to 3 pm. $2.50 per space. 25¢ admission antiques, jewelry, furniture, plants and household goods.

DULUTH-PROCTOR - 7th Annual Swap Meet & Flea Market, at the So. St. Louis County Fairgrounds. Sponsored by the Studebaker Drivers Club. ANNUAL - August 13th, 8 am to 5 pm. 500 dealers, $5 per space. Indoor and outdoors. 5000 avg. att. Shirley D. VanDell, P.O. Box 1004, Duluth, Minn. 55810. Ph: (218) 624-5932.

FAIRBAULT - Flea Market, open Sat. & Sun., 10 am to 5 pm. Fee $3.50 per day. Rance English, Fairbault, MN. Ph: (507) 334-5159.

LITCHFIELD - Meeker Co. Swap Area, located 1 mile west of Dairy Queen, on 11th St. Open April thru Oct., On Sat. & Sun. Dealers fee: $5 on Sat., $3 on Sun. Outdoors. Jerry Kramber, 501 Pleasant Ave., Litchfield, Minn, 55355. Ph: (612) 693-7698.

MANKATO - Smitty's Flea Market, National Guard Armory, No. 2nd St. Open Sept. thru April (one weekend a month). Indoor, 64 dealers. Fee: $10 per table. Att: 2,000-3,000. Jim Schmidt (Smitty, P. O. Box 585, 56001.) Ph: (507) 931-2449.

MINNEAPOLIS - Flea Market, Lyndale & Glenwood. Open every Sat. 9 am to 3 pm. $3 per space. Free admission. Antiques and 2nd hand merchandise.

MINNEAPOLIS - Flea Market, Midway Shopping Center, off Snelling Ave. and Hwy 36. Open every Sat. 9 am to 3 pm. $4 per space. Discounted new items and junk.

MONTICELLO - Orchard Fun Market - Rt. 1, Box 373. 3 miles west of stoplight in Monticello, ¼ mile on Orchard Rd. Open April thru Nov. 9-5, on Sat. & Sun. & 4-9 on Fri. Indoors and outdoors. Tables supplied. Dealers fee $6 Sat. $7 Sun. Joseph Osowski, Rt. 1, Box 373, Monticello, MN 55362.

NEW ULM - New Ulm Antique Show and Sale. 1st South and State St. Ph: (507) 354-3507. Mailing address 107 N. Jefferson, New Ulm, MN 56073. Indoor facilities, July 31 and Aug. 1st. 70 dealers, 1000 attendance. Dealer's fee $5 per table per day, entrance fee 75¢. Ample parking, home style dinner and lunch.

OGEMA - Wild Cat Swap Meet 1½ miles south of Ogema. Open Sat. & Sun. June to the end of Oct. Over 100 sellers, $3.50 per space. Dave Mertens, P.O. Box 94, Ogema, MN. Ph: (218) 983-3325.

OTTERTAIL - Carol's Flea Market. 9 miles south of Perham on 78. Indoors. Carol Coulter, Rt. 1, Ottertail, Minn., 56571. Ph: (218) 367-2742. Res. sug.

PINE CITY - Flea Market. Open on Wed. during the summer. Handmade jewelry, antiques and good 2nd hand items.

REDWING - Flea Market, Gibson's Store-parking lot. Open every Sun. 9 am to 3 pm. $3 per space. Household items and junk.

ST. PAUL - Flea Market, E. St. Paul National Guard Armory. 1530 E. Maryland Ave. Open 3 weekends per Mo. Sat. 7 am to 5 pm. Sun. 8-5. Sellers 90-200. Fee: outdoors $5 day, indoors $7. Ph: (612) 457-4999 for information.

ST. CLOUD - Flea Market, at the National Guard Armory, 8th St. Open Sept. thru March, usually last weekend of mo. -No show in Dec. 1981. 75 to 80 dealers, $27 per weekend. 3 to 500 avg. att. Indoors. Ken Bromenschenkel, RR 1 - St. Cloud, MN. 56301. Ph: (612) 251-9189.

WINONA - Flea Market, Levee Plaza Mall. Open every Sat. 7 am to 3 pm. Antiques, junk and a farmers market.

MISSISSIPPI

COLUMBUS - Possum Town Flea Market, Hwy 69 S., at the Lowndes Fairgrounds. Open the 3rd weekend of the month (except Sept). Sellers fee: $5 per day or $9 for the weekend. Phone (601) 328-1911.

JACKSON - Antique Fair & Flea Market. Fairgrounds. Free parking. July 18-19, Aug. 15-16, Aug. 29-30, Sept. 19-20, Oct. 31, Nov. 1, Nov. 28-29, Dec. 19-20. Hines Enterprises, Inc. P. O. Box 5423, Pearl, Miss. 39208. Phone (601) 939-3040.

JACKSON - Quality Antique Flea Market, at the State Fairgrounds. Dates for 1981 are: April 25-26, May 23-24, July 25-26, Sept. 12-13 & 26-27, Nov. 21-23, Dec. 12-13. At the Trademark Blvd. June 27-28, Aug. 22-23. 200 dealers $20 per weekend, except for Trademark Blvd. $25 per weekend. Larry or Betty Emery, 1617 McDowell Rd., Jackson, Miss. 39204. Ph: (601) 939-8596.

NATCHEZ - Thieves Market, on Canal & State St. Open every Sat., 9 am to 6 pm. and Sun., 1 to 6 pm. Indoor & outdoor. 45 dealers, $7 on Sat., $5 on Sun. 2500 avg. att. Ph: (601) 445-4034.

PASCAGOUL - Hwy 90 East. Hwy East of Searstown. Ph: (601) 875-2981. Mailing address 139 Souwan Ave., Ocean Springs, Miss. Indoor and outdoor facilities. Indoors daily, outdoors weekends. Dealer's fee $3. Ample parking.

RIPLEY - First Monday Trade Day, Hwy 15 south. Open first Sat. & Sun. of the first Mon. weekend of each mo. 200 to 300 dealers, $5 per day or $7.50 for the weekend. Wayne Windham, Hwy 15 So. Ripley, Miss. 38663. Ph: (601) 837-4250.

MISSOURI

BONNE TERRE - Trading Island Inc., Hwy. 67 south from St. Louis to Bonne Terre Exit, then north on old 67. Open Fri., Sat. & Sun. 200 dealers indoor and out. $4-$6 fee. Tables inside. Walter & Barb Davis, P. O. Box 68, Bonne Terre, MO., 63628. Ph: (314) 358-2288 or 358-2289.

COLUMBIA - Morton's Flea Mkt., on Hwy 63 south. Held on Sat. & Sun. 9 am - 5 pm, indoors and out. Avg. daily att. 300. Avg. 25 dealers. Dealers fee 1 table - 2 days $10, 2 tables - 2 days $15, 1 table - 1 day $8, 2 tables - 1 day $12. Held in a spacious building - heated & air cond. Phone (314) 449-6306.

HANNIBAL - Bonanza Flea Market, 110 Church Street. Every Sat. & Sun. 9-6. Inside and outside. Phone (314) 248-1505 or 221-7801.

JOPLIN - Joplin Flea Mkt., 1200 Block Virginia Ave., 80 plus indoor and out. $5 fee, tables available at $2 each. Open Sat. & Sun. Avg. atten. 4000-5000. LaVerne Miller and Ed Frazier, 1200 Block Virginia Ave., Joplin, MO 64801. Ph: (417) 623-3743 or 623-6328. New market, room for 120 inside spaces.

KANSAS CITY - Things Unlimited, 817 Westport Rd., Kansas City, MO 64111. Indoor facilities, every Sat. & Sun. 10-5. 75 dealers, 1-3000 atten. Dealer's fee $22 per space per weekend. Ample parking, food concessions.

KANSAS CITY - Waldo Flea Market, 75th & Broadway. Open daily-year round. 20 dealers, indoors. $20 a day per space. Good atten. on Sat. & Sun. David Boote & Ramon Wright, 226 W. 75th St. Kansas City, MO. 64114. Ph: 333-8233.

KANSAS CITY - Heart Swap and Shop a Bazaar. 6401 E. 40 Hiway. Open year round. Indoorss open 6 days. outdoors, Sat. & Sun. $2 and up dealers fee. Avg. Sun. att: 6,000. Michael Maturo, 6401 E. 40 Hiway, kansas City, Mo. 64129. Phone (816) 924-7885. No food, drinks or hand guns.

KANSAS CITY - Nate's 63rd St. Swap Shop, 63rd St. Drive-in theatre. U.S. 350 East I-435. Open all year from 7 a.m. to 3 p.m. Sat. & Sun. Outdoors avg. 500 sellers, 5000 buyers. Sellers, $3 to $10. Attendance fee 50¢. Snack shop, playground, electrical outlets. Nate Shurin, P. O. box 5374, Kansas City, Mo 64131. Phone (816) 523-0965. A tram will take buyers around perimeter of swap shop. Stop any place to load or unload. No charge.

KNOB NOSTER - Knob Noster Flea Market, 600 Allen Street. Open every Sat. & Sun. Indoors and outdoors. Avg. dealers: 70. Dealers fee: $6 indoors and $3 outdoors. Free attendance. Tables for rent. Avg. att: 3000. George Magee, 310 W. McPherson, Know Noster, Mo. 65336. Phone (816) 563-2031. No food, no alcohol. Res sug.

KANSAS CITY - Heart Bazaar Flea Market, 6401 E. 40 Hiway. Open Tue. thru Sun. Auction every Tue. 7 pm. Dealers, 65. Indoors. Dealers fee $35 per week. Attendance free. Michael Maturo 6401 E. 40 Hwy., K.C., MO 64129. Res. sug.

LEBANON - The Country Corner Flea Market, 585 N. Jefferson on I-44. Open daily. Phone (417) 588-1430.

MT. VERNON - Mt. Vernon Flea Market, Rt. 1 Box 1B Mt. Vernon, MO 65712. Ph: (417) 466-2422. Indoor and outdoor facilities, 9-5 week days, Sunday 1-5, closed Wed. Dealer's fees: outside, Mon-Fri. $1 per booth, Sat. and Sun. $1.50 per booth, inside available by the week.

NEOSHO - Ozark Garden, Bus. Rt. 60 East and Alt. 71. Sat. & Sun. 6 till dark. Indoors and outdoors. Avg. dealers 50. No att. fee. Avg. att: 5000. Mgr. Gharles Bull, Rt. 5 Box 97, Neosho, Miss. 64850. Ph: (417) 451-4379.

OSAGE BEACH - Americana Flea Market, State Hwy. 54. Open daily, indoors, also outdoors on weekends. 20 to 38 sellers. $5 per weekend. $45 monthly. Rt. 1, Box 101-10, Osage Beach, MO 65065. Ph: (314) 348-2144.

SEDALIA - Red Rooster Hyl 65 & Winsor, Mo. Jct. 52. Open year round. Outside. Fee: $2.50. Bill Copp, 1706 S. Osage, Sedalia, MO. 65301. Ph: 827-2368.

SIKESTON - Tradewinds, 875 W. Malone Ave. Open Thur., Fri., Sat. Dealers: 140. Att: 5,000. Fee $5 day. Daniel Byrd, 875 W. Malone Ave., Sikeston, MO 63801. Ph: 471-8419 or 471-3956.

SPRINGFIELD - Viking Flea Market, 626 W. Chase. Weekends. 100 dealers. Ph: (417) 869-4237. Carnival & Depression glass.

SPRINGFIELD - Park Central Flea Market, 429 Boonville. Open 10-5 Mon. thru Sat. Noon to 5 on Sun. 30 indoor dealers. Monthly rental dealers fee. Admission free. Avg. att: 200-300. Helen M. Smith, 429 Boonville, Springfield, Mo. 69806. Phone (417) 866-9629.

SPRINGFIELD - Olde Towne Flea Market, 600 Boonville. Open every day but Thur. Phone (417) 831-6665.

ST. LOUIS - 8370 North Broadway. 200 dealers. 10-4. Free admission. Phone (314) 569-3309. Betty Roberts.

ST. LOUIS - Gypsy Caravan, St. Louis Arena, Oakland Blvd. Annual, open Monday, Memorial Day, 9 am to 6 pm. 300 sellers, $35 outdoors and $75 indoors. Over 30,000 attendance, $1 admission over 12 years. Reservations required. St. Louis Symphony Society, Powell Symphony Hall, 718 N. Grand Blvd., St. Louis, MO. 63103. Ph: (314) 533-2500 ask for Carol Brumm.

ST. LOUIS - St. Louis County Flea Market. Outdoors - 9 acres. Every Sat. & Sun. For info: TMT, 7711 Walinca, Clayton, Missouri 63105. Phone (314) 863-7776.

ST. LOUIS - Northland Flea Market, V.F.W. Hall, 7208 W. Florissant St. Open Oct. thru May, 1st weekend of month. Indoors, 40 sellers $8.50 per table. Over 2000 attendance. Billie Dickemper, 8559 Mora Lane, St. Louis, MO 63147. Ph: (314) 383-1912.

WESTPORT - Page St. and Hwy. 270. Open 4th Sun. of the month, 10 am to 5 pm. 40 sellers. $20 for a two table booth. Betty Roberts, 8588 Forest Dr., St. Louis, MO 63134. Ph: (314) 521-5544.

MONTANA

BEATRICE - Town & Country Flea Market on U.S. 77 Hiway, ½ mile south of Beatrice. Open Sat. & Sun. July 25-26, Aug. 22-23, Sept. 5-6, Sept. 19-20, Oct. 3-4, Oct. 17-18, Nov. 7-8, Nov. 21-22, Dec. 5-6, Dec. 19-20. Free parking and admission.

GREAT FALLS - Great Falls Flea Market, 5700 2nd Avenue North. Open Sat. & Sun. May-October. Avg. 25 outdoors. Dealers fee: $10 per weekend. Free attendance. Avg. att. 300-500. Edward Baily, 2805 2nd Ave. North, Great Falls, Mont. 59401. Phone (406) 453-4615.

GREAT FALLS - Kat's Swap Mart, 112 Central Ave. Open 10-5:30 daily. Indoors. Fee: $3 day. Kathleen Rodgers, 112 Central, Great Falls, Mont. 59401. Ph: 761-9401. Res.

NEBRASKA

COLUMBUS - Columbus Flea Market, Platte County AG Park, Ph: (605) 332-4554. P.O. Box 236 Sioux Falls. S. Dak. 57101. Indoor facilities. Oct. 16-17 third of three per year. 100 dealers. 2000 attendance. 50¢ admisstion fee, $8 dealer's fee.

NORFOLK - Norfolk Flea Market, Municipal Auditorium, Ph (605) 332-4554. P.O. Box 236 Sioux Falls. S. Dak. 57101. Indoor facilities. Sept. 11-12. 100 dealers. 2000 attendance. 50¢ admission fee, dealer's fee $8.

OMAHA - New City Flea Market. Int. State 80 at 84th St. Ph: (402) 339-0800. New City Flea Market, 4095 S. 84 St., Omaha, Neb. 68127. Outdoor facilities. May 1 to Sept. 1, every Sat. & Sun. Fruit market, antiques.

OMAHA - Omaha Swap and Flea Mart, 5610 Redick. Open Sat. & Sun, Apr. 1 thru Dec. 31. Indoors and outdoors. Fee: $5 day. 700 spaces avail. Att: 200-3,000. Reservations. V.R. Mullin, 6826 N. 56, Omaha, Neb. 68152. Ph: (402) 571-5712 or 895-6351.

VALENTINE - 2nd Sunday Flea Mkt., Sandhills Drive-In Theatre on West Hwy. 20. Open 2nd Sun. of month, May thru Aug. 40 sellers outdoor, $4 fee, avg. atten. 500. National Advertising (Skip Schlueter), 520 Elenora Dr., Valentine, NB 69201. Ph: (402) 376-3711. Res. suggested.

NEVADA

CARSON CITY - Carson Flea Market, 9000 E. Hwy. 50. Open yr. round, every Sat. & Sun. 50 dealers. $3 to $6 per day. Indoor and out. Tables supplied. 2500 avg. att. Don Erickson, P.O. Box 787, Dayton, NV. 89403. Ph: (702) 882-4692.

DAYTON - Dayton Flea Market, Hwy 50 near Railroad St., Ph: (702) 882-3980. Mailing address, P.O. Box 75, Dayton, Nev. 89403. Outdoor facilities, every Sat.-Sun. April-Oct.. 40 dealers, dealer fee $3 per day. Ample parking.

FERNLEY - Fernley Fun Fair Flea Market U.S. 40 West. Exit 46 off I-80. Open Fri. noon, Sat., Sun. Dealers: 30. Att: 5,000. Fee: $4 to $10 day. Indoors and out. Vern Heater, P.O. Box 481, Fernley, Nev. 89408. Ph: (702) 575-4774.

LAS VEGAS - 1981 Heldorado Days Rodeo in Las Vegas at the Las Vegas Convention Center. From May 10 thru May 17. 900 Las Vegas Blvd., North, Las Vegas, Nevada 89101.

LAS VEGAS - Big Country Swap Meet. From Rawlins 18 mi. W. Riner Rd. N. from U.S. 80-30. 10 miles to Pipeline Rd. Turn right for 3 miles. Turn left. Look for Swap Meet signs. Sellers: $1 weekdays, $2 weekends. Overnight $1. Admission 25¢ adults. Free parking. AGTGC, P. O. Box 3607, N. Las Vegas, Nev. 89030.

LAS VEGAS - Tanner's Worldwide Flea Market. 1626 E. Charleston Blvd. Open showtime 9 am to 6 pm. Dealers: 300 to 400 indoors. Att: 8000 to 10000. Dealers fee: $35. Att. fee $1.25. Clare Tanner, 1626 E. Charleston Ave., Las Vegas, Nev., 89104, Ph: (702) 382-8355. Reserv.

LAS VEGAS - European Style Flea Market, 1981 Dates for the Convention Center are: Nov. 7 & 8, for the Showboat Hotel are: Aug. 15-16, Sept. 5-6, Oct. 3-4 & 17-18, Nov. 21-22, Dec. 12-13 & 19-20, May 9-10 & 23-24, June 6-7 & 20-21. Space fee: $30 per day for 10 by 10 corner space. Don Cook, 5128 W. Charleston Blvd., Las Vegas, Nv. 89102. Ph: (702) 878-4394.

LAS VEGAS - I-15 Swap Meet, I-15 & Cheyenne Ave. Open every weekend, 8-4. Indoors and out. Fee: indoors $10.00 day. Outdoors, $5 day. 5128 W. Charleston Blvd., Las Vegas, Nev. 89102. Ph: (702) 870-6922.

LAS VEGAS - Las Vegas Swap Meet, Sunset Drive-In. Open Sat. 6:30 am to 3 pm. Sun. 5:30 am to 3 pm. 150 sellers. $2 on Sat. $4 on Sun. 2000 attendance 35¢ admission (car load). Ph: (702) 648-7550.

NORTH LAS VEGAS - Broad acres, 2930 Las Vegas Blvd. North. Open every Sat. & Sun. Sunrise to ?, and week before XMAS. 400 dealers, $6 per day. 4000 avg. att. Dolph Bowman, P.O. Box 3059, No. Las Vegas, Nv. 89030. Ph: (702) 642-3777.

RENO - Harrah's Swap Meet and Car Show. Box 10 Reno, Nev 89504. Ph: (702) 786-3232. Outdoor facilities. 1300 dealers. 15,000 atten. Dealer's fee $25 per space. $5 for car show. Car Show and banquet. Annual.

RENO - Super Flea Market and Swap Meet, 555 El Rancho Dr., Sparks (El Rancho Drive-In Theatre). Open Sat. & Sun. from 7-4 pm. $6 fee, avg. atten. 800-1000. Michael Pontrelli, 2695 W. Plumb Lane, Reno, NV 89509. Ph: (702) 329-7109.

RENO - Tanner's World Wide Flea Market, held at the Reno Convention Center. April 12, May 31 - Oct. 25, Nov. 22, Dec. 20. $35 per space per day. 1626 E. Charleston Blvd., Las Vegas, Nev. 89104. Ph: (702) 382-8355.

SPARKS - Super Flea Market and Swap Meet, 555 El Rancho Dr. Open Sat. & Sun. 7-4, except Dec., Jan., & Feb. Outdoors. Fee: $6. Dealers: 40. Att. 800. Michael and Jeanny Ponrelli, 2695 W. Plumb Lane, Reno, Nev. 89509. Ph: (207) 7109.

NEW HAMPSHIRE

AMHERST - Outdoor Antiques Market, on Rt. 122. Open April thru Oct., 8 am to 4 pm. Sundays and Holidays. Indoors and out. 100 to 200 dealers. Outdoor fees $8 per Sun. or $30 for the month. Inside space is $40 per month. Admission is 50¢ per person. Richard Douglas, RFD 2, Milford, NH 03055. Ph: (603) 673-2093. Antiques, collectibles, crafts and quality merchandise.

CANTOOCOOK - Cornetts Farm, Penacook Rd. Follow signs 2½ miles east from Cantoocook Village. Open Sun. May 1 thru Oct. 15. Outdoors. Dealers: 30. Fee: $4. Att: 400. Bertha Cornett, RFDI Cantoocook, N.H. 03229. Ph: (603) 746-3960.

DERRY · Grand View Farm Flea Market. Jct. of Rt. 28 and Bypass 28S. Open year round, 8 am to 4 pm on Sundays. Indoors and out. 150 avg. dealers, outdoors in summer is $6; indoors $8. Winter indoor rate is $12. Tables are supplied. Reservations are required. Admission is 50¢ per person. Children free. Henry A. Weber, Box 13A RFD 2. Derry. NH 03038. Ph: (603) 432-2326. Junktiques to Antiques, new stuff to oldies.

HOLLIS · Hollis Country Store & flea Mkt. 436 Silver Lake Rd. Open April thru Nov. Sun. & Holidays. Outdoor. Dealers: 150. Att: 5,000. Gilbert & Alice Prieto, RFD No. 3, Milford, N.H. 03055. Ph: (603) 465-7813 or 882-6134. Res.

HUDSON · Hudson Antique Show & Sale. Rt. 111 at Lions Club & Holt Halls. Open Oct. thru April, 9 am to 4 pm, on Sundays. Indoors. 100 or more dealers. $4 per day (3 tables included). Admission: 50¢ per person. Don Hold, 16 Melendy Rd., Hudson, NH 03051. (603) 883-6770. Choice antiques, tools, crystal and china.

MEREDITH · Burlwood Antique Market, U.S. Rt. 3 between Meredith & Weirs Beach. Open Fri., Sat. & Sun. June to Labor Day. Sat. & Sun. Labor Day to Oct. 15th. Dealers: 35. Indoor and out. Fees: $6 day, $11 2 day, $14 3 day weekend. Att: 800-1200. Tom & Nan Lindsey, Rd 2, Meredith, N.H. 03253. Phone (603) 279-6387. Res. Sug.

MERRIMACK · Merrimack Flea & Antique Market, off Rt. 3 Exit 8. Open year round, 7 am to 5 pm. Sundays and holidays. Indoors and outdoors. 50 to 100 dealers. $10 indoors w/tables, $5 outdoors. Admission: 50¢ per person. Walter Lang, 175 Amherst St., Nashua, N.H. 03060. Ph: (603) 882-6962.

NORTHWOOD · Northwood Flea Market, Rt. 4, east of Concord, at Noel's Sport Shop. Open April thru Nov., 10 am to 6 pm. Sat., Sun. and Holiday weekends. Outdoors, about 10 to 15 dealers, $5 per day, $8 for two days. Grace V. Zibell, RFD 1, Durham, N.H. 03824. Ph: (603) 2703.

SWANZEY · Knotty Pine Antique Market. Rt. 10 West Swanzey. Open 7 days a week. Indoors and out. Joan Pappas, P.O. Box 96, West Swanzey, N.H. 03469. Ph: (603) 352-5252.

WEST SWAHZEY · Knotty Pine Antiques. 120 shops under one roof. Rt. 10. Open 7 days a week - year round - 9-5. 120 dealers indoors. Joan E. Pappas, P. O. Box 96, West Swahzey, N.H. 03469. Only antiques and collectables allowed.

NEW JERSEY

AVENEL · The Village Commons Flea Market. 1490 Rahway Avenue. Open Wed., Sat. & Sun. Avg. dealers: 35-40. 9 shops open all year. Dealers fee: $5. Free attendance. Tables supplied. Avg. att: 400. Bernadette Pirone, 1490 Rahway Avenue, Avenel, N.J. 07001. Phone (210) 574-8599.

BERGENFIELD · Annual, 80 S. Prospect Ave., at the Bergenfield High School. Indoors. Held on March 13th. Spon: Jr. Women's Club, Gloria Rothstein, 12 Chatham St., Suffern, N.Y. 10901. Ph: (914) 357-8410 or (301) 529-3896.

BERLIN · Berlin Farmers Market, 41 Clementon Rd., N.J. Turnpike exit 4 to Rt. 73 south to Rt. 30. Open year round. Sat. & Sun., 9 am to 5 pm. 100 dealers outdoors. Fee from $6 to $15. No Res. No tables. Louis Chimento, Berlin Farmers Market, 41 Clementon Rd., Berlin, NJ 08009. Ph: (609) 767-1284. Anything old.

BRIDGETON · Flea Market, 33 N. Laurel St. Open every Monday, 15 to 20 sellers. Ph: (609) 455-0865.

BROOKLINE · Cubby's Cozy Corner, 130 W. Proctor Hill Rd. Fri., Sat. & Sun. 11-5. Phone (603) 673-6963.

CHESTER · Lions Flea Market, on Rt. 206 in Chester. Open on Sun., 9 am to 5 pm. June thru Oct. 200 sellers. $12 per day. 3000 avg. atten. Lions Club, P.O. Box 126, Chester, NJ 01930.

CINNAMINSON · House of Antiques Flea Market, on Rt. 130, in the Cinnaminson Mall. Open every Fri., 12 to 10 pm. Sat. 10 am to 10 pm. Sun., 12 to 6 pm. Ph: (609) 829-9711.

CLIFTON · Boy's Club of Clifton Flea Market. 802 Clifton Ave. Clifton. N.J. Third Sun. of every month. Sept. thru May.

CLINTON · Colonial Clinton Fleatique, north of Clinton on Rt. 31. Open Sat. and Sun. April thru Nov. Outdoors, 250 spaces. Ph: (201) 638-8716.

COLUMBUS · Columbus Farmer's Market, Rt. 206, Columbus, N.J. N.J. Turnpike to Exit 7, Bordentown exit, head south on 206, 5 miles. Open every Thurs. from 1st Sun. in April to last Sun. before Christmas. Elwood Hammitt or Jack Benson, Rt. 206, Columbus, N.J., 08022. Ph: (609) 267-0051.

DEMAREST · 3rd Annual Antique and Collectible Show. Northern Valley Regional High School, Knickerbocker Rd. Ph: (914) 357-8410, (201) 529-3896, mailing address: Gloria Rothstein Shows, 12 Chatham St., Suffern, NJ 10901. Indoor facilities. Dealer's fee $20/sponsor, Jr. Women's Club of Harrington Park. Nov. 7, 11-6.

DORCHESTER · Bailey's Flea Market, Rt. 47 & Mauricetown Rd. Open daily, (best days are Sat. and Sun.) Outdoors. 90 to 100 sellers. Ph: (609) 825-0277.

EAST BRUNSWICK · Rt. 18 Indoor Market. 290 Rt. 18, East Brunswick, N.J. 08816. Fri. 12-9; Sat. 10-9. Sun. 10-7. Indoors. Free admission and parking. Phone(201) 254-5080.

EAST KEANSBURG · Rt. 36 Flea & Antique Markets, Inc., 100 Rt. 36. Open Fri. 10-10, Sun. 10-6. Indoors. Dealers: 40. Res. Al Golden, 100 Rt. 36, East Keansburg, 07734. Ph: (201) 495-9066.

EAST ORANGE · Brick Church Flea Market, Main & Prospect Ave. Open every Thur., Fri., and Sat. 10:30 am to 6:30 pm. Ph: (201) 674-2226.

EAST ORANGE · Village Flea Market, 356 Glenwood Ave., near Upsala College; off Garden State Pkwy. Exit 145. Open year round, Sat. & Sun., 10 am to 5 pm. 40 dealers indoors in winter, room for 75 outdoor, summer. Fee $8 day or $12 two days indoor; $5 day or $8 two days outdoor. Reservations needed. Greg Hubert, Rocky Way, West Orange, NJ 07052. Ph: (201) 325-3935. Antiques, collectibles, household, crafts, greenery.

EDISON · New Dover United Methodist Church Flea Market, 690 New Dover Rd. Open year round on Tues. 8 am to 5 pm. Indoors and out. 32 to 80 sellers. Ph: (201) 381-9478. ·

ENGLEWOOD · Annual, at the Congregation Ahavath Totah, 240 Broad Ave. Held on Feb. 6th Spon: Sisterhood of Congregation, Gloria Rothstein, 12 Chatham St., Suffern, N.Y. 10901. Ph: (914) 357-8410 or (201) 529-3896.

ENGLISHTOWN · Englishtown Auction Sales, Inc., 90 Wilson Avenue. Take N.J. turnpike Exit 9 . . . rt. 18E . . .Rt. 527 South. Open year round Sat. 5-5. Sun. 9-5. 150 dealers indoors. Several hundred outdoors. Dealers fee starts at $4. Free attendance. Tables supplied. Inquiries: Main Office, 90 Wilson Ave., Englishtown, N.J. 07726. Phone (201) 446-9644. Food items restricted.

FLEMINGTON · hwy. 31. Opening April 1. Flemington Fair Flea Market, R.D. 1, Box 486, Flemington, N.J. 08822. Open Wed. 9-3, Sun. 7-4. Indoors and outdoors. Free admission & parking. Phone (201) 782-7326, after 6 pm.

FORT LEE · Annual, at the Fort Lee High School. Held on Feb. 27. Spon: Children's Aide and Adoption Society. Gloria Rothstein, 12 Chatham St., Suffern, N.Y. 10901. Ph: (914) 357-8410 or (201) 529-3896.

FRENCHTOWN · Frenchtowns Merchants Market. Milfore - Frenchtown R. Indoors - Fri., Sat. & Sun. Outdoors - Sat. & Sun. Free admission and parking. Phone (201) 526-4620 and 996-4991.

FRENCHTOWN · Pastore's Flea Market, Frenchtown & Milford Rds. Open Wed., Sat. and Sun. year round. Indoors and out. 25 sellers.

HACKENSACK · Annual, at the Holy Trinity Church, Maple Ave. & Pangborn Place. Held on March 6. Spon: Holy Trinity Church School. Gloria Rothstein, 12 Chatham St., Suffern, NY 10901. Ph: (914) 357-8410 or (201) 529-3896.

HAWTHORNE · Flea Market, Antiques & Crafts, American Legion Post 199, Legion Place. Open 4th Sun every month, 10 am to 5 pm. 25¢ admission. Indoors. Ph: (201) 525-5618.

HAWTHORNE · Flea Market, Antiques & Crafts, Hawthorne Boys Club, Franklin Ave. Open 3rd Sun. every month, 10 am to 5 pm. 25¢ admission. Indoors. Ph: (201) 525-6518.

HOWELL · Howell Antique Village & Flea Market. 2215 Hwy. 19, Howell, N.J. Open Fri., Sat. & Sun. year round and Mon. holidays. Dealers 300-400. Indoors and outdoors Dealers fee: $5 for 1 table $2 for second. Free attendance. Avg. att: 3000. Bobbi Horowitz, P. O. Box 564, Howell, N.J. 07731. Phone (201) 367-1105.

JOBSTOWN · Jobstown Antiques & Flea Market. Rt. 537. Open Wed. thru Sat. 12 noon to 6. Sun. 2-6. Free adm. & parking. Phone (609) 597-1017.

LAKEWOOD · Rt. 70 Flea Market, east of Rt. 9 on Rt. 70. Fri. 12 noon to 6; Sat. & Sun. 9-6. Phone (201) 370-1837.

LAMBERTVILLE · Governor's Antique Market. Rt. 179 (1½ miles north of Lambertville. Open every Sat. & Sun. year round. Avg. dealers: 60-90 indoors and 50-200 outdoors. Free attendance. Tables supplied. F. S. Cad, P. O. Box 242, Lambertville, N.J. 08530. Phone (609) 397-2010. Restrictions: collectibles only. Res. sug.

LAMBERTVILLE · Lambertville Antique Flea Market. Rt. 29, 1½ mi. south of Lambertville; off I-95. Open year round, Sat., Sun., and holidays from 8 am to 5 pm. 16 permanent shops indoor, 100 dealers seasonal, 50 in winter. (Less on Sat.) Fee with two tables. $7 Sun. $4 Sat. Ed and Florence Cook, RD 2, Box 199, Lambertville, NJ 08530. Ph: (609) 397-0456. Antiques, collectibles, arts & crafts, produce & flowers.

LAMBERTVILLE · Golden Nugget Antique Flea Market, Rt. 20, 2 mi. south of Lambertville; off I-95. Open year round, Sat. 8 am to 6 pm. Sun. 6:30 am to 6 pm. Indoor shops, outdoor dealers around 120 on Sat., 220 on Sun. (spring thru fall). Fee $3 one table, $5 two tables on Sat; $6 one table, $10 two tables on Sun. Mrs. Judith K. Brenna, 10 Seven Oaks Lane, Trenton, NJ 08628. Phone (609) 882-1499. All types, especially pewter, brass, Hummels, silver. Free adm. & parking.

MANAHAWKIN · Manahawkin Mart "Peddler's Paradise", 657 Bay Ave. Open every Fri. & Sat. 10-8, Sun. 10-6. New outdoor market. Free admission & parking. Phone (609) 597-1017.

MANVILLE · Manville Flea Market. Fire Co. No. 2 Firehouse, Washington Ave., Corner South 13th Ave. Open 1st Sun. of each month 9-5. Indoors and outdoors. Free admission and parking. Phone (201) 526)2519.

MEYERSVILLE · Meyersville Grange Flea Market, Meyersville Rd., Gillette, N.J. Every Sun. 9-5 Oct. thru May. Info: (201) 832-7422 or 376-5772.

MICKLETON · Mickleton Flea Market. South of Harmony Rd. Exit on I-295. Sat. & Sun. 9-? Indoors and outdoors. Dealers info: (609) 423-3253.

MONTCLAIR · Montclair Historical Society Antiques Market. Lackauana Plaza, Montclair, N.J. 07042. Open Tue., Wed., Thur. & Fri. 10:30-3:30, Sat. 10-5. 10 indoor dealers. Mrs. June Emrich, 574 Grove St., Upper Montclair, N.J. 07043

MT. ARLINGTON · Hopatchong Elks Flea Market, on Howard Blvd. Open on Sun., 10 am to 5 pm. 25 indoor spaces, outdoors limited. Ph: (201) 398-9835.

NESHANIC STATION · Neshanic Station Flea Market, off Rt. 202. Open Sat. and Sun. 300 spaces, reservations required. Ph: (201) 369-3188. Mid-March to Mid-Dec.

NEW BRUNSWICK · U.S. #1 Flea Market and Antiques, Rts. 1 & 18 New Brunswick, NJ 08901. Indoor and outdoor facilities, Fri. noon-10, Sat. 10-10, Sun. 10-8. 500 dealers, 10,000 atten. Dealer's fee $39 per weekend (new merch.). $25 per weekend (antiques, used collectibles) $8 per day outdoors. Ample parking. Food Concessions.

NEW BRUNSWICK · Brunswick Bazaar, Rt. 27, 710 Somerset Avenue. Fri. 12-9; Sat. 10-9; Sun. 10-7. Free admission and parking. Phone Joann for info at (201) 846-9838 or (201) 238-0765 eve.

NEW DOVER · New Dover United Methodist Church Flea Market. 690 New Dover Rd., Edison, N.J. 08820. Tue. 6 a.m. - 2 p.m. Free admission. Info: (201) 381-9478.

NEWTON · Super Flea Market, Rt. 537. Newton Drive-in Theatre 1 mi. north on Rt. 206. Open May thru Oct. Wed., Sat. & Sun., 9 am - 5 pm. Avg. 80 dealers outdoors. Fee $6 day or $10 wknd. Ann Carol Perry, 328 Franklin Rd., Dover, NJ 07801. Phone (201) 366-4955. All types of produce in season.

NEW EGYPT · New Egypt Auction & Farmers Market, Rt. 537. From N.J. tpke: take Exit 7-A to Allentown, turn right on Main, follow Rt. 539 to Rt. 537, turn right go 1 mi. west of intersection. Open Sat., Sun., & Wed. Indoor and outdoors. Fee: $4 Sun., $3 Wed., Sat. free. Att: 3,000. Esler G. Miller. Rt. 537, New Egypt, N.J. 08533. Ph: (609) 758-2082. Res.

OLD BRIDGE · The Pushcart Palace. On Rt. 9 & Ernston Rd. 100,000 sq. ft. of indoor space, fully air conditioned and heated. Phone (201) 721-4930, 10-4, 7 days a week.

PALMYRA · Swap-N-Shop, Rt. 73 Tacony-Palmyra Drive-In Theatre, Palmyra NJ 08065. Ph: (609) 829-3001. Outdoor facilities, Sun. and holidays 8-4. 350 dealers, 4,000 atten. Dealer's fee $6. Ample parking, parking fee 60¢.

PALISADES PARK · Antique Flea Market at St. Michaels School, Central Blvd. at 1st St. Held on March 27. Spon: St. Michael's C.Y.O., Gloria Rothstein, 12 Chatham St., Suffern, Ny 10901. Ph: (914) 357-8410 or (201) 529-3896.

PATTERSON · Flea Market, Antiques & Crafts, at Patterson Catholic High School, 11th Ave. & Rt. 20. Open 2nd Sun. every month, 10 am to 5 pm. 25¢ admission. Indoors. Ph: (201) 525-5618.

PENNSAUKEN · The Bicentennial Mart, Rts. 130 & 73. Open on Fri. & Sat. 8-9. Sun. 8-6. Phone (609) 662-7800 or (215) 922-7095. Fleas, antiques & collectibles.

PENNSAUKEN · Pennsauken Flea Mart, east side Pennsauken Mart grounds. Rt. 73 & 130. Fri. & Sat. 8-9; Sun. 8-6. Indoors and outdoors. Free parking and admission. Phone (609) 662-9838.

RAHWAY · Rahway Italian-American Club Friday Flea Mkt. New Brunswick and Inman Ave. Fri. 8-4 indoors and outdoors. Free parking and admission. Phone (201) 634-3936.

RAHWAY · Delancey Street, 1507 Main St. Indoors and outdoors. Thur., Fri. & Sat. Phone (201) 574-8696.

RAHWAY · Friday Flea Market, at the Italian-American Club, New Brunswick & Inman Aves. Open every Fri. 8 am to 4 pm. Indoor and outdoors. Phil & Mary Lima. Ph: (201) 634-3936.

RAHWAY · Rahway Italian-American Club, corner of Inman and New Brunswick Aves., off St. Georges Ave. Open year round, Wed. from 9 am to 4 pm. 29 dealers indoor from Nov. to mid-April, more outdoor April thru Oct. Fee $5 indoor w/table, $4 outdoor no table. Mrs. Dorothy Bacon, 132 Willow St., Colonia, NJ 07067. Ph: (201) 382-7828. Antiques, collectibles, depression glass, brass, pewter, copper, primitives, coins, stamps, etc.

RANCOCAS WOODS · William Spencer Flea Market, Creek Rd. 1 mile off the I-295, Rancocas Woods Exit. 1981 dates: May 14, June 11, July 9, Aug. 13, Sept. 10, Oct. 8. 75 dealers, $15 per space. William Spencer - Rich Slawinski, Creek Rd., Rancocas Woods, NJ 08060. Ph: (609) 235-1830.

RIO GRANDE · Rodia's Flea Market, on Rt. 9. Open Sat. and Sun. 9 am to 6 pm. 50 sellers indoors. Ph: (609) 465-9767 or 465-5662 after 5 p.m.

RIO GRANDE · Rodia's Flea Market, on Rt. 9. Open Sat. & Sun. 8 am - ? 50 sellers indoors. Phone (609) 465-9767 or 465-5662 after 5 pm. Free admission and parking.

ROBBINSVILLE · Robbinsville Auction Market, North 2325, Rt. 33. Open Mon., Wed., Fri. and Sun., 9 am to 6 pm. Antiques, glass, primitives, furniture, tools and hardware.

ROCKAWAY · Rockaway Indoor Mkt. Rt. 46, Rockaway, N.J. Fri. 11-9; Sat. & Sun. 10-6. Free admission & parking. Dealers call (201) 627-1030.

RUTHERFORD · Super Flea Market, Rt. 3 Drive-in Theatre. Across from Meadowlands Sports Complex. Open Sat. & Sun. 9-5. Tue. & Thur. eve. 6 p.m. to midnite. Avg. dealers: 200. Outdoors. Dealers fee: $15 1 day, $25 weekend; $15 1 evening, $25 for 2. 75¢ carload; Senior Citizens free. Avg. att: 5,000-10,000. Philip LaPorta, 454 Park Ave., Rutherford, N.J. 07070. Phone (201) 933-4388. Restrictions: no food or beverages. Res. sug.

RUTHERFORD · Rt. 3 Drive-in Flea Mkt. Sat. & Sun. 9-5. Also Tue. & Thur. 6-midnite. 75¢ parking. Sr. Citizens free. (201) 933-4388 weekdays at 939-4033.

SOMERVILLE · Packard's Farmers Market, on Rt. 206. Open year round Wed. and Fri. 12 noon to 10 pm Fresh meats and produce, new & used books and magazines and a lot of general merchandise. Ph: (201) 725-1045.

SPRINGDALE · Springdale Farmers Mkt. Rt. 206 and Stickles Pond Rd. Sat. 10-5, Sun. 9-6. Indoors. Free admission and parking. Phone (201) 383-9997.

SPRINGTOWN · Tron's Grove Flea Mkt. Municipal Drive & Still Valley Rd. Sat. & Sun. 10-5. Phone (201) 359-0430 or 454-4951.

UNION · The Union Market, Springfield Ave. & Rt. 24 (Exit 50-B). Open year round - indoors. Fri. 12-9:30; Sat. 11-9; Sun. 11-6. Free admission and parking. Phone (201) 688-6161.

VINELAND · U-Sell Flea & Farm Market. 08360. Delsea Dr. & Grant Ave. Open Fri., Sat. & Sun., 8-4 year round. Outdoors, 80 sellers. Phone (609) 691-9562 or 691-0998. Free adm. & prk.

VINELAND - Rovers Flea Market, So. Delsea Dr. Open Fri., Sat. and Sun. March to Dec., starts at 8 am. 30 tables, $2 per space. Ph: (609) 691-7654.

WARREN - Washington Valley Fire Co., 140 Washington Valley Rd., 2 mi. north of Bound Brook, between Rts. 78 and 22. Open May thru Oct., Sun. 8 am to 4 pm. 300 dealer capacity outdoor. Fee $5, table rental $1. Reservations suggested. Richard Carlson, 25 Christy Dr., Warren, NJ 07060. Ph: (201) 356-5122. all types of merchandise.

WAYNE - Flea Market, Antiques & Crafts, Wayne PAL, North Cove Rd. Open 1st Sunday every month, 10 am to 5 pm. 25¢ admission. Indoors. Ph: (201) 525-5618.

WEST CREEK - Norman C. Cramer's Flea Market, on Rt. 9. Open Fri., Sat. and Sun. 8 am to 5 pm. 65 sellers. Indoors and out. Ph: (609) 296-3351.

WOODBRIDGE - Woodbridge Auction Market on Rt. 9. 1 mile south of the Hess Bldg. Outdoors. Open Wed., Fri. & Sat. About 100 sellers. Phone (201) 634-9760. Ask for Andy or Joe.

WOODSTOWN - Cowtown, Rt. 40, 8 mi. east of Delaware Memorial Bridge. Open year round. Tues. dawn to dusk. 250-350 dealers indoor and outdoor, depending on weather. Fee $10 up w/tables. Cowtown, Rt. 40, Woodstown, NJ 08098. Ph: (609) 769-3000. All types of merch.

NEW MEXICO

ALAMOGORDO - Larry's Flea Market, Hwy. 70 west, 5 miles west of Alamogordo. Open 9-6 daily. Dealers: 20. Indoors and outdoors. Fee: $2.50. Att: 100-150. Larry Dobour, P.O. Box 3572 Boles Acres, N.M. 88310. Ph: (505) 434-1050.

ALBUQUERQUE - State Fairgrounds. Open every Sat. and Sun. 7 am to ? 200 sellers. $3 per space. Attendance 2000 plus. Jewelry, turquoise and silver and many crafts.

ALBUQUERQUE - Flea Market, 6770 4th St. Open Sat. and Sun. 9 am to late afternoon. 50 sellers, $3.50 per space. 600 to 800 atten. Flea Market, Inc., 6770 4th St: Ph: (505) 345-2223.

ALBUQUERQUE - Flea Market, on S. Coors Rd. Open every Sat. & Sun., 4 days on holidays.

FARMINGTON - Flea Market, Axtex-Farmington Hwy. Open every Sat.

LAS CRUCES - Amador Swap Center & Flea Market, 1510 W. Amador. Open every Sat. & Sun. & holidays, 6 am to 6 pm. Outdoors, $2 sellers fee per day. Josie A. Balizan, 1510 W. Amador, Las Cruces, N.M. 88001. Phone (505) 524-2330.

ROSWELL - Trader's Village of Southeastern New Mexico, 2000 S. Sunset, at Sunset & Poe. Open every Sat., Sun. & holidays. 50 dealers, $2 for outside space, $3 under shed. 1000 avg. att. Dalton & Nell Ross, Ph: (505) 623-6953.

SANTA FE - Trader Jack's, Cerrillos Rd. at Truck by-pass. Open every Sat. and Sun. 8 am to late afternoon. 300 to 400 sellers, $3 per day or $5 for the weekend. 5000 atten. Turquoise and silver jewelry and southwestern collectibles.

NEW YORK

AKRON - Newstead Auction & Flea Market, 13311 Main Rd., Rt. 15; between Buffalo and Batavia. Open year round. Sun. from 6 am to 6 pm. 65 dealers, 20 plus outdoor in summer. Fee w/tables, $6 one table, $10 two tables. John Goodman, 73 Parkridge Ave., Buffalo, NY 14215. All types of merchandise.

167

FLEA MARKET AMERICA

ALBANY · Mohawk Drive-In Flea Mkt., 1814 Central Ave., Sat. & Sun. 9-5. 60 dealers outdoor. Spaces $5 (exit 2-W off 87 Northway). Jerry Hayes, 1814 Central Ave., Albany, NY 12205. Ph: (518) 456-2551.

BALDWIN · Baldwin Antiques Center, 906 Merrick Rd., off Sunrise Hwy. (Rt. 27). Open late April thru Nov., Thurs. 9 am to 3:30 pm. 20-40 dealers outdoors. Fee $2, no tables, no res. Eleanor Dahl, 906 Merrick Rd., Baldwin, NY 11510. Ph: (516) 223-9842. Antiques and collectibles.

BATAVIA · Kiwanis Flea Market, East Main St. Rd., 1 mile east of Batavia at Genesse County Fairgrounds. Open Sundays from the second week in June until cold weather, from 7 am to 5 pm. 90 dealers indoors. Fee $4 w/table. Bernard Kowalski, 24 Richmond Ave., Batvia, NY 14020. Ph: (716) 343-1594. Antiques, collectibles & misc.

BAY SHORE · LONG ISLAND · U.A. Bayshore Trade 'N' Sell Market, Bay Shore Drive-In, Sunrise Hwy. Open Sun., 8 am to 4 pm, and Wed., 9 am to 4 pm. $5 per space. 350 sellers. 2000 atten., $1.50 per car. Outdoors. Ph: (516) 665-1784.

BLOOMINGBURG · Indoor Flea Market, on Main St. Exit 116, Rt. 17. Open every Sat. and Sun., 8 am to 6 pm. Ph. (914) 773-4141.

CHEEKTOWAGA · Super Flea & Farmers Market, 2500 Walden Ave., east of Union Rd., off NY Turnpike 52E (Walden-Depew) Open year round. Sat. and Sun. 9 am to 6 pm. 300-500 dealers indoors and outdoors. Fee starts at $8 a day indoor, $6 outdoor. Joe Grossman, 2500 Walden Ave., Cheektowaga, NY 14225. Ph: (716) 683-9679 or 9680. All items, including grocery & baked goods.

CHEEKTOWAGA · Airport Plaza Flea Market, Union Rd., at Genesee St. Ph: (716) 631-5897, mailing address; 168 Ellen Dr., Cheektowaga. NY 14225. Outdoor facilities, every Sunday May-Oct. 9-5. 50-70 dealers. 20,000 atten. Dealer's fee $6 space.

CLARENCE · Hickey Flea Market, 10511 Main St. Rt. 5. Open Sundays from mid-March to the end of October, 6 am to 6 pm. 200-300 dealers outdoor, 30 indoor. Fee $6, reservation needed. Norman Orts, 10745 Park, Clarence, NY 14031. Ph: (716) 542-9600. All types of merchandise.

CORAM, LONG ISLAND · Coram Drive-In Flea to 4 pm. 80 dealers outdoor. Fee $3, car and walk-in admission. Barry Harsch, Ph: (516) 732-6200. All types of merchandise.

EAST GREENBUSH - East Greenbush Flea Market. Greenbush Fair Shopping Center, junction Rts. 4, 9 & 20. Open every weekend year round. Air-cond. & heat. dealers 65 indoors. Dealers fee: $20 per weekend. Free admission and parking. Tables supplied. Jean Goldman, Gilligan Road, East Greenbush, NY 12061. Res. sug.

FARMINGDALE · Long Island, Rt 110 Flea Mkt., located at 1815 Route 110. Held on Fri. Sat. & Sun. 10 am - 6 pm. Avg. wkend att. 25,000. 300 spaces inside and 100 outside. Dealers fee $5 Fri., $25 per day Sat. & Sun. Inside. $15 per day outside. Held in a heated/air conditioned building. Camping available for dealers. The largest indoor market in the Metro NY area. Phone (516) 454-0405.

FLUSHING · Flushing Flea Market, Fri., Sat. & Sun. Exit 14 on Van Wyck Expressway. Indoors, year round. Free admission and free parking. Phone (212) 358-1332.

GREENWOOD LAKE · Flea Market, American Legion Post 1443, on Monroe Rd. Open the 3rd Sat. of each month, April thru Oct. Over 100 sellers, $10 space fee. 6000 avg. atten. Ph: (914) 477-2288.

GUILDERLAND · Route 20, Antique & Flea Market, 2555 Western Turnpike (Rt. 20); 10 minutes west of Albany City Line. Open year round. Sat. & Sun. from 10 am to 6 pm. 20 dealers indoor, 20 or more outdoor. Fee $8 indoor, $5 outdoor. One month advance notice needed. William E. Gladwish, Jr. P.O. Box 43, Guilderland. NY 12084, or call Dorothy at (518) 456-4216. Antiques, collectibles & crafts only.

HOPEWELL JUNCTION · Parker's Robinson Lane, off Rt. 376; 2 mi. south of Dutchess County airport. Open year round. Sundays from 7 am on. 50 indoor spaces, many more outdoors. Write for costs. P.O. Box 458, Hopewell Junction, NY 125333. Ph: (914) 266-2424, ext. 126. All types of merchandise.

INWOOD · Inwood Flea Market, on Taft Ave. Open every Wed., 3 pm to 10 pm, Sat. and Sun., 8 am to 6 pm. Have over 400 spaces, $5 aisle space. New Market. Admission 50¢ per person, $1 car load. Inwood Flea Market, Inc. 475 Northern Blvd., Great Neck, N.Y. 11021. Ph: (516) 487-8333.

ITHACA · Martha's Flea Market, 619 Five Mile Dr.; Rt. 13A, ½ mi. from Rt. 13. Open Memorial Day thru Oct., Sat., Sun., and Mon. holidays from 9 am to 5 pm. 15 dealers outdoors. Fee $5 per day, no reservations needed. Martha Mobbs, 619 Five Mile Drive, Ithaca, NY 14850. Ph: (607) 272-3289. Household to old goodies.

KIRKLAND · Kirkland Galleries, on Rt. 5. Open every Sat. and Sun., 10 am to 5 pm.

KIRKLAND · Peddlers Market, on Rt. 11. Open every Sun. Mary Dyer, Mgr.

LOWMAN · Lowman Flea Market, off of Rt. 17. Open every Sat., Sun. and Holidays, 9 am to 5 pm. 50 to 70 sellers, $8 for 1 day, $11 for 2 days and $15 for 3 days. $1 for tables. 6000 to 8000 avg. atten. Ph: 734-1038.

MANHATTAN · Essex Street Flea Market, 140 Essex Street. Fri. 10-4, Sat. & Sun. 10-6. Indoors, year round. Free admission. Phone (212) 673-5934.

MAYBROOK · Maybrook Swap-N-Shop, Rt. 208, 1 mi. south of Rt. 84, exit 5. Ph: (914) 427-2715, mailing address, 131 Pike St., Port Jervis, NY 12543. Indoor and outdoor facilities, Sat and Sun. 300 dealers. $5.

MIDDLEPORT · Pattie'S, Rt. 31 and Carmen Rd. Open year round, Sun. 9:30 am to 5 pm. 10-20 dealers, more in winter. Fee $2 per table, no res. needed. Mr. Darnley, Pattie's Rt. 31 and Carmen Rd. Middleport, NY 14105. Ph: (716) 735-9995. All types.

MIDDLETOWN · Middletown Drive-In Flea Market, at Bradley Corners, Rt. 6 and 17. Open Sat. and Sun., 9 am to 4:30 pm. Sellers fee $2.50. 25¢ admission per car full. Ph: (914) 343-5551 or 778-1914.

MONSEY · Rockland Flea Market, on Rt. 59. Open every Sat. and Sun., 10 am to 6 pm. 100 to 150 sellers. Indoors and outdoors, $5 per space outdoors. Ph: (914) 352-2637. E. & P Promotions, P.O. Box 252, Monsey, N.Y. 10952.

MONTICELLO · Monteco Antique & Craft Flea Market. Off Rt. 17. Open June to Sept., Fri., Sat. and Sun. from 9 am to 6 pm. Res. sug. Free security overnight if more than one day. Al Bagon, Box 790, S. Fallisburg, NY 12779. Ph: (914) 434-5513. All types.

NEW CITY · Davies Lake Flea Market, 255 Little Tor Rd. Open every Sat. and Sun. 40 sellers, indoors and outdoors. Ph: (914) 634-7250.

NEWBURGH - Mid Valley Mall Flea Market. Open Sat. & Sun. 10-5 & holidays. Arthur Alt, Frank Monachelli, Tri State Flea Market, inc., Mid Valley Mall, Rt. 32 & 9 W, Newburgh, NY 12550. Phone 561-9300.

NEW LEBANON - Quick's Hut Flea Market, on Rts. 20 & 22. Open every Sat. & Sun. 8-dusk. (518) 794-8084.

NEW YORK - Greenwich Village, 252 Bleecker St. Flea Mkt. Between 6th & 7th Avenues. Open every Thur. - Sun. - 12-8. indoors, air cond. Mr. Burns, Phone (212) 255-0175. Antiques, jewelry, crafts, old and new collectibles, good junque, plants.

NEW YORK - Sixth Avenue Flea Mkt. at Sixth Ave. & 25th St. Every Sunday 10-7. Free parking. Admission 75¢. Children under 12 free. Phone (212) 243-5343.

NEW YORK - P. S. 183 Farmers & Antiques Flea Mkt. at Public school on 66th St. between York & 1st Aves. NY, NY 10021. Sat. 9-5. Phone (212) 737-8888.

NEW YORK - Soho Canal Flea Market, 369-71 Canal Street. Open Thur. & Mon. 11-6. Closed Tue. & Wed. Avg. dealers: 40. Indoors. Dealers fee: $50 wkly. Admission free. Avg. att: 300-1000. J. Mathieson, 10013. Phone (212) 226-8724. Restrictions: no new merchandise. Res. Sug.

NEW YORK CITY - N.Y. East Antique & Flea Market, 145 East 23 St. open Wed. thru Sun., 11 am to 7 pm. Indoors. 25 plus sellers, free admission. Sellers fee $8 and up. (212) 777-9609.

NEW YORK CITY - New York Flea Market, 25th St. and Ave. of the Avenues. Open Sun. from the second week of April thru the end of June, and from the week after Labor Day thru mid-October, noon to 7 pm. 85-120 dealers outdoors. Fee $40 for 10 by 13 space, or $20 for half the space. Reservations needed. N.H. Mager, 11 Warren St., NY 10007. (212) 233-6010. Merchandise has artistic or historic merit, quality.

NEW YORK CITY - So-Ho Canal Flea Market, 369 Canal St. off West Broadway. Open year round, seven days a week, 11 am to 6 pm. 25 dealers indoor, more outdoor. Fee $35 per week indoor, $5 per day outdoor (during the week) $15 Sat. or Sun. $25 for whole week. So-Ho Canal Flea Market, 369 Canal St., NY 10013. Ph: (212) 226-8724. Nostalgia, collectibles, interesting junk.

NEW YORK - 52nd Street Festival, on 9th Ave. to East River. ANNUAL, 1981 date: June 18 (rain date June 25). Over 1000 dealers, $60 per space. Atten. is over 200,000. N.H. Mager, 233 Broadway-17 floor, N.Y.C., N.Y. 10007. Ph: (212) 233-6010. Arts. Crafts, Antiques, Food ONLY.

NEW YORK CITY - Elmhurst - Jackson Heights F.M. 81-16 45th Ave., off Queens Blvd; Elmhurst Open year round, Fri. and Sat. 10 am to 10 pm. Sun. 10 am to 5 pm. 100 plus indoors. Free $10 one day, $25 three days. One week's notice required. H. Ingbar, 40-10 Junction Blvd., Corona, NY 11368. Ph: (212) 426-9500. All types of merchandise.

NEW YORK CITY - 29th St. Flea Market. 39 W. 29th S. Midtown Manhattan. Open Tues. thru Sun. (11 am to 6 pm) Indoors and outdoors. Dealers: 75. Fee: from $50 per week. Res. John Ghedini, 39 W. 29th St., NY, NY 10001. Ph: (219) 679-7002.

NEW YORK CITY - The Canal Street Flea Market, 335 Canal Street, corner of Canal and Green Street. Open Sat. & Sun., April thru December. Avg. dealers: 65. Outdoors. Dealers fee: $25 per day. Avg. Att: 10-15 M. Joel Kaufmann, 8 Greene Street, NYC, NY 10013.

NIAGARA FALLS - Super Flea Market, 3035 Niagara Falls Blvd. (Amherst). Open every Sat. and Sun. 9 am to 6 pm. 100 or more sellers, $8 indoors, $6 outdoors. 5000 avg. atten. A good antique market. Ph: (716) 691-9893.

NORTH ROSE - Country Squires "Super Flea", on Rt. 41 Open every Sunday. Indoors and outdoors. 300 to 500 sellers. $3 outside, $7 and up inside. 7000 avg. att. Phone (315) 587-2689. Pat or Chuck Squires.

ORANGEBURG - Trade 'N' Sell, 303 Drive In Theatre. Open Sat. and Sun., 8 am to 5 pm. year round. 300 sellers, $5 per day. Admission 50¢ per car load. 18,000 attendance. Jim Picariello, Ph: (914) 359-3686.

PATTERSON - Patterson Grange Farmers F.M., Rts. 22, off I-84. Open April thru Nov., Sundays from dawn to dark. 60 plus dealers indoors and outdoors. Fee $5, tables rented $1. Phyllis or Tom Prisco, Rt. 22, Patterson, NY 12563. Ph: (916) 878-660. All types of merchandise including livestock.

QUEENS - Barterama - Aquaduct Flea Market, Belmont Flea, 108th St. & Rockaway Blvd. Open, Aqueduct, every Tues. Mar—Xmas. Every Sun. May-Oct. Belmont, Sun. Mar. - May, Oct. - Dec. Dealers: over 1,000. Outdoors. Fee: $15. Att: 50,000. 257 Hempstead, Elmont, N.Y. 11003. Ph: (510) 775-8774. Res.

ROCHESTER - Super Flea, 2080 Chili Ave. in Westgate Plaza. Open sat. & Sun. 9-5. Dealers: 60 indoors. Dealers fee: $18 per weekend. Attendance fee. Tables supplied for 50¢. Avg. wknd att. 5,000. Gregory A. Vieira, 2080 Chili Ave., Rochester, N.Y. 14624. Phone (716) 247-8366. Restrictions: no food items. Res. sug.

ROCHESTER - Collector's Marketplace, 1439 Buffalo Rd. (Rt. 33). Open on Sundays, Oct. thru May, 9 am to 5 pm. 30 sellers, $8 per space. 1000 avg. atten.

SARATOGA SPRINGS - Greater Saratoga Flea Market & Antique Sales, corner of Broadway (Rt. 9) & Crescent Ave. Ph: (518) 584-7422. Mailing address RD 1 Nelson Ave. Saratoga Springs, NY 12866. Outdoor facilities, Sat-Sun May-Oct. 50-80 dealers, 3-5000 atten. Dealer's fee $10 per day, $18 per wknd.

SCHENECTADY - Dutch Mill Antique & Flea Market, 3633 Carman Rd., (town of Guilderland-Albany Co.) Ph: (518) 355-3420. Mailing address, 3633 Carman Rd., Schenectady, NY 12303. Indoor and outdoor facilities, every Sat. and Sun. year round. 50-150 dealers. Dealer's fee $5, 6, 7, 8 per day.

SCHENECTADY - Jerry's Trading Post, 1671 Crane St. Open year round, daily from 9 am to 9 pm. 20 dealers indoors, more outdoors. Fee $8 per day, one week's notice required. Jerry and Nancy Haley, 1671 Crane St., Schenectady, NY 12303. Ph: (518) 355-9800. Household, furniture & antiques.

SHRUB OAK - Sunnyside Antiques, Rt. 6 and Barger St., off Taconic State Pkwy. Open summer, Sundays from 9 am to 5 pm. 20-40 dealers outdoors. Fee $10. William Kelly, Locust Ave. Peekskill, NY 10588. Ph: (914) PE9-4103. Bric-a-brac, odds and ends, collectibles & misc.

SHORTSVILLE - Davis Auction House, 5 E. Main St. Open 7 days a week except Wed. aft. from 10-5. 40 sellers indoor, also room outdoor. $6-$10 fee includes tables. Avg. atten. 300-2000. Otis M. Davis, Jr., Box 294, Shortsville, NY 14518. Ph: (716) 289-3611.

SLOATSBURG - Sloatsburg Flea Market, on Rt. 17. Open every Sat. and Sun. Indoors and outdoors. Ph: (914) 753-5109.

SPRING VALLEY - Antique, Craft, Collectible Flea Market, Spring Valley High School, Rt. 59, Ph: (914) 357-7410, (201) 529-3896. Mailing address: Gloria Rothstein Shows, 12 Chatham St., Suffern, NY 10901, Sunday 11-6, Nov. 21, $15 per space.

SOUTH FARMINGDALE, LONG ISLAND - Columbus Lodge Flea Market, Intersection of Boundary Ave. and Broadway. Open year round, Sun. from 10 am to 5 pm. 76 dealers indoors. Fee $7, includes 8 table and two chairs. One week's notice required. Columbus Lodge, 2143 Boundary Ave., S. Farmingdale, NY 11737. Ph: (516) 799-1652, or 4588, or 293-8545. Miscellaneous old & new.

STORMVILLE - Stormville Airport Show & Flea Mkt. 1982 show dates are: May 30, July 4, Sept. 5. Rain or shine. Avg. dealers: 600-750. Outdoors. Dealers fee: $25 prepaid, $30 day of show. No attendance fee. Avg. daily att: 15,000. Pat Carnahan, Box 85, Stormville, NY 12582. (914) 226-6561. Restrictions: no food. Opens to public 5 a.m. Sunday- 6 p.m. Dealer set up 2 p.m. Sat.-6 a.m. Sun.

SYRACUSE - Regional Mkt., 1 block down on Park St. Open Sundays April thru Oct. 60 sellers indoor. Contact Regional Market, Park St. Syracuse, NY 13206.

VALLEY STREAM - Sunrise Flea Market. Sunrise Hwy. NY 11582. Ph: (516) 825-6110. Outdoor facilities, Sat., Tues., and Thurs. 600 dealers, 8,000 atten. Attendance fee $1.50 per car, dealer's fee $3 weekdays, $5 Sat. Ample parking.

WEBSTER - Antiques Flea Market, American Legion, 818 Ridge Rd. Open every Sunday. Indoor & outdoors. Exceptional variety of antiques.

WEST BERNE - Fox Creek Auction Arena Flea Market, Rt. 443, 25 mi. west of NY Thruway Albany exit. Open Sundays from Memorial Day weekend thru the last week of Sept., 9 am to 6 pm. 36 dealers indoors, 60 plus outdoors. Fee$7 indoors, $5 outdoors, res. for inside only. Paul Cornwell, Box 46, Gallupville, NY 12073. Ph: (518) 872-9921. Antique, junk, crafts, produce.

WEST WINFIELD - Birmingham's. Corner Rt. 20 & 51 - North. Open May thru Nov., 10-6. Avg. dealers: 15-50, outdoors. Dealers fee: $6. Kathleen Lindfield, West Winfield, New York 13491. Ph: (315) 822-6870.

NORTH CAROLINA

ASHEVILLE - Dreamland Flea Market, 91 S. Tunnel Rd. Open every Fri., Sat. & Sun., 7 am to 4:30 pm. 300 dealers, $3 Fri., $5 Sat. & Sun. 15,000 avg. att. Outdoors. Paul J. Pless, Jr., P. O. Box 5936, Asheville, N.C. 28803. Phone (704) 255-7777 or 254-7309.

BESSEMER CITY - Toney's Trade Post. Hwy. 29-74 West near I-85. Open Sat. & Sun. Avg. dealers: 130, outdoors. Mgr. Clyde Toney Sr., Rt. 3, Box 323, Bessemer City, NC 28016.

CHARLOTTE - Piedmont Flea Market, 101 E. Kingston. Open every Sat. & Sun. 30 to 50 dealers. $6 per day, indoors. $4.50 outdoors. 500 avg. att. W. E. or Christine McManus. P.O. Box 367, Mutthews, N. Car. 28105. Ph: 334-3618

CHARLOTTE - Serendipity Flea Mkt. & Trade Lot. Metrolina Fairgrounds Hwy. 21 N, Statesville Rd., Charlotte, N.C. 3rd weekend of each mo. Sat. & Sun. 8-5. Free adm. & prk. Phone (704) 663-5252 or 596-4645.

GREENVILLE - The Greenville Collectors Club Flea Market. Meadowbrook Drive-in Theatre, Mumford Rd. Annual Market usually held in Sept. The Greenville Collectors Club, 105 N. Jarvis St., Greenville, NC 27834. Ph: (919) 752-3456.

GOLDSBORO - Fairground Flea Market, 117 S. Goldsboro, New Market, room for 120 sellers, Ph: (919) 731-2854.

HICKORY - Hickory Livestock & Flea Mkt. Sweet Water Road. Open all day Thur. Avg. dealers: 157. Dealers fee: $4 & $5. Free admission. Avg. att: 7500. George Hahn, R. 6, Box 754, Hickory, N.C. 28601. Phone (704) 256-2673. Restrictions: no food or drinks.

JACKSONVILLE - Cinema Drive-in Flea Mkt. Belfork Rd. Open Fri., Sat. ? Sun. Avg. dealers: 150. Outdoors. Dealers fee: $4. 50¢ per car for shoppers. Tables rented $1.50 each. Avg. att: 3000. Bill Jensen, P. O. Box 5043, Jacksonville, N.C. 28540. Phone (919) 353-0911. Restrictions: no dogs, no alcohol.

LEXINGTON - Farmers Market & Flea Market, on old Hwy 64 W. Open on Tue. afternoon and all day Wed. Sellers fee: $2 on Tue., $3 to $5 on Wed. 100 to 150 dealers. Avg. att. is around 10,000. Outdoors and under sheds. Overnight camping is available for sellers. Phone (704) 246-2157.

WAYNESVILLE - Rag Mill Mall & Flea Market, 108 Allens Ck. Ext. Seven days 8 am to 6 pm. Avg. dealers 40 indoors. Dealers fee $5 a day, free admission. Phone (704) 456-8627.

NORTH DAKOTA

MINOT - Magic City Flea Market, on the State Fairgrounds, Hwy 2. Open year round, 2nd Sun. of each mo. 275 dealers, $6 per space. 3000 avg. atten. Indoor & outdoors. Richard W. Timboe, 823 4 th Ave. S.E., Minot, N.D. 58701. Ph: (701) 839-6595.

OHIO

AKRON - Montrose Drive-in Theatre Flea Mkt. 4030 W. Market St. (Jct. Rt. 18 & I-77) West Akron. Open Sat. & Sun. from April 1 to Nov. 30. Avg. dealers outdoors: 350. Dealers fee: $3 Sat. & $5 Sun. 50¢ per car. Avg. att: 8000. Louis Ratener, P. O. Box 5346, Akron, Ohio 44313. Phone (216) 666-3000. Food sold by our refreshment stand.

ALLIANCE - Alliance Farmers Auction and Flea Market, on Rte. 62, 18 miles NE of Canton. Open every Sat. and Sun. Indoors. Tables furnished. Ph: (216) 823-8242.

AMANDA - Flea Mkt. Located on Hwy. 159. Held on Sat. : Sun. 10am - 6pm.

AMHERST - Jamie's Flea Market Inc., Rt. 113, ½ mi. W Rt. 58. Ph: (216) 986-4402, mailing address, 48590 Telegraph Rd. Amherst, Ohio 44001. Indoor and outdoor facilities, year round Wed. and Sat. 300 dealers, 5000 atten. Dealer's fee $7.   Ample   parking.

AURORA - Aurora Flea Market, on Rt. 43 S of Aurora. Open every Wed. & Sun. 7:30 am to 4 pm. 300 dealers, $4 per space. 2000 to 4000 in attendance, free adm. Ph: (216) 562-7800.

BATH - 6th Annual Hale Farm Meet, 2686 Oak Hill Rd. Ph: (216) 861-4573, mailing address, 10825 East Blvd., Cleveland, Ohio 44106. Outdoor facilities, August 14-15. Attendance fee $3 Adults, $1 child. Dealer's fee $10 both days. Two day car show, separate flea market.

BELLEFONTAINE - Bellefontaine Flea Mkt., Lake Ave. Entrance to Logan City. Fairgrounds. Open wknds with 20-30 dealers. Tables supplied. W.S. Meyer, 616 Hilltop Dr., Bellefontaine, OH 43311. Ph: (513) 592-1626. Res. sugg.

BETHEL - Flea Mkt., 1095 Union St. Phone (513) 734-6928.

BRUNSWICK - 42 Drive-In Flea Market, Rt. 42. Sun. 7-4. Phone (216) 225-3200.

BRYAN - Flea Market, on U.S. 6 & S.R. 10, between Bryan and Edgerton. Open every 3rd Sunday of the month.

BRYAN-MONTPELIER - The Exit 2 Flea Market. Holiday Inn, Rte. 15 south turnpike exit. Open every Sun. 10 am to 6 pm. Reservations req. Ph: (517) 764-1247 or (419) 485-5555.

BURLINGTON - Antique Flea Market, Bonne County Fairgrounds. Open Sun. 9 am to 5 pm. Don Nehring, Mgr.

CAMBRIDGE - Weekly Flea Market, Salt Fork Jct. I-77 & U.S. 22. Open Sat. & Sun. April thru Oct. Ph: (614) 439-4241.

CANFIELD - Annual Flea Mkt., sponsored by Womans Club. No Dates at this time. Phone (216) 553-4626.

CANTON - Canton Flea Mkt. Meyers Lake Plaza on Whipple Rd. Every Sat. 9 - 4:30. Phone (216) 477-3259.

CANTON - Flea Market, every Sat. & Sun. 10 am to 4 pm. Year round. Phone (216) 364-6089.

CANTON - Stark County Fairgrounds. 305 Wertz, N. W. Antique Show & Flea Mkt. Indoors & out.

CHILLICOTHE - Ross County Fair Flea Market, 344 Fairgrounds Rd. Held at 9 am till ? Avg. daily attendance 500 avg. 60-70 dealers. Dealers fee: $4 per space indoors $3 per space outdoors unlimited space. Both inside & out. Have our own state approved campgrounds w/electric, sewage & water. This Mkt. is a new Mkt. held on 53 acre fairgrounds. Phone (614) 775-0012.

CINCINNATI - Cassinelli Square Mall, Princeton Pike. 10 am - 9 pm. Mon. thru Fri. 12 noon - 5 pm Sun.

CINCINNATI - Ferguson Hills Drive-In Flea Market, 2310 Ferguson Rd. Sat. & Sun. Phone (513) 451-1270.

CINCINNATI - London Village Shopping Center Flea Market, located on Hamilton & Ash Tree. Every Fri., Sat. & Sun. Phone (606) 342-8076.

CINCINNATI - Pisgah Flea Market, 8882 Cincinnati -Columbus Rd. (St. Rd. 42). Sat. Phone (513) 777-2310 or 777-9866.

CINCINNATI - Finneytown Flea Mkt. 1047 North Bead Rd. Wed., Fri., Sat. & Sun. Phone (513) 681-7250.

CINCINNATI - Midtown Flea Market, 3421 Montgomery Rd. Fri., Sat. & Sun.

Cincinnati - Tom's Mini Flea Mkt. 3713 Eastern Ave. Phone (513) 871-8319.

CINCINNATI - Kellogg Flea Mkt. 3742 Kellogg Ave. Open on Sat. & Sun. Phone 321-7341.

CINCINNATI - Village Flea Market, 2100 Losantville Ave., Cincinnati Ohio 45237. Ph: (513) 351-3151. Indoor and outdoor facilities, Sat. and Sun 11-6. 70 dealers, 1500 attendance. Dealer's fee, $7.50 and up.

CINCINNATI - Paris Flea Market, 2310 Ferguson Rd., Ferguson Hills Drive-In Theatre. Open every Sunday 7 am to 5 pm. 250 to 350 dealers. Avg. atten. 7000. Ph: (513) 223-0222 or 451- 1271.

CLEVELAND - Memphis Drive-In, 10543 Memphis Ave. Sat. 7-4 outdoors. Phone (216) 941-2892.

CLEVELAND - Auto Drive-In, 11395 Brookpark Rd. Sun. 7-4 outdoors. Phone (216) 267-6660.

CLEVELAND - Cloverleaf Drive-In, Rt. 17 & 22, Sat. & Sun. 7 -4 outdoors. Phone (216) 524-2929.

CLEVELAND - East Lake Drive-In. 34280 Vine St. Sat. & Sun. outdoors. Phone (216) 942-2663.

CLEVELAND - Lee Rd. International Market. 4115 Lee Rd. Fri., Sat. & Sun. Indoors. Phone (216) 491-9058.

CLEVELAND - Grant Flea Mkts., 7000 Aetna Rd. Phone (216) 441-4799.

CLEVELAND - Silver Mkt. Ridge Rd. Phone (216) 398-5283.

COLUMBIANA - On Rt. 164 at Theron's Country Store & Restaurant. Open Wed. & Sun. year round, indoors and out. Jack Brown. Ph: (216) 369-5973. Mostly antiques.

COLUMBUS - Cleveland Ave. Flea Market, 2481 Cleveland Ave. Open every Sat. and Sun. 9 am to 6 pm.

COLUMBUS - Rainbow Giant indoor flea Mkt. 3454 Cleveland Ave. In the Amos Shopping Center. Every Fri. 12 noon to 9 pm every Sat. & Sun. 9 am to 6 pm all year. Attendance 3000 to 4000, 200 dealers spaces available. Dealers Apx. $15 per space per weekend. Doug Hott, Manager. Mailing address 865 King Ave. Columbus, Ohio 43212. Phone (614) 444-2313.

COLUMBUS - Flea Market, 1063 W. Broad St. Open every Sat. & Sun. 10 am to 6 pm. Norma Harper. Ph: (614) 228-1949, or 262-0110.

COLUMBUS - Eastside Drive-In Flea Market, 3811 E. Main St., on Rt. 40 E. Open every Sunday, 9 am to 6 pm. Adm. 50¢ per car. Ph: (614) 444-2313.

COLUMBUS - South Swap Shop & Flea Mkt. So. Twin Drive-In Theatre, 3050 So. High St. Rt. 23 South. 1 mile No. of I-270. Every Sat. 7 am to 4 pm. April through Oct. Avg. visitors 3500 to 5000. Avg. dealers 350 to 500. Sellers $2 per space. Doug Hott. Mailing address 865 King Ave., Columbus, Ohio 43212. Phone (614) 444-2313.

COLUMBUS - CCC Swap Shop & Flea Mkt. CCC Twin Theatre. 1375 Harrisburg Pike Rt. 62 So. Just ½ mile No. of I-270 on Harrisburg Pike. Every Sun. 7 am to 4 pm. April through Oct. Avg. visitors 2500 to 3000. Avg. dealers 150 to 200. Sellers $2. Doug Hott. Mailing address 865 King Ave., Columbus, Ohio 43212. Phone (614) 444-2313.

COLUMBUS - 40 East Swap Shop Flea Mkt. 40 East Twin Drive-In Theatre on east Main St. (Rt. 40) 1 mile east of Reynoldsburg. Every Sun. from 7 am to 4 pm. April through Oct. Avg. visitors 2500 to 3000. Avg. dealers 150 to 200. Sellers $2 per space. Manager Steve Valentine. Mailing address 865 King Ave., Columbus, Ohio 43212. Phone (614) 444-2313.

COLUMBUS - Bob & Marie's Flea Market, 2448 Cleveland Ave. Held on Mon. thru Sat. Phone (614) 261-0353.

COLUMBUS - Trader Ned's Thieves Mkt. & Dealer's Auction. Franklin County Fairgrounds. Open thrid wknd. Space available for 350 indoor and 1000 outdoor dealers. Inside 12' x 15', $30 wknd. or $20 day. Outside $15 wknd or $10 day. Tables available for $7.50 ea. for wknd. Mkt. hrs. 10-7 Sat., 9-6 Sun. Set-up anytime after 4 pm Fri. before. B. S. Enterprises, P. O. Box 21347, Columbus, Ohio 43221. Phone (614) 876-8883. Res. sug. inside. Free overnight parking. Camping facilities nearby, $5 nite for elect. hook-up. Dealers auction every Mkt. Sat. at 8 pm. Live entertainment all day.

DAYTON - Shop Keepers Fair Flea Mkt. 3998 Salem Ave. Held Mon., Tue., Fri., Sat. & Sun.

DAYTON - Yesterday's Flea Market, held at 222 Romington Pike. Tue. - Sat. Phone (573) 252-2844.

DAYTON - London Flea Market. Forest Park Plaza Shopping Center. Fri., Sat., Sun. Ph: (513) 276-9536.

DAYTON - Paris Flea Market, 6201 N. Dixie, Dixie Drive-In Theatre. Open every Sun. 7 am to 5 pm. 200 to 300 dealers. Avg. Atten. 6000. Ph: (513) 223-0222 or 451-1271.

DEFIANCE - Wheel & Deal indoor Flea Market. Every Sat. & Sun. Phone (419) 782-0593.

DELAWARE - The Country Bazaar, on U.S. 23 between Columbus and Delaware. Open every Sun. 10 am to 7 pm. Indoors, $8 per space, tables $2. Ph: (614) 548-7034.

DUBLIN - Flea Market, Dublin Drive-In Theatre, 4148 W. Granville Rd. Open every Sun. 7 am to 5 pm. 50¢ to buy or sell. Ph: (614) 889-9195. Bill Reese, Mgr.

DUBLIN - Dublin Flea Mkt. & Swap Shop, 4148 W. Granville Rd., Sun.

EATON - Flea Market, Frederick Bldg. Open last Sat. & Sun of the month.

ETNA - Park 'N' Swap Flea Market, at the Lions Park. Held monthly. Ernest Bowers. Ph: (614) 927-5763.

FREMONT - Fremont Flea Mkt. located 4 mi. south of Ohio Tpk. exit 6 in N.W. Ohio. At the Fremont Fairgrounds. Indoors & outdoor spaces available. Held on the 2nd weekend of every month year round. Sat. & Sun. from 10 am to 5 pm. Avg. daily attendance 2,000. Admission free. Avg. 60 dealers. Dealers fee $10 a day, per table. Camping available for dealers. Free - no hookups. Auto racing at Fairgrounds on Sat. evening in summer. Phone (419) 332-1200 or 332-6937.

FAIRBORN - Fairborn Flea Mkt., 136 N. 1st St. Fri., Sat. & Sun. Phone (513) 878-0606.

FAIRHAVEN - Flea Mkt. Annual, no dates at this time. Antiques. Phone (513) 796-3191.

FRANKLIN - Schomy Flea Market, 1½ miles on Dayton-Oxford Rd. Sat. Phone (513) 746-1371.

GALLIPOLIS - French 500 Flea Market, Gallia Co. Fairgrounds, on U.S. 35 & 60. Open 2nd weekend of month. April to Oct. (except Aug.) Fri. & Sat. 9 am to 6 pm, Sun 9 am to 5 pm. Largest market in S.E. Ohio. Ph: (614) 446-2656 or 446-4200.

HAMILTON - AAA Overpeck Flea Market, 2075 Jackson Rd., (Take State Rt. 127 to New Miami, 1st traffic light in New Miami; turn right on Augsburger Rd. to Jackson Rd.). Held indoors & out on Fri., Sat. & Sun. 9 am - 8 pm. Room for 150 dealers. Phone (513) 896-4782.

HARRISON - Harrison Flea Market, 1110 Harrison Ave. Open Fri. 12-8, Sat. 8-5 & Sun. 10-5. Indoors & outdoors. Dealers fee $3 outside & $6 inside. Admission free. Tables supplied. Henry Furguson, 1110 Harrison Ave., Harrison, Ohio 45030. (513) 367-9162. Overnight parking & camping facilities nearby.

HARRISON - J.R.'s Flea Market. U.S. 52 East of Harrison. Sat. & Sun. Ph: (317) 647-6308.

HARTVILLE - Farmers Flea Market, 1 mi W. of Hartville on Rt. SR 619. Open year round on Mon. $3 per space.

HARTVILLE - Hartville Flea Mkt., 788 Edison St. Held Mon. Daybreak till 5 pm : Thur. 8 am- 5 pm. Indoors & out. Avg. daily attendance 2-10,000. Free admission and ample parking. Avg. 500 dealers Mon. & 100 dealers Thur. Dealers fees. Mon. $5 & Thur. $3. Full restaurant & snack bars on premises. Campgrounds near-by. Phone (216) 699-3952.

HILLIARD - Hilliard Antique Show & Flea Market, Franklin Co. Fairgrounds. Open Sun. May 10, June 14, Aug. 9, Sept. 13, Oct. 11. Indoors & out. Dealers fee: $8 outside, $17 inside. Att. fee: $1 per car. $5 table rental. Steve Stockwell, 4214 N. High St., Columbus, Ohio 43214. (616) 267-8163. Res. sug.

LAKESIDE - Fort Firelands Flea Market & Campground, 5650 E. Harbor Rd. State Rt. 163, held Fri., Sat., Sun. & holidays Memorial Day thru Labor Day. Indoors & Out. Avg. daily attendance 300. Free admission & parking to the Flea Mkt. Avg. 25 dealers. Daily, weekly, monthly & seasonal rates, restaurant & small grocery on premises. Campground has 212 spaces & tent area, showers. Unique setting. Phone (419) 734-1237.

LIMA - Lima Antique Show & Flea Market, Allen County Fairgrounds. Open 9 am to 6 pm. Sept 4-5, Oct. 2-3, Nov. 20-21. Indoors & outdoors. Fee $13 indoors, $5 outdoors. Johr R. Jervis, 2451 Harding Hwy., Lima, Ohio 45804. Ph: (419) 224-7961.

LOVELAND - Flea Mkt., located on Maderia Rd. Fri., Sat. & Sun. Phone (513) 683-1350.

MALVERN - Flea Market, open every Sat. & Sun. 9 am to 5 pm. Indoors. Ph: (216) 862-1659.

MANSFIELD - Mansfield Flea Market, Richland County Fairgrounds. Open last full weekend of the month 9 am to 6 pm. 300-500 dealers. $30 for double space. Reservations needed. John Stark, 564 E. Townview Circle, Mansfield, Ohio 44907. Ph: (419) 756-0655.

MARION - Antique Show & Flea Market, Marion County Fairgrounds, at the Coliseum. Open Aug. 28-29, Sept. 11-12, Oct. 23-24, Nov. 13-14, 9 am to 6 pm. Fee: Inside main room $14 wknd, side room $7 wknd; Outside $6 wknd. 25¢ admission. Ronald Hilbert, P.O. Box 67, Unionville Center, Ohion 43077. Ph: (614) 873-4552.

MASON - 770 Reading Rd., Mason, Ohio, 45040. Sat. & Sun. 9-6. Ph: (513) 398-3532.

MEDINA - Medina flea Mkt. located at 735 Lafayette Rd. (U.S. 42 So.) held on Sun. Avg daily attendance 5,000. Avg. 150 dealers free admission. Dealers inside $7, $9 & 10 outside space $6. Ample free parking. Food concession on premises, camping near by. Phone (419) 945-2296.

MIDDLEFIELD - Middlefield Flea Mkt. & Farmers Mkt. Rt. 608 & Nauvoo Rd. Mon. Phone (216) 632-1001.

MIDDLETOWN - Dixie Flea Mkt., 3009 South Main. Sat. & Sun. (513) 423-2431.

MILAN - Firelands Flea Market 2 mi So. of Ohio Turnpike - Exit 7. Open every Sun. 9 am to 6 pm. 40 booths indoors, $5 per space, plenty of spaces outdoors at $3 each. Ph: (419) 499-4254.

MILFORD - Open Air Flea Market, Milford Shopping Center on Rt. 50, 2 miles east of Milford. Open every Sun. 7:30 am to 6 pm. No res. needed. $5 per space. Jacob Rosenzweig, Mgr.

MILFORD - Milford Flea Market, Sept. 13. Hours 9-4. Downtown Mainstreet. Sponsor: Milford Histortical Society. Free admission.

MONROE - Congress Inn Antiques & Flea Market. I-75 & Route 63 Monroe, Ohio. 10-5. Admission 50¢. Sept 26-27, Oct. 24-25, Nov. 21-22, Dec. 12-13.

NEWARK - Fiberglass Field House Flea Market. 840 Hollander st. Sat. March 28, 10 am - 5 pm, Sun. March 29, 12 am - 5 pm. Sponsored by Fiberglass Club. Mgr., Ernie Decker, 763-2125 or 763-4390. Call if you want to have an auction.

NORWICH - Stagecoach Antique Mall - 2nd weekend of each month. 9 miles east of Zanesville at I-70 Norwich Exit #164. ½ mile west on Rt. 40. (614) 872-3720.

PERRYSBERG - Flea Market Lakeview Hall behind I-75 Holiday Inn. Perrysberg-Fremont exit. Sun. 10-5. Ph: (419) 874-5012.

PIQUA - Flea Market, I-75 at Rt. 36. Open Sat. & Sun. S. Hurney, Mgr.

PISGAH - Flea Market, on Rt. 42, 3 mi. N. of Sharonville. Open Sat. 10 am to 5 pm. and Sun. 11 am to 5 pm. Ph: (513) 777-2310.

PORTAGE - Flea Market, on Rt. 25, 1 mi. west I-75. Open 1st & 3rd Sunday of the month. Ph: (419) 352-1861.

RAVENNA - Auction & Flea Market open every Fri. noon till auction ends. Auction starts at 6:30 pm. Col Norm Root, 5555 Newton Falls Rd., Ravenna, Ohio 44266. Ph: (216) 678-4000.

RAVENNA - Midway Drive-in theatre. 2736 St. Rt. 59, between Kent & Ravenna. Every Sat. & Sun. 8-4. Dave Delin, Mgr. (419) 296-9829.

ROGERS - Rogers Community Auction & Flea Mkt., located 8 miles east of Lisbon on St. Rt. 154. Held Fri. nights 4:30 - 11 pm. Set up 7:30 am. Avg. daily attendance 5,000. Free admission. Ample free parking. Dealers fee $6, $7. Auction of produce, poultry & misc. Restaurant on premises. Camping nearby. Phone (216) 227-3233.

ROSS - Strickers Grove, Exit 128 off 126. Oct. 18, 11-5.. Nov. 15, 11-5. Adm. 50¢. Mrs. Gladys Jordan. (513) 733-5885.

SHARONVILLE - Paris Flea Market, 2081 Kemper Rd., Jolly Roger Drive-In Theatre. Open every Sun. 7 am to 5 pm. 200 dealers. Avg. attendance 5000. Ph: (513) 223-0222 or 771-8358.

SOUTH AMHERST - Jamie's Flea Market, 48590 Telegraph Rd. Open every Wed. & Sat. 280 dealers, $5 outdoors, $7 indoors. 5000 avg. atten. Stan Ingersoll, 48590 Telegraph Rd., Amherst, Oh. 44001. Ph: (216) 986-4402.

SOUTH VIENNA - Crawfords Mkt. & Campground. 7968 E. U.S. 40. Between 62 & 66 off I-70. Held every Fri. & June 27-28, July 25-27, Aug. 29-31, Sept. 26-28, Oct. 24-26. Free admission, dealers fee: $3.50 outside, $5 inside. (If dealers pay for camping they get free market space). Food concessions on premises. Cold meats - fruits & vegetable market is held on level well kept campground. Phone (513) 568-4266.

SPRINGFIELD - Sellers Swap Meet, Exit 62 off I-70 - ½ mile on 40. Every Sat. & Sun. Phone (513) 568-4266.

SPRINGFIELD - The Springfield Antique Show & Flea Market. Clark County Fairgrounds. Exit 59 off I-70. 250 dealers year round inside - 400 dealers outside. 2nd & 3rd weekend of each month. Oct. 17-18 inside & outside, Nov. 14-15 inside, Dec. 5-6 inside. Admission 50¢, children under 12 free. For info call Knight-Magill, Mgrs. (513) 399-2261, write 5140 Morris Rd., Springfield, Ohio 45502.

SOUTH AMHERST - Jamie's Flea Mkt., Inc. Rt. 113, ½ mile west Rt. 58. Wed. & Sat. Market held inside & out. Free admission, ample parking. Camping nearby - contact Jamie's Flea Market, Inc. 48590. Telegraph Rd., Amherst, Ohio 44001. Phone (216) 986-4402.

STRASBURG - Lynheart Drive-In. Rts 125 & 21. Sat.

TOLEDO - Giant Outdoor Fleam Mkt. Secor Rd. Westgate Shopping Center. We.. Sat. & Sun. 8-4. No reservations needed. Mgr., Mr. Harper.

TROY - Miami County Fairgrounds, 25 AN Dixie. No dates at this time. Phone (513) 773-3780.

TROY - Open Air Market, at the Troy Mini-Mall 1375 So. Union St. Open Sat. & Sun April thru Oct. 11 am to 6 pm. Fee $4. Room for 400 dealers. Ph: (513) 335-7294.

URBANA - Urbana Flea Mkt. & Antiques. 1st Sat. & Sun. of each month at fairgrounds. Phone (513) 653-6013 or 653-6945.

WARREN - Warren Flea Market, located at 428 South Main St., held year round, every Tue. & Sat., 8 am - 5 pm indoors and outdoors. Dealers fee $5.50 and up inside. All tables furnished. $3 per set-up outdoors. Sanck bar on premises. Reservations advised. Phone 399-8298. "A good line of High quality mdse., including a meat & See Display ad.

WASHINGTO COURT HOUSE - Flea Mkt. located at 1270 Rt. 22 West, open Sat. & Sun. Over 1 acre, inside, air conditioned. Free admission and parking. Food available. Phone (614) 335-9780.

WILMINGTON - Caesars Creek Flea Mkt. State Rt. 73. Open Sat. & Sun. Avg. dealers: 350. Dealers fee: $25 per weekend. Indoors and out. 25¢ adm over 12 yrs. (513) 382-1669. Overnight parking and camping facilities nearby.

WOODSFIELD - "Lil Rebel" Flea Mkt. 1st & 3rd Sat. every month. Indoors and out. Radson Shopping Center.

OKLAHOMA

CRESCENT - Old Barn Swap Meet and Flea Market, 201 W. Van Buren. Open every Sat. and Sun. 9 am to 5 pm., 10 to 50 sellers, $2.50 per space. 2000 avg. atten., free admission. Bill Dansby. Ph: (405) 969-2768 or 969-2765.

LAWTON - Lawton Flea Market and Farmers Market, 1130 E. Gore Blvd. Open third Sat. by the calendar. Fri., Sat., Sun. Farmers Market is open each Sat. and Sun. Outdoors. Dealers: 225. Att: 3,500. Fee $3 per day. Joseph B. Reynolds, 910 B Avenue, 73501. Ph: 355-1292.

MARLOW - Flea Market, Hwy. 81 North of Duncan. Open 1st Sat. and Sun of every month.

MANGUM LABOR DAY FLEA MKT. - Held downtown around the square. Held Labor Day weekend. Spaces $5, 100-200 dealers. Retail Merchants, Blake Bratton, 222 W. Jefferson, Mangum OK 73554.

OKLAHOMA CITY - Mary's Old Time Flea Market, Hwy. 62, east at Spencer City limits. Open every wknd, outdoors. 200 sellers. 2000 atten.

OKLAHOMA CITY - Old Paris Flea Market, 1111 S. Eastern. Open Sat. & Sun. 9-6. Dealers: 350. Indoors and out. Fee: $11 day indoors, $3 out. Att: 10,000 wknd. Res. Ken or Norma Wise, 1111 S. Eastern, Okla. City, 73129. Ph: 670-2611 or 670-2612.

OKLAHOMA CITY - Farmer's City Public Auditorium. Open every Thur. thru Sun., indoors.

OKLAHOMA CITY - Antique World & Flea Mkt. 405 N. Meridian. Held on Sat. & Sun. inside. Set up time 7am - 6pm. Avg. daily att. 4,000. Avg. 150 dealers. Dealers fee $10 per day. Camping nearby. Phone (405) 946-3948.

OKLAHOME CITY - Harrisville Flea Market 3101 S. E. 15th St. Open Thur., thru Sun. (405) 677-4056.

OKLAHOMA CITY - Odom's Capital Hill Flea Market, located at 403 SW 25th. Held Sat. & Sun. 3 am - 6 pm. 10 x 10 spaces inside. Dealers fee $7.50 per day. Avg. daily att. 2-3,000. Avg. 100 dealers. Dealers may camp over night. Phone (405) 631-9233 or 636-4265.

FLEA MARKET AMERICA

SPENCER - East Side Flea Market, located at 8424 N.E. 23 Rd. Open every Sat. & Sun. 8 am - 6 pm. 40,000 sq. ft. Avg. daily att. 8,000. Avg. 125 dealers. Dealers fee $10 per day 10 x 10 space. A.C., dealers may camp over night. Phone (405) 427-0304.

TAHLEQUAH - Tahlequah Open Market, open the first Sun. of April thru Sun. before Thanksgiving. Avg. daily att. 2,000. Avg. 50 dealers. Dealers fee $3. A lot of shade trees to park up under. Phone (913) 456-6478.

TOEAU - Public "Flea" Market, Hwy 271-59 North, Ph: (918) 647-4790, mailing address, P.O. Box 195, Poteau, OK 74953. Indoor and outdoor facilities, open 7 days a week. 30 dealers, 1500 atten. Dealer's fee $3.50 outside, $5 inside.

TULSA - Flea For All, 6921 E. Admiral Pl. Open every Fri., 6 pm to 10 pm., Sat., 9 am to 6 pm., Sun., 10 am to 6 pm. 160 dealers, fee $20 for the wknd. Indoors. Bruce Rotherford, 6921 E. Admiral Pl., Tulsa Okla. 74115. Ph: (918) 836-6571.

TULSA - Tulsa Flea Market, held at the Fairgrounds, Touth Building. Open every Sat. 8 am to 6 pm. Seller spaces, 10 by 12, $10, tables $1.50. Drive in and unload. P.O. Box 4511, Tulsa, OKLA 74104. Ph: 936-1386.

WAURIKA - Flea Market, Nancy's Antiques, Hwy 70 (south of town), Ph: (405) 228-2575, mailing address, Nancy's Antiques, Hwy 70, Waurika, OK 73573. Outdoor facilities, every 4th Sat. and Sun. 50 to 75 dealers, 300 to 1000 atten. Dealer's fee $2 day.

OREGON

BANDON - Bandon Flea Mkt., 735 3rd St. E. (off Hwy. 101). Open Fri., Sat., & Sun. June, July, Aug. & Sept. Open wknds all other months. 60 dealers indoor and out. Tables supplied. W. Smith, 735 3rd St. E., Bandon, Ore. 97411. Ph: (503) 347-9941.

BEAVERTON - 11595 S.W. Canyon Rd., Beaverton, Ore. Every Sat. & Sun., 10-6. No admission charge, free parking. Call fro details or reservations 646-2936 or 644-4062.

BEND - Bend Flea Market Hwy-97 on Cooley Rd. Open May thru Sept., every Sat. & Sun. & Holidays. 30 to 40 dealers. $5 fee, tables supplied. 2000 avg. att. Dave Roberts, 18952 Baker Rd., Bend, Org. 97701. Ph: 382-4960.

CORVALLIS - Heart of the Valley, Flea Market and Bazaar, Banton County Fairgrounds, Ph: (503) 929-3825 mailing address, Rt. 1 Box 436, Philomath, Ore, 97370. Indoor facilities, 1st Sun. each month, Sept.-June. 56 dealers, 1000 attendance. Dealer's fee, $5, attendance fee 15¢. Good food, excellent parking.

EUGENE - Piccadilly Flea Market, 830 W. 7th, Lane Co. Fairgrounds City Center. Indoor. Dealers: 275-500. Att: 2,000-3,000. Fee: $7.50. Rosemary Major, 830 W. 7th, Eugene, Ore. 97402. Ph: (503) 345-7931. Res.

EUGENE - Eugene Flea Market, at the Lane Co. Fairgrounds. Held 1 Sun of each month. Tables $5 each. Max Larkin, 1858 Garfield St., Eugene, OR 97405. Ph: (503) 343-5226 or 686-9569.

GAINBALDI - Old Cow Barn Flea Mkt. Open weekends until Nov. 68 tables. Miami - Foley Creek Jct. Hwy. 101 N. Gainbaldi, Ore. 97118. Phone (503) 322-3328.

GRANT'S PASS - Flea Market, 8th E. Open Sat. & Sun. Dealers: 40. Indoors. Fee: $4. Att: 800. Res. Darrel Bell, 421 S.E. 6th St., Grants Pass, Ore. 95726. Ph: (503) 479-7450.

HERMISTON - Rainbow Flea Market. Located on Hwy 395 & Baggett Lane, 2 miles north of town. Held indoors on Sat. & Sun. 9 am - 5 pm year round. Avg. daily att. 300. Avg. 25 dealers. Dealers fee $5 per talbe. Camping nearby. Phone (503) 567-2889 anytime for information.

KLAMATH FALLS - Deeland Park Flea Mkt. Located 3½ miles north on Hwy 97. Held outdoors every Sat. & Sun. May thru last weekend of Sept. Avg. daily att. 300. Avg. 16 dealers. Free admission. Dealers fee $3.50 per space, tables $1 extra. Camping nearby. 10th year in business with a good local following as well as tourist attraction. Phone 883-2960 or 882-8222.

KLAMATH FALLS - Linkville Flea Market. 3531 S. 7th St. Dealers: 90. Att: 800 to 1,000. Dealers fee: $5 per 3 by 6 table. Att. fee: 25¢. Elizabeth Boorman, 5420 Cottage, Klamath Falls, Ore. 97501. Ph: (503) 884-4352.

LEBONON - Del Vonne's Flea Markets are fun, at the Armory. Held twice a year., call for dates. DelVonne Roberts. P.O. Box 24, Garibaldi, Ore. 97118. Ph: (503) 322-3250.

LINCOLN CITY - Flea Market, at the Masonic Temple. 1981 date: July 15-16. $6 per space per day. Capital Prom.. 5724 Aetna St., S.E., Salem, Ore. 97301. Ph: (503) 585-1263 or 362-1063.

MEDFORD - The Original Flea Market, at the Medford Armory. Open year round, once a month. Next dates are: April 12, May 3-31, June 14-28. 180 sellers, $6 for a table, $4 per space. 1800 avg. atten. 25¢ admission. Call collect to confirm dates. Dee Nelson, 2687 Griffin Creek Rd. Medford, Ore. 97501. Ph: (503) 772-8211.

NEWPORT - Del Vonne's Flea Markets are fun, at the armory, 1981 dates are: April 4-5, May 9-10 & 23-24-25, June 6-7, July 3-4-5 & 18-19, Aug. 1-2 & 8-9 & 15-16 & 29-30, Sept. 5-6-7 & 26-27. DelVonne Roberts, P.O. Box 24, Garibaldi, Ore. 97118. Ph: (503) 322-3250.

PHILOMATH - Valley Flea Market, 934 Main St. Open every Sat. & Sun. 9 am to 6 pm. 30 to 40 sellers, indoors, $5 with table. 1000 avg. atten. Frank Miller. Ph: (503) 928-3603.

PORTLAND - Sandy Barr's Flea Market, 8725 N. Chautauqua, at the Portland Sports Arena. Open every Sun. 7 amto 3:30 pm. 800 dealers, $5 per table. 6000 avg. atten. Sandy Barr, P.O. Box 17202, Portland, Ore. 97217.

PORTLAND - Saturday Flea Market, at the Memorial Coliseum. Open year round, Sat., 11 am to 5 pm. 100 sellers, $5 per table. 1500 avg. atten. Don Wirfs, 7928 S.W. 30th, Portland, Ore. 97219. Ph: (503) 246-9996.

PORTLAND - Memorial Coliseum. Open every Sun. 10 am to 5 pm. 100 to 200 sellers, sellers fee, $7.50 - single booth, $15 - 3 table booth, $20 - 4 table booth. 2,000 to 4,800 attendance. 25¢ admission. H.C. Stadelman, 3610 N.E. Knott, Portland, OR 97212; Ph: (503) 282-6467.

PORTLAND - Springers Flea Market, 18300 S.E. Richey Rd. Open every Sat. and Sun., 10 am to 5 pm. 100 sellers, $6 for a small table, $12 for a large table. Jack Fox Ph: (503) 665-3568.

PORTLAND - Holgate Flea Mkt., 103rd & S.E. Holgate. Open wknds all year. 90 dealers indoor. Tables supplied for $6 space fee. Daily atten. 2500. Rick McDonald, 4916 S.E. 66th St., Portland, Ore. 97206. Ph: (503) 771-3234.

RICKREALL - Rickereall Flea Market, Polk County Fairgrounds. Open year round, 1st Sun. of the month, 9:30 to 4:30. 150 to 200 sellers, $5 per table. 15¢ admission. 1620 River Loop Rt. 1, Eugene, OR 97404. Ph: (503) 688-6709.

SALEM - Salem Flea Market at State Fairgrounds. 1981 dates: Apr. 22, May 13-27, June 10, July 3-4, Sept. 9-23, Oct. 6-7 & 28, Nov. 11-25, Dec. 9. Over 450 tables. Indoors. Fee: $6. Att: 2,000-3,000. Frank & Elizabeth Haley, 4795 Rivercrest Dr. North, Salem Ore. 97303. Ph: (503) 393-2897. Res.

SUMPTER - Eastern Oregons Outdoor Thievs Market, Mill Street. Open 8 am - 5 pm Next shows, July 3, 4, 5; Aug. 7, 8, 9; Sept. 5, 6, 7. Avg. dealers: 90-170. Outdoors. Dealers fee: $5 per space per day. Free admission. Kelly L. Olson, Box 546, Sumpter, Ore. 97877. Phone (503) 894-2235. Restrictions: animals & rummage clothes. Res. req.

PENNSYLVANIA

ADAMSTOWN - Black Angus Antique Mall, Rt. 222, North of PA Turnpike, exit 21. Open year round, every Sun., 8 am to 5 pm. 90 dealers. Ph: (215) 484-4655. American Primitives, dolls, coins, glass and china.

ADAMSTOWN - Black Angus Antique Mall, Rt. 222, 1 mi. No. of PA Turnpike exit 21. Open year round on Sun., 8 am to 5 pm. 100 dealers, indoor Pennsylvania Dutch area features quality antiques and collectibles, no "junque". Coins and stamps also Ed Stoudt, Box 277, Adamstown, PA 19501.

ADAMSTOWN - Renninger's No. 1 Rt. 222, north of PA Turnpike, exit 21. Open year round Sun. from 8 am to 5 pm. 500 dealers indoors, up to 300 outdoors depending on weather. Claims to be largest every Sun. antiques market in the U.S. known for quality merchandise. Look for Renningers No. 2 in Kutztown. Resrvations needed for indoor section, but not for outdoor (cost $10). Terry Heilman, Box 107, Adamstown, PA 19501. Ph: (215) 267-2177.

ALLENTOWN - The Peddler's Cove. 1038 N. Sherman St. Tue. - Sat. 10 - 5.

ALLENWOOD - Outdoor Flea Mkt. Major Rt. 15, 1 mile north of Allenwood. Sat. & Sun. 8-5. Phone (717) 538-1401.

ARDMORE - The Ardmart Antique Village, 44 Greenfield Ave., Ardmore, Pa. 19003. Open Fri. 11 am - 1 pm, Sat. & Sun. 11 am - 6 pm. 100 dealers indoors. Free attendance. Dottee Kohlen, Phone)215)642-1000. Restrictions: no new mds.

BARNESVILLE - Lakeside Flea Market, Lakeside Park, Rt. 54, midway between Tamaqua and Mahanoy City. Open year round, Sundays from 9 am to 5 pm. Indoors and out. 30 plus dealers. Sites avail. for self contained campers: E.J. McGrath, P.O. Box 376, Mahoney City, PA 17948. Ph: (717) 467-2411. 6 to 9 pm. Antiques, collectibles, misc. oddments.

BATH - Klein's Grove, 1½ miles north of Bath, off Rt. 987 North, follow red & white arrows. Open from may until weather gets cold. Thursdays from 9 am to 5 pm and Sundays from 9 am to 5 pm. Indoors and out. No advance reservation needed. 25 dealers, auctions held Thurs. at 6 pm. Fees: indoors $4 per space; $1 ea. additional table. Outdoors $3 bring your own tables. Rudolph Klein, P.O. Box 3, Bath, PA 18914. Ph: (215) 837-0088. Antiques and collectibles, arts and crafts, misc.

BLOOMSBURG - Hoffman's Flea Mkt. 1 mile off exit 34 of I-80. Every Sat. & Sun. 10-5. Phone (717) 784-9534.

BOALSBURG - 13th Annual Antique Flea Market, at Boalsburg Firehall Grounds, on Rt. 322. 50¢ admission. 52 sellers.

BUCK - The Jocky Lot Farm & Flea Mkt. Rt. 272, Buck Pa. Sat. 8-5.

CEDARS - Up Country Flea Market, Rt. 73, between Center Point and Skippack, 21 miles from Phila. Open May thru Oct. third Sat. each month from 10 am to 6 pm. Outdoors. Rain dates the following Sat. 100 dealers. Fees $9 and $15, tables can be rented at $1.50 ea. Advance reservations necessary. Robert and Faith Dibbe, Rt. 73, Cedars, PA 19423. Ph: (215) 584-4238. Antiques, good crafts, furn., country primit.

CENTRAL CITY - Martha's Flea Mart & Snack Bar. 3½ mi. east of Reels Corners on Rt. 30. 18 miles west of Bedford, PA. Open Tues. thru Sun. 10 am to 6 pm. Martha Eastwood, Rt. #1, Box 129 B, Central City, PA. 15926. Ph: (814) 754-5803. Antiques, Collectibles & Junque.

CHAMBERSBURG - Sunset Farmers Antiques & Flea Mkt. at Sunset Drive-in Theatre. 2 miles north on Rt. 11. Sun 9-4. Phone (717) 264-2855.

CHESTNUT HILL - Twelve West. 12 West Willow Grove Ave. Indoors. Wed. - Sat. 11-6. Sun. 12-5. Free admission (215) 242-1600.

COATESVILLE - Poser House Flea Market, Rt. 30, 7 mi. west of Coatesville. Open year round on Sat., Sun. & holidays. Indoors & out. Joe McCoy, RD Charlesburg, Pa. 19365.

COLLEGEVILLE - Power House Flea Market Rt. 29 N. Near intersection of Rt. 422 & Rt. 29 between Norristown and Pottstown. Open Sun. all year. Dealers: 30. Indoors and out. Dealers fee: $10-$12. Erv Shainline or Janet McDonnell, 45 First Ave., Box 101, Collegeville, PA 19426. Ph: (215) 489-7388. Res. sug.

COLUMBIA - The Market House, 3rd St. Farmers & Variety Market, Fri. and Sat. 9 am to 4 pm. Flea Market, Sun. 8 am to 4 pm. Ph: (717) 684-2468 or 684-2121.

CREAMERY - Creamery Corner Antiques & Flea Market, Rt. 113 between Collegeville and Harleysville. Open daily 10 am to 5 pm.

CRESCO - Rt. 191 north. Outdoor Flea Mkt. Antiques & Collectibles only. Sat. & Sun. Phone (717) 595-7155.

DALLASTOWN - Dallastown Collectors Mall-1W, Mail St. Rt. 74 off Rt. 83 exit 6, 7 mi. so. of York. Open 1st Sunday in Sept., every Sun. till the end of June, 9 am to 5 pm. Indoors and out. 20 dealers. Fees $10, $8, and $7 advance notice required. James E. Knislev. RD. 2, Dallastown, PA 18313. Ph: (717) 244-6394 or 244-9614. Sun.

DENVER - Hummers, Rt. 222 north pa Turnpike Exit 21. Open year round from 8 am to 5 pm. Indoor and out. 60 dealers indoors, reservations needed, fee $5. Thomas Carlock, 19 Running Pump Rd., Lancaster, PA 17603. Ph: (717) 394-2884. Mostly antiques & coll., some old tools & primitive woodenware.

DENVER - Shupp's Grove, from PA Turnpike exit 21, go 1 mile north on Rt. 222, 1 mile right on Rt. 897. Open Spring, Summer & Fall. Sat. & Sun. 8-5. Shupps Grove, Farm Rt. 1, Denver, Pa. 17512. also P. O. Box 384, Adamstown, Pa. 19581 (215) 267-9975.

DENVER - Texter's Antiques Flea Mkt. Rt. 272 - 2 mi. south of Pa. Tpke. Sun. 7-5. 30 indoor stands. Phone (215) 267-9975.

DERRY - Latrobe Plaza Shopping Centre, Rt. 30 between Greensburg and Ligonier. Open Sun. from last week in April to end of October 8 am to 5 pm. Outdoors. 30 dealers. Free $5, no reservation, bring your own tables. Charles F. Crispin, 110 Walter St., Derry PA 15627. Ph: (412) 694-9806. Little bit of everything.

DOWINGTOWN - Downington Farmers Mkt. Fri. & Sat. 10-10:30, Sun. 10-6. Free admission & parking. Phone (215) 269-6000.

DUNCANNON - The Cove Barn Antique & Flea Market, on Rt. 11 & 15. Open Mon. thru Thur., 9 am to 5 pm, and on Sun., 9 am to 6 pm. Sellers fee: $4. Jack Ford, P.O. Box 97A, Rd. 3, Duncannon, PA. Ph: (717) 834-4088.

DUNCANSVILLE - Flea Market, at the Duncansville Community Center, on Rt. 22. Open every 2nd Sun. of the month, 9 am to 5 pm. Ph: (814) 695-3982.

EASTON - 19th Annual Y.M.C.A. Antique Show Renee Moss, Mgr. Bos 222, Easton PA 18042.

EDINBORO - Edinboro Indoor Fleam Mkt. Edinboro Mall. Rt. 6 N & Mill St. 10-4. Open every Wed. & Sat. Free parking & free admission. (814) 734-4366.

EDINBURG - Michaelangelo's, Rt. 422, 5 mi. west of New Castle, 6 mi. from Ohio border. Open year round, Fri. from 4 pm to 10 pm, Sun. 9 am to 5 pm. 100 dealers indoors, 300 outdoors. No reservations outside. Fee $3 indoor for 8 foot table & 1 chair, outdoor $2 day, bring your own tables. Mr. & Mrs. Michael Carbone, Rd. 1 Box 211, Edinburg, PA 16116. Ph: (412) 658-0382. Antiques, collectibles, coins, stamps, depression glass, etc., crafts & farmers market items. Auction every Fri. at 6:30 pm. (household to antique).

ELIZABETHTOWN - Trading Post Center, 451 W. High St. Open wknds 9-5. 265 dealers mostly indoor. Tables supplied. Overnites ok. Tony & Donna Szafranic, 451 High St., 17022. Ph: (717) 838-5278. Res. required indoor.

EPHRATA - Green Dragon Farmers Market, North State St., 1 mile north of Ephrata, Rt. 272 south from PA Turnpike exit 21. Open year round, Fri. 1 am to 10 pm. Indoors and out. 60 flea market dealers. 130 farmers market merchants. indoor and out auctions also. One week notice required. Fee $7 indoor, $8 outdoor. Green Dragon Ephrata #3, Pa. 17522. Phone (717) 733-2334.

ERIE - Penninsula Drive-In Swap, Rt. 20 to K-Mart, then north on Penninsula Dr. to drive in theatre. Open Sun. from the first Sun. after to November, 10 am to 5 pm. Outdoors, attracts 150 dealers good weather, no reservation. 50¢ per car, sellers or buyers, just come & set up. Frank Herring, 303 Penninsula Dr., Erie, PA 16505. Ph: (814) 833-0924 or after 7:30 pm 6941.

FAYETTEVILLE - Fields & Sollenberger Antique & Flea Mkt. Sat. & Sun. 8-5. Rt. 30, 2½ miles west of Caledonia St. Park. Phone (717) 352-7571 or 263-2371.

FRAZER - Frazer Mall Flea Market, Rts. 30 and 352, 33 mi. west of Phila. on Lincoln Hwy. (Rt. 30). Open year round, Sat. & Sun. 10 am to 5:30 pm. Indoors. 26 dealers inside & room for overflow in corridor. Fee: $20 per month and up. Some tables. Florence Wilhelm, 328 Abbey Rd., Berwyn, PA 19312. Ph: (215) 414-4883. Furniture, guns, antiques, collectibles & misc.

GETTYSBURG - Country Flea Market, old Rt. 15, 4 mi. north of Gettysburg. Open year round, Sat. 11 am to 6 pm, Sun., 9 am to 5 pm. Indoors and out. James Sizemore. RD 6, Gettsburg, PA 17325. Ph: (717) 334-7430 or 334-6354.

GETTYSBURG - Gettysburg Unlimited Antique, 4th & Water St. 17325. Open every Sunday. 10 am to 5 pm. Phone (717) 334-6400. Free adm & prk.

GILBERTSVILLE - Zerns Farmers Market, Rt. 73, PA turnpike to Downingtown exit. Rt. 100 north to Rt. 73, turn right ½ mile. Open Fri. 2-10, Sat. 11-10. Dealers: 335. Inside and out. Fee: $10. Att: 15,000. John Speca, Rt. 73, Gilbertsville, PA 19525. Phone (215) 367-2461. Res. Free adm & prk.

GLENMORE - Conestoga Trail, Rt. 401, 2½ mi. west of Rt. 100, 6 mi. north of PA Turnpike Downington exit. Open Memorial DAy thru mid-October, Sun. 8 am to 4:30 pm. Indoors and out. 30 dealers. Dealers set up is free because market attracts customer to the furniture complex. William Kilpatrick. Rd. 1, Box 182, Glenmoore, PA 19343. Ph: (215) 458-5747.

GREAT BEND - Endless Mts. Antique & Flea Mart, Rt. 11 off 181 exit 68, south of Binghamton, NY. Open year round Sat. & Sun. 10 am to 5 pm. 24 dealers indoors, no limit outdoors. Reservations inside. Fee: $10 one day, $17.50 for the wknd., $50 by the month. Outdoors fee is $1.00. Gerald and Alyce Wilmot, Box 56, Main St., Great Bend, PA 18821. Ph: (717) 879-4129. All types of merchandise.

HARRISBURG - Rt. 22 Flea Market. 6305 Allentown Blvd. Sat. & Sun. 8-5. For information (717) 766-2300 days or (717) 652-7003 evenings.

HARRISBURG - Silver Spring Antique & Flea Mkt. Rt. 11, 7 mi. west of Harrisburg. Sun. 8-5. Free parking and adm. Anna Smith, 6416 Carlisle Pike, Mechanicsburg, Pa. 17055. Phone (717) 249-8378.

HATFIELD - R. & S. Flea Mkt. Rt. 309 Wed. & Sun. 9-? Over 120 dealers, Tree adm & parking. $5 per space. Phone (215) 675-5232.

HORSHAM - Bazaar Flea Mkt. Rt. 611. Fri 3-dark, Sat. & Sun. 9-6. Outdoors. (215) 443-8070.

HORSHAM - Stephenson's Village Weekend Antique Mart, at Rt. 611 and 463 west. Open year round, Fri., 5 am to 9 pm., Sat. 9 am to 5 pm., Sun. 10 am to 5 pm. Indoors and out. Ph: (215) 947-1922.

HULMEVILLE - Olde Mill Flea Market, 1 mi. from PA Turnpike Exit 28, north of Phila., at intersection of Bellvue Ave., Hulmeville Rd. (Rt. 513) and Trenton Rd. Open year round Thurs. & Fri. nights from 6 to 10, Sat. from noon to 10 pm., Sun. noon to 6 pm. Mostly indoors. Avg. 15-20 dealers, more outdoors in summer. Reservations required. Fee: $15 weekend. Kathy Loeffler, Mill Mart, Bellevue, Hulmeville, Trenton Aves., Hulmeville, PA 19047. Ph: (215) 757-1777. Antiques and collec., some misc., used & antique furniture.

HUMMELSTOWN — Dutch Village, Hummelstown-Middletown Rd., 1½ miles south of Rt. 322, 4 mi. west of Hershey. Open year round, Sun. 9 am to 6 pm. 40 dealers indoors. Fee $28 per month, reservations. Farmers market on Fri. & Sat. & auctions on Fri. nights. John Banks, 17 Runyon Rd. No. 3, Hummelstown, PA 17036. Ph: (717) 566-8681. Fleas, furniture and antiques.

HUMMELSTOWN - Outdoor Flea Market, off Rt. 322 at Indian Echo caverns. Open on Sun. until Mid Oct. 9 am to 6 pm. Ph: (717) 566-8131.

INDIANA - Curry Run House, Rt. 422, 6 mi. west of Indiana. Open year round, Sun. 11 am to 5 pm. 14 inside dealers, 10-20 outside. Fee $4 per day or $3 outside. Tables indoors. Zenas Hoover, P.O. Box 1, Indiana, PA 15701. Ph: (412) 465-4923. Antiques & collectibles, coins & guns.

KIMBERTON - Kimberton Village, on Kimberton Rd. Open every Sat. & Sun., 10 am to 6 pm. Sellers fee: $5 outdoors, $20 wknd inside. 100 dealers. Lucy & Pete Lensi or Al & Jeanette DiEnna. Ph: (215) 933-3202.

KUTZTOWN - Renninger's No. 2, Nobel St., 1 mi. south of center of town, between Reading and Allentown. Open year round, Sat. 8 am to 5 pm. 250 dealers indoor, outdoor varies, open spring thru fall. Reservation indoors required and fee varies. Outdoor is $10. Terry Heilman, Renninger's Box 107, Adamstown, PA 19501. Ph: (215) 267-2177. Produce, household, antique.

LAHASKA - Antique Ctr. & Flea Mkt. Rt. 202, across from Peddler's Village. Open year round, every day Wed. thru Sun. Outdoors, weather permitting. All indoor shops open Sat., Sun. & holidays. Free adm. & prk. (215) 794-5000.

LANCASTER - Park City Farmer's Mkt. Lower Level, Park City Shopping Center, Lancaster, Pa. 17601. Thur. & Fri. 10-9; Sat. 9-5. Free adm. & prk. (717) 392-7314. Call for reservation.

LANCASTER - The Barn Yard & Flea Market, 2323 Lincoln Hwy. East, Lancaster PA 17602, Ph: (717) 393-2323. Indoor and outdoor facilities, seven days a week during summer. Dealer's fee, $5-$8.

LANGHORNE - Roosevelt Drive-in Flea Market, open Mar.-Dec. Res. Avg. dealers 250. Att. 10,000. Norm Shore, 48 Fallenrock Rd., Levittown, PA 19056. Ph: (215) 943-0670 or 934-9523.

LEBANON - Sunset Flea Mkt. Rear Bargaintown. North 7th St. Sat. & Sun. 10-6. Phone (717) 273-2665.

LEESPORT - Leesport Market and Auction, east off Rt. 61 at north end of Leesport. Open year round, Wed., from noon to 9 pm. Indoors and out. 100 dealers. Cattle sale every Wed. Fee $5. John U. Weist, Leesport Market and Auction, Leesport, PA 19533. Ph: (215) 926-1307. Produce & plants, antiques, new & used clothing.

LEMOYNE - West Shore Antique Center & Flea Market, 900 Market St. Open Tues., Fri., Sat. & Sun. 10 am to 5 pm. Ph: (717) 9837.

LEOLA - Meadowbrook Antique Center, 339 West Main St. Open Fri., 9-8, Sat., 8-4. Dealers: 110. Indoor. Wayne Stauffer, 339 W. Main St., Leola, PA 17540. Ph: (717) 656-2226. Res.

LEONA - Meadowbrook Farmers Mkt. 345 W. Main St., Leona, PA. 17540. Fri. 9-8; Sat. 8-4. Free adm. & prk. (717) 656-2226.

LEWISBURG - Big Flea Market 5 miles S. of I-80, Rt. 15 above. Open every Sun. 8 am to 6 pm. Over 60 sellers. Collectibles & antiques. Andy & Tom Shingara, P.O. Box 95, Dewart, PA 17730. Ph: (717) 538-9148 or 538-1005 or 286-7948.

LEVITTOWN - Center Antique & Collectible Flea Mart, Rt. 13 Levittown Parkway. Open Fri., 10 am to 9 pm, Sat. 10 am to 6 pm., Sun. 11 am to 5 pm. year round, indoors. 16 plus sellers. Ph: (215) 945-9849.

MAINLAND/HARLEYSVILLE - terry Homes Flea Mkt. Free admission. Every Fri. & Sat. 8-5. Indoor and outdoor. Off Rt. 63 at 254 Freed Rd. (215) 584-9394 or (215) 256-6523.

MECHANICSBURG - Silver Spring Flea Market, Rt. 11, 7 mi. west of Harrisburg. Open year round on Sun., 8 am to 5 pm. 100 dealers indoors, 75 outdoors in good weather. Fee $20 per month indoors, tables, outdoor $5 bring tables. J.C. Smith, 14 Carlisle Pike, Mechanicsburg, PA 17055. Ph: (717) 732- 9394. Antiques, collectibles, furniture, some new merchandise.

MONTOURSVILLE - Montoursville Flea Market, Rt. 87 off of 220, at Fireman's Social Hall. Open 1st and 3rd Sun., 9 am to 5 pm. Free admission. M & K Antiques. Ph: (717) 322-0407 or 322-0806.

MORGANTOWN - Twin Slope Flea Market, Rts. 10 & 23. Open every Fri. 11 am to 9 pm, and Sat. 9 am to 3 pm. Sellers fee: $7 for the wknd., table included. Phone (215) 286-9164 or 286-9800. Collectibles, antiques, jewelry, bottles, tools, crafts, Produce, furniture. Free adm. & prk.

MORTON - The Village Mall, 1 Morton Ave., Morton, PA 19070. Ph: (215) 543-5566. Indoor and outdoor facilities. Fri. evenings 6-10, Sat. and Sun. 12-6. 60 dealers. Collectibles, antiques, music museum.

MT. JOY - Mt. Joy Flea Market, east Main St., Rt. 230. Open Sat. and Sun., 10 am to 8 pm. Ph: (717) 653-8301. Antiques and collectibles.

NAZARETH - Al Loquastro's Mammoth Antiques Show & Flea Market, Rt. 191 and 248. Open Sundays 7 am to 5 pm. 200 to 300 sellers, indoors and outdoors. Ph: (215) 865- 3880.

NEW CASTLE - 5 miles west, Michaelangelos, Rt. 422 West. RD No. 1 Edinburg. Open Sun. 7-5. Dealers: 150, indoors and out. Fee: $4 outside & $5 inside. Att: 3,000. Michael Carbone or Brenda Lipsey, RD No. 1 Box 211 Edinburg, PA 16116. Ph: (412) 654-0382. Res.

NEW FREEDOM - Annual Flea Mkt. and Arts Fair. New Freedom playground. Exit 1 off I-83. Open 2nd Sat. in Aug. Dealers: 110. Outdoors. Daniel H. Sides, RD }1 Box 193-B2, New Freedom, Pa. 17349. Phone (717) 235-4438. Restrictions - no food to be sold. Rew. Req.

NEW HOPE - Rice's Market Place, Green Hill Rd. Open every Tues. 200 sellers, indoors and outdoors. Ph: (215) 297-5816.

NEW HOPE - Country Host Flea Market, Rt. 202, 1 mi. north of Holiday Inn. Open Sat., Sun. and holidays from the last week of March to December, 8 am to dusk. 45 dealers outdoors. Fee: includes 2 tables, Sat. $5, Sun. $8. G. Kohler, 7311 Woodcrest Ave., Philadelphia, PA 19151. Ph: (215) 477-4541. Antiques, collectibles, arts & crafts.

NEW KINSINGTON - Gateway Drive-in theatre. 133 Logans Ferry Rd. Every Sun. 9-5. Phone (423) 335-1111. Alice Laporte, Mgr.

NEW OXFORD - Indoor Flea Market. ½ mile south of U.S. 30 on PA 94. Every Sat. & Sun. 8-5. (717) 624-2362.

NEWRY - Leighty's Fea Mkt. on route 222. Sat. & Sun. 8-6. 16 acres of dealers and parking. Phone (814) 695-9533.

PARKSBURG - Wrights Flea Mkt. Rt. 10, 2 mi. south of Parksburg. Phone (215) 857-9960. Sun. 12-6 Tue. 1-10.

PARKESBURG - McCoy Flea Market, RD-2, Box 345. Open Sat., Sun. & Mon. holidays. Dealers fee: $4 a day outside. Tables supplied. Joseph McCoy, Box 345, Parkesburg, Pa. 19365. Phone (717) 442-4355. Restrictions: no animals or livestock.

PARKESBURG - Blackhorse Flea Mkt. RD-2. Open Sat., Sun. & Mon. holidays. Dealers fee: $4. Tables supplied. Joe McCoy, RD-2 Box 345, Parkesburg, Pa. (717) 442-4355. Restrictions: livestock.

PENNSBURY-CHADDS FORD - Antique Mall and Flea Market, south on U.S. Rt. 1. Open year round, Fri., 6 pm to 10 pm., Sat., 11 am to 6 pm Sun., 11 am to 6 pm. Indoors. Box 174, Chadds Ford, PA 19317. Ph: (215) 692-6311.

PERKIOMENVILLE - Perkiomenville Auction, South of Allentown, east of Reading, ½ block east of Rt. 29, off PA Turnpike. Open year round, every Mon. except Christmas day Mon. from dawn to 10 pm. 350 dealers indoors and outdoors, 50 dealers in winter. Also six auctions going on simultaneously, from 8 am. Fee is $6 per 8' table. Reservations needed. John Dulin, 262 Main St., Red Hill, PA. Ph: (215) 679-9461. Little bit of everything.

PHILADELPHIA - Manayunk Sub-Station, Main & Green Lane, Belmont Exit off Schuykill Expressway. Open year round. Sat. & Sun. from 10 am to 6 pm. 20 dealers indoors and outdoors, more on Sun. Fee $20 indoor for weekend, bring tables, $3 outdoor Sun. Reservations needed. Carl & Marvin Bornfriend, Manayunk Sub-Station, Main & Green Lane, Philadelphia, PA 19127. Ph: (215) IV2-9604 or 828-2000. Crafts, antiques, good collec., wide variety of collector's items.

PHILADELPHIA - Roosevelt Mall Flea Market, 2329 Cottman Ave. Open every Sunday, $5 per space.

PHILADELPHIA - Aramingo Mkt., bounded by Aramingo, Castor & Venango Sts. Open Sat. & Sun. 6-4. Call (215) 245-1793 or 739-2463.

PHILADELPHIA - Hackerts State Road Flea Mkt. Fri. 5-9:30; Sat. 8-5; Sun. 8-4. Rain or shine. Indoors or outdoors. Sponsored by Bridesberg VFW Post }2. Free admission & parking. (215) 335-1800.

PHILADELPHIA - Reading Terminal Mkt. 12 & Filbert St., Phil., Pa. Sat. 8-6. Indoors Dealer info (215) 922-2317 or 922-2340.

PHILADELPHIA - Quaker City Flea Market, Tacony and Conly Sts. Open Sat. & Sun., 10 am to 5 pm. Dealers: 160. Att: 2,000, Fee: $8 outside. Indoor and out. Kay Williams, Joe Breish, Tacony & Conly Sts., Phila., PA 19136. Phone (215) 744-2022. Res. Sug. Free adm. & prk.

PHILADELPHIA - Penn's Landing Antiques Market, 16 South Front St., overlooking the Delaware River. Open Mid-Sept. to mid-May, Sun. from 11 am to 6 pm. 65-70 dealers indoors. Reservations needed. Milton Calesnick, 18 South Front St., Philadelphia, PA 19106. Ph: (215) WA3-6845. Antiques only, no crafts or "junque". Fourth floor to be added for furniture.

PHILADELPHIA - Old City Antique Market, 139 2nd St. Open daily year round, 10 am to 7 pm. Indoors 40 dealers. Outdoor market on Sun. Ph: (215) 627-7093.

PHILADELPHIA - The Big Bash Flea Market, D & Tioga Sts. Open every Fri. 12 to 9 pm. Sat. & Sun. 10 am to 5 pm. Indoors and out. Bill Larkin Ph: (215) 427-3700.

PITTSBURG - Keystone State Grand Flea Mkt. 1500 Penn Ave., Pittsburg, Pa. Sat. & Sun. 9-5. Adm.25¢. Free parking. (412) 232-3338.

PITTSBURGH - Pittsburgh Merchandise Mart, 258 Monroeville Mall. Cliff Sutton, Collector's Cabinet, 258 Monroeville Mall, Pittsburgh, PA 15146. Ph: (412) 373-1233. Antiques & collec.

QUAKERTOWN - Quakertown Flea Market, PA Turnpike to Quakertown exit, Rt. 663 to Rt. 309 south to KMart sign. Open year round, Fri., and Sat. from 10 am to 10 pm. 94 indoor, room for 40 outdoor, (under shelter). Fee $5 indoors w/table or $12.50 wknd. Outdoor w/ table $3. Richard W. Siebert, 201 Station Rd., Quakertown, PA 18951. Ph: (215) 536-4115. Discount dept. store, farmers market & flea.

READING - Reading Fairground Antique & Flea Market, 2924 N. 5th St. Highway. Ph: (215) 921-9072, mailing address 8 Upland Rd. Reading, PA 19609. Indoor and outdoor facilities. Sun. 8-5. 40 dealers, 750 atten. Dealer's fee, $10. Ample parking. Races Sundays.

READING - Dell's Flea Market. 1018 Windsor St. Daily except Sun. & Mon. from 11-5. Phone (215) 376-7957 or 374-8298.

READING - Reading Terminal Mkt. 12th and Filbert Sts. Phil., Pa. Sat. 8-6 Indoors. (215) 922-2317, or 922-2340.

REEDSVILLE - Big Valley Auction Center, Rt. 655 off Rt. 322, between Lewistown and Milroy. Open year round, seven days a week from 8 am to 5 pm. Nine permanent shops. 22 regular dealers, room for more. Indoor and outdoor. 30 days notice required. Fee $10 w/tables. Ray Clark, Church Hill Manor, Reedsville, PA 17084. Ph: (717) 667-6383 or 2940 or 3357. Antiques, collectibles & crafts.

SCIOTA - Collector's Cove, on Rt. 33. Open every Sun. 9 am to 5 pm. Indoors, 76 booths. Ph: (717) 992-9161 or 421-7439. New Market. Antiques & collectibles only.

SHADY GROVE PARK - Antiques & Collectibles Outdoor Market, Exit 21-PA Turnpike-1 mi. north on Rt. 222. turn left on Rt. 897-north ¼ mile. Open Sat. 8 am to 9 pm. Ph: (215) 484-4225.

SHIPPENSBURG - King's Antique & Flea Market, 710 E. King St. off Rt. 81. Open year round, Sun. early to dusk. 200 capacity indoors and outdoors. Fee: $5 indoor or out, bring tables or rent them. Harold Swidler, 180 York Rd., Box 399, Carlisle, PA 17013. Ph: (717) 243-1200, after 5 pm. 243-4000. More antique & collectible than flea.

SOLEBURY - Rice's Sale & Co. Mkt. Green Hill Rd., Solebury, Pa. Every Tue. dawn - ? Indoors and outdoors. Free adm. & prk. (215) 297-5808.

SOUDERSBURG - Ted Mertz Flea Market, Rt. 30, 8 miles east of Lancaster. Open year round, Sat. and Sun., 10 am to dark.

SYBERTSVILLE - Hal's Antique Flea Market, Rt. 93, off I-81 Exit 41. Open year round from 10 am to 6 pm., on Sun. Indoors, 60 to 75 dealers, $5 for three tables per Sunday. Harold E. Welsh, Box 40, Sybertsville, PA 18251. Ph: (717) 788-1275. Antiques to the flea market fare.

WEST MIDDLESEX - Mentzer's Flea Market, Rt. 18 at I-80 at I 180, exit 1-N. Open year round, Wed., Sat., and Sun. 8 am to 5 pm. 100 sellers indoors, unlimited outdoor space. Free admission. Ph: (412) 981-6067 or 528-2300. Featuring antiques, collectibles, crafts, primitives, etc.

WEST MILTON - Silver Moon Flea Market, Rt. 15, 2 miles north of Lewisburg Open Sun. and Mon. and holidays, 8 am to 5 pm., from May until cold weather sets in. Outdoors, 35 or more dealers, $3 per space. Thomas L. Shingara, Box 95, Dewart, PA 17730. Ph: (717) 538-2877. Quality merchandise, antiques and collectibles.

WILLIAMSPORT - Goldy's Antique & Flea Market, 1½ miles north of Williamsport on Rt. 15. Open year round, Sat. 10 am to 6 pm., Sun. 8 am to 5 pm. Indoors and out, over 100 dealers. Ph: (717) 323-2552 or 494-9983.

WORCESTER - Barn Stripes Village, off Rt. 73 between Center Pt. & Skippack. Open year round, Sat. & Sun., 10 am to 6 pm. Outdoors, $5 per weekend, tables supplied. Ph: (215) 584-4635.

RHODE ISLAND

ASHAWAY - Ashaway Flea Market, at Ashaway Recreation Center. Open May to Oct., 8 am to 5 pm. on Sun. Outdoors, $6 per space, 15 to 50 dealers. John Marley, 2 Juniper Dr., Ashaway, RI 02804. Ph: (401) 377-4947. Antiques, collec., crafts, clothing and furniture.

ASHAWAY - Ashaway Flea Mkt. P & H Variety. Rt. 3 Ashaway, R.I. 02804. Sat. & Sun. 9-5. Free parking and admission.

CHARLESTOWN - Ye Olde General Stanton Inn, Rt. 1A, Ph: (401) 364-8888, mailing address Box 222 Charlestown, RI 02813. Outdoor facilities, May 1 - Oct. 1 weather permitting. 70 dealers. Dealer's fee $8. Unlimited parking. Food concessions.

EAST GREENWICH - Rocky Hill Americana Flea Market, Rt. 2, at Rocky Hill Fairgrounds. Open April thru mid-Dec. (except August) 4:30 am to 5 pm on Sundays. Outdoors, 150 to 400 dealers, $7 per space. 5000 buyers. Reservations are preferred. Christie Mercurio, Box 175, North Kingstown, RI 02852. Ph: (401) 737-0480.

PORTSMOUTH - Island Park Flea Market, Park Ave., off Rt. 138. Open year round, 9 am to 5 pm. Sat., Sun. and holidays. Indoors and out. 15 plus dealers, $15 per wknd for outside sellers, inside seller fees vary. Shorty Brosseau, 88 Cove St., Portsmouth, RI 02871. Ph: (401) 683-9081 or 683-2898.

PORTSMOUTH - Tex's Auction House Flea Market, 1678 E. Main Rd. Open year round, Fri., 1 to 5 pm. Sat., Sun. and holidays, 8:30 am to 5 pm. Indoors and out. Sellers fee $4 for one day, $7 for two. Henry F. Violette, 113 Cedar Ave., Portsmouth, RI 02871. Ph: (401) 683-9870 or 683-9594.

TIVERTON - Rt. 177 Flea Mkt. 1560 Bulgarmarsh Rd. Open all year. Dealers: 80. Indoors and out. Fee: $8. Att: 5,000. Tom Ouielette, 1560 Bulgarmarsh Rd. Tiverton, R.I. 02878. Ph: (401) 624-9354.

SOUTH CAROLINA

ANDERSON - Jockey Lot, 9 miles north of town on Hwy 29. Open all day on Sat., Sun. 1 pm till ? 800 to 1000 sellers, fee: $2.50 outside, $5 under shed. Over 20,000 avg. att. Phone (803) 224-2027.

ANDERSON - Melvins Trade Lao, on Hwy 29, across from the Jockey Lot. Open every weekend. Phone (803) 226-6852.

CHARLESTON - Old City Market, Market St. Open Sat. and Sun. $4 per day sellers fee. Free admission.

CHARLESTON - Antique Fair Flea Market, 63 State St. Open Mon thru Thur 10 am to 5 pm. Fri. and Sat. 9 am to 5 pm. 7 to 20 sellers. Indoors. John Ward. P.O. Box 1016, Charleston, SC 29402. Ph: (803) 556-5371.

CHARLESTON - North 52 Drive-in Theatre Flea Market and Swap Meet. Ph: (803) 747-7624. 400 selling spaces. Come early for space. Open Sat. & Sun. 8 am till 5 pm. Snack bar & rest rooms open. Thousands of shoppers. Open 12 months a year! On Highway 52 just off I-26 - just minutes to the coast.

CHARLESTON - Municipal Auditorium, 77 Calhoun St. Open 3rd weekend of the month. 9 am to 6 pm. 75 to 125 sellers, $12.50 per space. 5 to 7000 attendance. 50¢ admission. Nelson Garrett, Inc., P.O. Box 4031, Columbia, SC 29240. Ph: (803) 788-5269 or 577-7400.

FLORENCE - Florence Market Place, on Hwy 301N & 327. Open every Fri. & Sat. 20 to 50 dealers, sellers fee $3 and up. 1000 avg. att. Phone (803) 669-5503.

GREENVILLE - Augusta Road Drive-in Theatre Flea Market & Swap Meet. Phone (803) 277-9846. 400 selling spaces. Come early for space. Open Fri., Sat, & Sun, 8 am till 5 pm. Snack bar, rest rooms, playground open for the children. Open 12 months a year! Thousands of shoppers. Highway 25 & I-85 intersection. 15 minutes to mountains.

MONCKS CORNER - Swamp Fox Drive-in Theatre Flea Market & Swap Meet. Phone (803) 899-2412. 200 selling spaces. Come early for space. Open Sat. & Sun. 8 am till 5 pm. Snack bar & rest rooms open. Open 12 months a year! On Highway 52 in Moncks Corner. Near beautiful, good fishing lake.

NORTH CHARLESTON - Fayes Flea Market, on Hwy 52 & 7319 Rivers Ave. Indoors and out. Open on Fri., Sat. & Sun. 150 dealers, $4 per day. 3000 avg. att.

N. MYRTLE BEACH - Smuggler's Cove Flea Market, Hwy. 1 N. Windy Hill area. Open 7 days June - Avg. weekends others. Fee $6 day. Susan Duke, P.O. Box 93, N. Myrtle Beach, S.C. 29577. Ph: Summer: 272-8221, Winter: 449-7947.

SPARTANBURG - Thunderbird Drive-in Theatre Flea Market & Swap Meet. Phone (803) 578-4141. 400 selling spaces. Come early for space. Open Fri., Sat. & Sun. 8 am till 5 pm. Snack bar, rest rooms & astro playground. Open 12 months a year! Thousands of shoppers. Ashville Highway just off I-85.

ROCK HILL - Rock Hill Flea Market, 1170 Saluda St. Open every Thur., Fri. & Sat. $5 per space sellers fee. Phone (803) 324-2129 or 324-0205.

SPRINGFIELD - Springfield Flea Market, at the Stockyards on Main St. Open Mon. & Sat. Outdoors. 300 dealers, $3 per space. 3000 avg. att. Phone (803) 258-3391.

WEST COLUMBIA - Airport Flea Market, on Hwy's 215 & 302. Open all day on Fri. & Sat. Around 100 dealers, $4 per space. 1500 avg. att. Phone (803) 794-0985.

SOUTH DAKOTA

RAPID CITY - Rapid City flea Market Antique Sale, at the Rushmore Plaza Civic Center. Open 1 weekend a mo. except Nov. & Dec. then twice. 150 dealers, $12.00 per table. Indoors. 1000 avg. att. 50¢ admission. Mrs. Robert C. Orelup. 2631 Lawndale Dr., Rapid City, S.D. 57701. Ph: (605) 342-2524.

RAPID CITY - Black Hills Outdoor Flea Market, on U.S. 16 on Mt. Rushmore Rd. Open on wknds, May thru Sept. 200 sellers, $5 per day or $7.50 for the wknd. 2000 avg. atten. Paul & Maybelle Ashland, Keystone Rt. Box 100, Rapid City, S.D. 57701. Ph: (605) 343-6477.

SIOUX FALLS - Downtown Mall Flea Market, Philips Ave., Ph: (605) 332-4554, mailing address, P.O. Box 236, Sioux Falls, SD 57101. Outdoor facilities, Sat. Aug. 7, 1981. 60-100 dealers, 2000 atten. Dealer's fee $8 per 8 ft. table.

TENNESSEE

CHATTANOOGA - Super Flea Market, 2395 Rossville Blvd., Chattanooga, Tenn 37408. Indoor and outdoor facilities, Fri., Sat. and Sun. year round. 150 dealers, 5000 atten. Dealer's fee $5 for a shed, $2.50 outside. Ferris wheel and kiddie rides.

CLARKSVILLE - Clarksville Plaza Flea Market. Open every Wed., March thru Nov. sellers fee $3. Limited merchandise. Jimmy Rodgers. Phone (615) 893-8854.

CLARKSVILLE - Clarksville Tennessee's 1st Indoor Flea Market, Kraft St. Flea Markte Mall, 161 Kraft St. Open Fri. & Sat. 7 am to 9 pm, Sun., 8 am to 6 pm. $5 sellers fee with table. Phone 645-5093 or 552-7725 between 6 and 9 pm.

CLEVELAND - Forest Fleas, Appalachian Hwy. (by-pass off 75). Open every Sat. and Sun. (also on Thurs. & Fri. - small crowds). 60 dealers, $2 per day, tables supplied, 15000 atten. per week. Louise Mills, 1106 Linda Dr., Cleveland, TN 37311. Ph: 472-4792.

CLINTON - 7 Acres Flea Market. Thurs., Fri., Sat. & Sun. $2 table for dealers. Up to 2,000 daily attendance.

CROSSVILLE - Super Flea Market. Open every Sat., Sun. & Holidays. 100's of spaces, open space, $2, sheds, $4 on Sat., $3 on Sun. Phone (615) 484-4083 or 484-2947.

CROSSVILLE - Shady Lake Flea Market. Highway 70 North across from the Stock Barn. Open Sat., Sun., holidays. Outdoor. Fee: $2. Att: 3,000 to 4,000. Tools, jewelry, antiques. No food or drinks sold by dealers.

FRANKLIN - Friendly Flea's Midweek Market, on 2nd Ave. & Franklin Rd., at the new shopping mall. Open on Wed., 7 am to 4 pm. March thru Oct. 45 dealers, $3 for 2 spaces. Ph: (615) 794-0313.

JACKSON - Antique City Mall Flea Market, Hwy 45 North. Open every 1st, 2nd, & 3rd weekends, on Sat. & Sun. Phone 784-3422.

KNOXVILLE - Knoxville Fairgrounds Antique Flea Market. 250 dealers indoors. Open 3rd Sat. & Sun. each month. 10-6. Att: 4000. Ralph Green, P.O. Box 9247, Knoxville, Tenn., 37920. Ph: (615) 573-7489. Res. sug.

KNOXVILLE - Green Acres Flea Market. 10,000 daily atten. Mgr. Jim Baldwin, Alcoa Hwy. Ph: 933-7325.

LEBANON - Parkland Flea Market, on Hwy. 231 South. Open Sat. & Sun. 100 to 150 dealers, 3 to 5000 avg. att. Phone (615) 444-0711.

MEMPHIS - Memphis Flea Market. Central Ave. Open: Write for info. Fee: $30. Att: 15,000. Tables rented $3. No food. Fred Hicks, Rt. 1, Fairview, Tenn. 37062. Ph: (615) 799-0084 or 799-2912. Res.

MURFREESBORO - Memorial Village Flea Market, on Memorial Blvd. Open every Mon., except in Dec. Phone (615) 893-8854, Jimmy Rodgers.

MURFREESBORO - Clarks Flea Market, on Memorial Blvd. Open every Fri., except 2nd Fri. preceding Christmas. $3 set up fee. Jimmy Rodgers, Phone (615) 893-8854.

NASHVILLE - Nashville Flea Market. Wedgewood Ave. Open 4th wknd each month except Sept. and Dec. Indoor and out. Fee: $15, $25, $30. Att: 20,000. Tables rented $3. Fred Hicks, Rt. 1, Fairview, Tenn., 37062. Ph: (615) 799-0084 or 799-2912. Res. Indoors.

OOLTEWAH - Ooltewah Flea Market, on Lee Hwy. 11-64. Open every Sat. & Sun. 175 spaces, $2.50 fee per day. Phone 238-4970.

SODDY DAISY - Soddy Daisy Indoor-Outdoor Flea Market, on Hwy. 27. Held every Sat. & Sun., 7 am to 6 pm. 50 dealers, $3 indoors, $1 outside. 5000 avg. att. Phone (615) 322-3864 or 322-9138 evenings.

SWEETWATER - Flea Market. Open every Thur. thru Sun., just north of the Sweetwater Livestock Auction.

TAZEWELL - Dogwood High Flea Market, on Hwy. 25E, 1 mile east of town. Open every Fri., Sat. & Sun. Phone (615) 626-4108.

TAZEWELL - Giles Flea Market. Att: 5000 to 10000. Open Sat. & Sun. and some holidays. $3 per table for dealers. Cecil Carter, Mgr.

TELFORD - Dee's Antique Flea Market, Hwy 11 East, 4 mi. west. Open every Sun. 8:30 am to 5 PM. 100 sellers. $2 per space. 3 to 4000 atten. Free admission. Outdoors. Ph: (615) 753-4241. Antiques, furniture, glass, collec. and produce.

TEXAS

ABILENE - Free Gigantic Flea Mkt. Old Abilene Town, East I-20 at north end of Loop 322. Open weekend before the second Mon. of each month. Sellers fee: $4.50 for outdoor spaces. W. S. Smith, Route 8, Box 896, Abilene, Tex. 79601. Phone (915) 677-2611.

ALVARADO - Bee Tee & Susie's Flea Market & Trading Post. Located on U.S. 67, 2 mi. west of I-35 & 8 mi. east of Cleborne. Held all day Fri. & Sat. 7 am - 5 pm. Closed Dec., Jan. & Feb. each year. Avg. daily att. 200. Avg. 50 dealers. Dealers fee $3 per space. Dealers may camp on premises. Phone (817) 738-3910. Owners Bee Tee & Susie Marchbanks.

AMARILLO - The Dollar Stretcher Flea Market, 2100 E. 10th Ave. Held indoors and out. 9-6. 7 days per week. Avg. weekly att. 2-5,000. Avg. 30 dealers. Dealers fee $15 per week. Camping nearby. Held in air conditioned building. Auction held 1st Sat. of each month. Phone (806) 372-1602.

AMARILLO - Amarillo Flea Market, held at the Sunset Drive-In Theatre. Open every Sat. and Sun. 10 am to 5 pm. 30 to 40 sellers, $3 per space or $5 for two. 2000 avg. atten. Free adm. P.O. Box 2572, Amarillo Tx. 79105. Ph: (803) 353-2034.

AMARILLO - East 3rd St. Flea Market. Open every Sat. and Sun. 9 am to 6 pm. 20 to 40 sellers, $3.50 per day. 1 to 15000 atten. Free admission with airconditioning. "Red" Bostock, 3008 S. Polk, Amarillo, Texas.

AMARILLO - T-Anchor Flea Mkt., 1401 S. Ross Blvd., Open Sat. & Sun. year round. 90 sellers indoor and out, room for more. $5 to $7 fee. Claudia & H.D. Blythe, P.O. Box 31182, Amarillo, Tx 79120. Ph: (806) 373-0430.

ARANSAS PASS - Flea Market of Aransas Pass. Hwy 35 North. North of Corpus Christi. Open Sat. & Sun. Dealers: 65. Indoors and out. Fee: $5 day. Att: 2,000. Jim Watkins, P.O. Box 363, Aransas Pass, Tx. 78336. Ph: (512) 758-2663 or 758-2749. Res.

ARKANSAS PASS - Shrimp Capital Boutique - Flea Mkt., 1242 No. Commercial. Held Fri., Sat. & Sun. each week, inside and out, avg. 40 dealers. Free admission and parking for the public, dealers fee according to size $4, $5, $6 or $7. Snack Bar on premises, camping nearby. Phone (512) 758-5812.

AUSTIN - Pirate's Den Flea Market, 11704 N. Lamar. Open Tues. thru Sun., 9 am to dark. Indoors and out. Sellers fees: $3 daily or $5 for the wknd. Monthly rentals $25 and up. Nick Spassky. Ph: (512) 836-4966.

AUSTIN - Austin Open Mkt., Hwy. 620 (2.2 mi. W. of Hwy. 183 on 620). Open year round, indoor and out. Tables supplied for $1. Room for 250 sellers. Bill Goodman & Amador DeLeon, P.O. Box 15221, Austin, Tx. 78761. Ph: (512) 258-0433.

BALLINGER - Ballinger Flea Market, Community Center. Open every 3rd weekend except in March, 4th weekend. Dealers fee: $9, wknd. Tables to rent. Buddy McQueen, 1000 10th St., Ballinger, Tex. 76821. Phone (915) 365-3262. Restrictions: new clothes. Res. req.

BEAUMONT - Larry's Antique Mall & Flea Market. 7150 Eastex Freeway. Open Sat. 9-6 & Sun. 1-6. Dealers 75, indoors & outdoors. Dealers fee: $5 outside. Free admission. Tables supplied. Larry & Justine Tinkle, 7150 Eastex Freeway, Beaumont, Tex. 77708. Ph: (713) 892-4000. Restrictions: no old clothes or shoes unless antique quality. Res. sug.

BEAUMONT - Beaumont Flea Market, 8 miles N. of I-10 at Pine Island Bayou on the Koutze-Silsbee Hwy. Open every Sat. and Sun. Sellers fees: $4 in the open, $5 covered space, 35 sellers. 500 avg. atten. Free admission. Tom Gibbons. Ph: (713) 886-5712.

BERTRAM - Trader's Paradise Flea Market, on State Hwy. 29. Open daily, indoors. New Market. Johnnie Mae Wheeler, Rt. 2, P.O. Box 63, Betram, Tx. 78605. Ph: (512) 335-2141.

BIG SPRING - May Belle's Flea Market, 1671 E. 3rd St. Ph: (915) 263-4222, mailing address, P.O. Box 1828, Big Spring, Tex. 79720. Outdoor facilities. Sat. and Sun. every 3rd wknd. 40 to 60 dealers. Dealer's fee $3. $3 per day for electricity.

BIG SPRING - May Belle's Flea Market, 1671 E. 3rd St. Phone (915) 263-4222, mailing address, P. O. Box 1828, Big Spring, Tex. 79720. Outdoor facilities. Fri., Sat. & Sun. every 3rd wknd. 40 to 60 dealers. Dealers fee: $3. $3 per day for electricity.

BONHAM - Bonham Trade Days, Box 58 W. Sam Rayburn Dr., Bonham, Tx. 75418. Indoor and outdoor facilities, weekends prior to second Monday. 30 dealers, dealer's fee $1.

BOWIE - Flea Market. Open the weekend before the 2nd Monday of each month. Over 300 sellers.

BRYAN - Peoples Flea Mkt. FM 2818 (west bypass). VFW Hall 4692. Open third Sun. of each mo. yr. round. Avg. dealers: 125. Indoors, airconditioned. Dealers fee $20, 8 x 10 space. Free attendance. Tables supplied. Avg. att: over 5000. Ronni Elmore, P. O. Box 4333, Bryan, Tex. 77801. Phone (713) 846-3679. Res. sug.

BUFFALO GAP - Buffalo Gap Flea Mkt., located 11 miles South of Abilene on Farm to Market Road, 89. Held the 3rd Fri., Sat. & Sun. each month. April thru Dec. Phone (915) 673-0249.

CANTON - First Monday Trade Day. 2 blocks north of courthouse. Open first Monday of each month and preceeding Fri., Sat. & Sun. Avg. dealers: 2000. Outdoors. Dealers fee: $11-$26. Admission free. Avg. att: 40,000. Gerald Turner, Box 245, Canton Tex. 75103. Ph: (214) 567-4300. Restrictions: No animals. Res. sug.

CHRISTOVAL - Christoval Park Flea Market. Every 4th weekend of each month. Outdoors, 50 dealers. $9 12' space for weekend. Avg. att. per day 1,000 - no admission - dealers must bring tables. Manager, Buddy McQueen, 1000 10th St. Ballinger, Texas 76821. Phone (915) 365-3262. Res. get best shades.

CLEBURNE - Burd's Flea Market, 926 E. Henderson. Open every Thur. and Fri. Mrs. Burd, P.O. Box 64, Cleburne, Tx. 76031. Ph: (817) 645-4468.

CORPUS CHRISTI - Swap-O-Rama, at the Viking Drive-In Theatre, 5333 Ayers. Open every Sat. and Sun. 50 to 150 sellers, $2 on Sat., $4 on Sun. 1000 to 3000 avg. atten., small adm. charge.

CORPUS CHRISTI - Shoppers City Mall, 2833 S. Padre Dr. Open every Sat. and Sun., 9 am to 6 pm. 15 to 20 sellers (still growing), $7 per table, $30 for a booth for the wknd. New Market. Indoors. 4800 avg. atten.

DALLAS - Bargain Market, 1501 Ft. Worth Ave. Open Fri. and Sat. 10 am to 9 pm and Sun. 10 am to 6 pm. 70 sellers. $3.50 to $4.50 sellers fee. 2-4000 atten. Wm Hamilton. Ph: (214) 747-9741.

DALLAS - Lou Ann's Flea Market, 3136 Routh, in Chelsea Square. Open every Sun. 9 am to 5 pm. Indoors. Ph: (214) 528-1728.

DENTON - Monday Trade Day, east of Denton on Lake Dallas. Held in Sept. and Dec. Over 100 sellers. Jim Runge, 2122 Chippendale, McKinney, Tx. 75069. Ph: (214) 542-2805 or 347-2330.

EL PASO - Ascarate Drive-In Theatre Swap-O-Rama, 6701 Delta Drive. Open Sat. and Sun. Seller's fee, $2 per space. 25¢ admission. Ph: (915) 779-2303.

EL PASO - The El Paso International Flea Mkt., 1500 E. Palsano. Open Fri. 12 to 9:30 pm. Sat. 9:30 am to 9:30 pm. Sun. 9:30 am to 7:30 pm. Indoors. 160 spaces. Free admission. Sam Deener, Ph: (915) 533-1605.

EL PASO - Indoor Flea Mkt., 8150 Dyers St. Open 7 days a week from 7 am to 10 pm. 80 sellers indoor and out. Outdoor setup free. Jamie and Leon, 8150 Dyer St., El Paso, Tx. 79904. Ph: (915) 755-9825.

EL PASO - Lakeside Swap Meet, at the Lakeside Shopping Center, 7000 Alameda. Open every Sat. and Sun. Outdoors.

EL PASO - Sunrise Swap Meet, at the Sunrise Shopping Center, 8500 Dyer. Open every Sun. Outdoors.

EL PASO - Vend-A-Rama, at the Fox Plaza Shopping Center, 5501 Alameda. Open every Sun. Ph: (915) 779-2803.

FOREST HILLS - Forest Hills Flea Market & Trades Day, on old Hwy. 287, 15 miles S. of Ft. Worth. Open every wknd. 200 sellers. 3000 attendance. Outdoors.

FORNEY - Paris Super Flea Market, on I-20, 20 miles E. of Dallas. Open every Sat. and Sun. 9 am to ?? $10 inside space, $5 outside space. 200 spaces. Ph: (214) 552-3839.

FORT WORTH - Plaza Flea Market, Hwy. 80 and Lancaster Blvd. Open every wknd. Indoors 100 stalls.

FORT WORTH - Flea Market, Will Rogers Memorial Center (barn #3), at 3301 W. Lancaster. Open every Sat. and Sun. Ph: (817) 335-0734.

GARLAND - Vikon Village Flea Mkt. 2918 Jupitor Rd. Open every Sat. & Sun. 10 am - 7 pm Dealers: 215. Indoors. Dealers fee based on sq. ft. Free att. 5,000 to 10,000 att. per wknd. Max Alford, 2918 Jupitor Rd., Garland, Tex. 75041. Phone (214) 271-0565. Res. sug.

GRAND PRIARIE - Grand Priarie Antique and Trade Fair, 4601 E. Main St. Open every Sat. and Sun. 160 dealers. $6 per day or $6 for the wknd. Indoor booth $45 per mo. Elaine Davis. Ph: (214) 263-7696.

GRAND PRAIRIE - Traders Village Flea Market, 2602 Mayfield Rd. Open every Sat. & Sun., 8 am to dusk. Over 400 dealers. Fee: $7 per day for open space, $11 per day for covered space, $115-145 per month for enclosed building space. 15,000 to 25,000 avg. atten. each wknd. Ph: (214) 647-2331.

GREENVILLE - Tradearama, on State Hwy 34. Open every 2nd and 4th (Monday) weekends. 50 sellers, $4 per day or $6 for the wknd. Trade-arama, P.O. Box 97B, Greenville, Tx. 75401. Ph: (214) 883-2558.

HARLINGEN - All-Valley Flea Market of Harlingen, H. St. & Expressway 77. Open Sat. and Sun., daylight to dark. 100 sellers. $1 per space on Sat., $2 per space on Sun. 1500 daily atten. 10¢ admission. Indoors and out. Harvey Bruns, P.O. Drawer 908, Mission, Tx. 78572. Ph: (512) 787-4200.

HARLINGEN - Harlingen Flea Mart, 4300 S. 83 Exp. Open Fri., Sat. & Sun. 9 am - 7 pm Avg. dealers: 50 outdoors. Dealers $3.50 fee. Admission free. Tables supplied. Avg. att: 1500. Fred Schurga, 4300 S. 83, Exp. harlingen, Tex. 78550. Phone (512) 423-4535.

HOUSTON - Trading Fair II, 5515 S. Loop East, Crestmont Exit North - South. Fri., Sat., Sun. & Mon. Dealers indoors. (713) 731-1111.

HOUSTON - 7 C's Flea Market, 7600 Airline Dr. Open year round, Wed. thru Fri. $4 on Sat., $5 on Sun. Indoors. Free admission, 2500 daily attendance. Ph: (713) 445-2791.

HOUSTON - Houston Flea Market, Inc., at 6116 S.W. Freeway. Open Sat. and Sun., 8 am to 7 pm. 350 sellers, $8 on Sat., $12 on Sun. 5000 avg. atten. Mary & John Wright. Ph: (713) 782-0391.

HOUSTON - Country Square Common Market, I-10 West, Addicks Exit, North on Hwy 6. Open every Sat. & Sun., 8 am to 6 pm. 160 sellers, $5 on Sat., $7 on Sun. 6000 avg. atten. John Wardell, 611 Ramblewood Rd., Houston, Tx. 77079. Ph: (713) 493-2320 or 497-0914.

HOUSTON - The White Elephant, 15660 East Freeway. Jackie Rice, Ph: (713) 452-9022.

JEFFERSON - Jefferson Flea Market, downtown area. Held on the 3rd weekend of the month. Sponsored by the Marion Co. Chamber of Commerce. Ph: (214) 665-2672.

KERRVILLE - Flea Market, Bolero Drive-In Theatre, Hwy. 27 N. Open 1st Sat. of every month. $2 sellers fee. Mamie Keith, 1108 E. Main, Kerrville, Tx. Ph: (512) 896-1413.

LONGVIEW - Trade Days. Open the 2nd wknd of the month. Sellers fee $3.50 outside, $7 inside.

LUBBOCK - Lubbock Flea Market. 2323 Ave. K. Open Sat. & Sun. year around. Dealers: 350 plus. Indoors and outdoors. Dealer fee depends on size of space. Attendance free. Tables rented when available. Avg. att: 5,000. Mrs. Pauline Gibbs, 1717 Ave. K, Suite 219, Lubbock, TexaS Gibbs, 1717 Ave. K, Suite 219, Lubbock, Tex. 79401.

LUBBOCK - Susie Q's Flea Market, 302 N. Ave. U. Open every Sat. and Sun., 7 am to 5 pm. 127 sellers, $3 on Sat., $4 on Sun. Susie Kirksey, 1906 Sixth St., Lubbock Tx. 79401. Ph: (806) 762-3140 or 762-1289.

MABANK - Gun Barrel City Flea Market, Hwy. 85 E. of 7 points. Mailing address, Rt. 3, Mabank, Tx. 75147. Indoor and outdoor facilities. Sat. and Sun. 8-6. 100 dealers. 3000 attendance. Dealer's fee $2 to $6.

MANSFIELD - Rodeo City Flea Market, at the "Y", 57 & U.S. 287. 12 mi. S. of Arlington. Open Fri. nights & all day Sat. & Sun. Avg. dealers 125. Fee $2 day. Avg. att. 4,000 to 5,000. Lock-up sheds $30 mo. Fred & Jan Faulkner, Rt. #2 Box 285, Alvarado, TX 76009. Ph: (817) 473-9488.

MANSFIELD - County Line Flea Market, on old Hwy. 287 20 miles S. of Ft. Worth. Indoors. 50 dealers.

McALLEN - The Flea Market, 2400 S. 23rd. Open every Sat. and Sun., 7 am to 6 pm. Indoor and out. 200 sellers. $2 to $5 per space. 3000 avg. atten. H.C. Gunter, Ph: (512) 687-4513.

McALLEN - All Valley Annual Garage Sale, 10th St. & Express 83. Sat. & Sun. 200 dealers indoors. 5,000 daily attend. Harvey Bruns, P.O. Drawer 789, Pharr, Tx. 78577. Ph: (512) 781-1911. Res. req.

MERCEDES - All Valley of Mercedes. Between Mercedes and Westlake on Expressway 83. Open Wed. thru Sun. 300-400 dealers. 8000 att: Jim Shawn, P.O. Drawer 789, Pharr, Tx. 78577. Ph: (512) 781-1911. Res. sug.

MINERAL WELLS - Brazos Trading Days Flea Market, on Hwy 281. Held every 3rd and 4th Mon., and the Fri., Sat., and Sun. before. Sellers fee: $2 per day. W.I. Thurmon, P.O. Box 340. Ph: (817) 325-1695.

NACOGDOCHES - Nacogdoches Flea Market, 5900 North St. Indoor and out. Sellers fee: $2.50 and up. Rudy Millard, Ph: (713) 564-3611.

NEDERLAND - Mid-County Flea Market, on Hwy. 69, S. of the airport. Open on weekends, 9 am to 5 pm. Sellers fee: $10 per wknd. or $30 for the month. Mrs. Richard Dixon, P.O. Box 400, Nederland, Tx. 77627. Ph: (713) 727-4012.

ODESSA - "O" Antiques & Flea Market, 404 W. University, Odessa, Tex. 79762. Ph: (915) 337-1775. Indoor and outdoor facilities. Sat. and Sun. 15 dealers, dealer's fee $5 indoors and $3 outdoors. Open weekdays 10-5.

ONALASKA - Flea Market, on Hwy. 190. Open every Sat. and Sun. Sellers fee: $10 for the wknd. James Justice. Ph: (713) 327-4601.

PEARLAND - Cole's Flea Market & Antique Village, 1022 N. Main. Open every Fri., Sat. and Sun., 7 am to ?? Over 300 sellers, $5 to $7 outdoors and $10 for indoors. 5000 avg. attend. E.J. & Diane Cole, 1022 N. Main, Pearland, Tx. 77581. Ph: (713) 485-2277.

PHARR - All-Valley Flea Market of Pharr, 807 E. Hwy. 83. Open Sat. and Sun., daylight to dark. 300 to 400 sellers. $1.50 per space on Sat., $2.50 per space on Sun. Summer attend.: 4000, winter attend: 8000. 10¢ admission. Harvey Bruns, P.O. Drawer 908, Mission, Tx. 78572. Ph: (512) 787-4200.

PHARR - Weekend Flea Market, 807 E. Hwy. 83, between Pharr & San Juan. Open every wknd. Harvey Bruns, Drawer 908, Mission, Tx. 78572. Ph: (512) 787-4200.

PORT ARTHUR - 26th Annual CavOil Cade. Thieves Mkt. Held on the grounds of Woodrow Wilson Junior High School. Located on Stillwell Blvd. at Lake Shore Dr. Avg. daily att. 2,000. Avg. 100 dealers. Free admission. Dealers fee $600. Electricity included if needed. This market held in conjunction with the 26th Annual CavOil Cade Celebration. Sponsored by Chamber of Commerce. Ph: (713) 982-3421.

PURDON - Purdon Flea Market, downtown Purdon. Open every third Sat. and Sun. Indoor booths. Dorothy Jones, P.O. Box 307, Purdon, Tx. 76679. Ph: (214) 872-1975.

SAN ANGELO - The Pack Rat Flea Market, 19 E. Concho St. Open every 2nd wknd of the mo. Sellers fee: $3 per space. Wayne Henson, 1403 S. David, San Angelo, Tx. Ph: (915) 655-2721.

SAN ANTONIO - Mission Drive-In Theatre Swap-O-Rama, 3100 Roosevelt St. Open every Sat. and Sun. Over 200 sellers, $3 per space. 25¢ admission per car load. John Cavender, Ph: (512) 532-3259.

SAN ANTONIO - Callagan Square Flea Market, 4394 Callaghan Rd. Open every Sat. and Sun., 8 am to 6 pm. Sellers fee: $10 for the wknd. Melvin Miller. Ph: (512) 432-9273.

SAN ANTONIO - San Pedro Drive-In Theatre Flea Market, 600 Bitters Rd. Open every wknd. Santikos Theatres, Inc. 4103 San Pedro. Ph: (512) 734-7263.

SAN ANTONIO - Colonies North Flea Market, at the Colonies North Shopping Center. Open every Sunday, 10 am to 6 pm. 175 sellers, $8 per table. Indoors. 5000 avg. attend. Manual Garza. Ph: (512) 691-1283.

SAN ANTONIO - Swapper's Park, 9906 Moursund. Open every wknd. and some holidays, daylight to dark. Sellers fee: $3 daily. 5000 att. H.R. Tharp, 610 E. Josephine. Ph: (512) 222-9985.

SAN ANTONIO - Flea Market & Fun Town, 18738 I-H 35 N. Held every Sat. & Sun. 9 am - 6 pm. Avg. daily att. 5,000. Avg. 120 dealers. Admission fee 25¢ per person. Dealers fee $5 on Sat. $7 on Sun. Ample free parking. 40 permanent dealers, 90 table spaces under cover. Specializing in antiques. (512) 651-6836.

SEVEN OAKS - 7 Oaks Flea Mkt. located 11 miles north of Livingston on Hwy 59. Every Fri., Sat. & Sun. Dealers fee $15 per weekend. Includes 3-8' tables. 7 am - Dark. Under shed. Trailer park with complete hookups. (713) 398-2409.

TIOGA - Western Trade Days, On the Square. Open 1st Mon. wknd. each mo. Avg. dealers: 150 indoors and outdoors. Att: 1,500 plus. James or Mignon Wendover, P. O. Box 176, Tioga, Tex. 76271. Phone (817) 437-2219 or (817) 668-7077. Res. sug.

UVALDE - Cactus Jack Flea Market (June) & Fall Arts & Crafts Festival (November). Fairgrounds. Number of dealers: 60-75. Outdoors. Bill Dillard, P. O. Box 706, Uvalde, Tex. 78801. (512) 278-3361.

VICTORIA - Victoria Flea Market, Victoria Regional Airport. Open every Sun., except 5th Sun. of month. Avg. dealers: 25-50. Indoors and outdoors. Dealers fee: $3 - $10. Free admission. Tables supplied if available. Avg. att: 1500. Lewis Vanorman, Rt. 5, Box 143A, Victoria, Tex. 77901. Phone (512) 578-8021.

FLEA MARKET AMERICA

WACO - Price's Unlimited Flea Market, 2722 La Salle (at I-35 at Valley Mills, 1 block so. of the Circle). Held every Sat. & Sun. year round. Good crowds. Avg. 150 dealers. Free parking and admission. Dealers fee $1.50 to $3 per day outside. Inside varies. Camping nearby. Phone (817) 662-9971.

WACO - Deep Elm Antique Mart, 2729 La Salle. Open Tues. thru Fri., 10 am to 5 pm. Sat. and Sun., daylight till dark. Over 200 sellers, $1.50 and up. Ph: (817) 662-4446.

WACO - J & J Flea Market, 1118 New Dallas Hwy. (Bellmead). Open daily. Indoor and out. $1.50 per space. Joe Adamson. Ph: (817) 799-4501.

WEATHERFORD - Flea Market, west of Ft. Worth. Open 1st wknd of month. 300 sellers, outdoors with shelters.

WICHITA FALLS - 2820 Holliday Rd. on Holliday Creek. Open Sat. and Sun. 7 am to 8 pm. 100 sellers $3 per space outdoors, $5 per booth indoors. 8 to 10,000 attend., free admission. Roy Parish, 4428 Sisk Rd., Wichita Falls, Tx. Ph: (817) 767-9038 or 692-0305.

WIMBERLY - Market Days. Held at Lions Memorial Field on Ranch Road. 2325 on the first Sat. May thru Oct. Avg. daily att. 5,000. Avg. 150 dealers. Free adm. Dealers fee $40 per season or $10 per day. 8th Year. Phone (512) 847-2391.

UTAH

OGDEN - The Swap & Shop Meet. Exchange Rd. Open Sun., soon will open Sat. 200 dealers indoors. Dealers fee: $3. Att. fee: 25¢ per person. Mgr. John Elizondo. P.O. Box 9692, Ogden, Utah, 84409. Ph: (801) 479-0252. "New Retail" dealers are welcome but charged more.

OGDEN - Ogden Flea Market, 3111 Wall. Open Sat. & Sun. Indoors and outdoors. Dealers fee: $3 to $8. Attendance fee 25¢. Avg. att: 600. Art Kolbek, 518 27th, Ogden, Utah 84403. Phone (801) 393-0383. No live animals sold. Res. sug.

SALT LAKE CITY - Intermountain Independent Flea Mkt., 3435 S. Main. Open year round. Sat. & Sun. 9 am to 5 pm. 75 to 100 sellers. Indoors. $10 plus $2 lic. fee. Up to 5000 Attend. Jim & Glennis Ponton, 2773 W. 7550 S. West Jordan Utah. 84084. Ph: (801) 255-4029.

SALT LAKE CITY - Swap Meet and Flea Market, 3700 S. Redwood Dr. at the Drive-In. Open Sat. and Sun., 8 am to 3:30 pm. $1 to $3 per space. Ph: (801) 973-7088 or 973-7089.

VERMONT

CHARLOTTE - Charlotte Flea Market, Rt. 7. Open May to Oct., 10 am to 5 pm., Sat and Sun. Outdoors. 20 dealers. Larry and Karen Larilette, Charlotte, VT 05445.

BENNINGTON - The 11th Annual Bennington Antiques Flea Market, on Rt. 7, 2 miles north of Bennington. Sat. Aug. 14, 9 am to 6 pm. Admission $1. Sponsored by Mt. Anthony Chapter No. 1, O.E.S.

BRUNSWICK - 1st Annual Bear Mountain Labor Day Flea Market & Auction. Rt. 105. Ph: (802) 962-3359, mailing address, Jack Brooks, Bear Mountain Inn Brunswick, VT c/o Po North Stratford, NH. Outdoor facilities, Dealer's fee and attendance free. Loads of free parking. Full restaurant and snack bars.

MANCHESTER - Manchester Flea Market, Rts. 11 and 30, 3 mi east of Manchester. Open last week in May to last week in Oct. 9 am to 5 pm, Sat. Outdoors 20 to 40 dealers, $40 per day. John P. Wessner, Manchester, VT 05255. Ph: (802) 362-1631. Antiques, crafts, livestock and household items.

MIDDLEBURY - Mitchell's Flea Market. Open May to Sept. 9 am to 6 pm. Sat. and Sun. Outdoors. 10 to 15 sellers. $5 per day. Mitchell's Rd. No. 3, Middlebury, VT 05753. Ph: (802) 388-7623. Antiques and collectibles.

MORRISVILLE - Mud City Antique Market, off Rt. 100, 1 mi. south of Morrisville. Open last week in June to Columbus Day weekend, 10 am to 5 pm. Sundays. Indoors and out. 23 to 45 dealers. $4 a day with tables supplied. Jeanette Lepine, Manchester, VT 05661. Ph: (802) 888-4076. Furniture and collectibles.

NEWFANE - The original Newfane Flea Market,. Rt. 30 2 mi. north of Newfane. Open May thru Oct. 9 am to 5 pm. Sundays. Outdoors. 85-90 dealers. $5 per day. Bill Morse, Jr., Box 55, Newfane, VT. 05345. Ph: (802) 365-7771. Furniture collectibles, crafts and produce.

WILMINGTON - Vermont Indoor Flea Market, Rt. 100. Open all year, 10 am to 6 pm. Sat., Sun. and holidays. Indoor and out. Avg. 50 dealers. $7.50 per day for indoor space, $5 per day for outdoor space. Harris King, Newfane, VT 05345. Ph: (802) 365-4482.

VIRGINIA

CHESAPEAKE - Oak Grove Flea Market, 910 Oak Grove Rd. Open every Sat. & Sun. 10 am to 6 pm. 38 sellers. Indoors and out. Bob or Winnie Larmore. Ph: (804) 547-1500 or 782-1030.

FARMVILLE - Farmville Drive-In Flea Market, Rt. 15 South. Open Sat. 8 am to 4:30 pm, Sun. afternoon. Seller's fee $2 each day. 25¢ admission. A.T. Kline, Jr., 4501 Stanbrook Dr., Richmond, VA 23234. Ph: (703) 898-1260 or (804) 275-1187.

FREDRICKSBURG - Flea Market, on U.S. 1 south of Fredricksburg. Open Sat. and Sun. 8 am to 4:30 pm year round. Sellers fee $2 onSat., $3 on Sun. 25¢ admission. A.T. Kline Jr., 4501 Stanbrook Dr., Richmond, VA 23234. Ph: (804) 275-1187.

GLOUCESTER - Carters Flea & Farmer Mkt. U.S. Rt. 17 South. Sat. 9-5 & Sun. 1-6. Free Adm. & prk. (804) 693-4530.

HILLSVILLE - VFW Labor Day Gun Show & Flea Market. Route 58. Open Sat. Sept. 5, 8-8; Sun. Sept 6, 8-8; & Mon. Sept. 7, 8-4. Flea Mkt. Dealers fee: $15 for 3 days. Att. fee: $1. Tables supplied inside only. Avg. att: 5000. Melvin Webb, Rt. 2 Box 39A, Hillsville, Va. 24343. Res Req.

MANASSAS - Manassas - Manassas Drive-In Flea Market, Rt. 28 North. Open Sat. and Sun., 8 am to 4:30 pm. Seller's fee $5 per day. 25¢ admission. (New Market). A.T. Kline, Jr., 4501 Stanbrook Dr., Richmond, VA 23234. Ph: (703) 368-2513 or (804) 275-1187.

MANASSAS - Law's Auction & Antiques, 7209 Centreville Rd. Open 2nd and 4th Sun. of the month, 9 am to 5 pm. 65 to 75 sellers, $10 per space. 5 to 10,000 attend. Free admission. Mrs. Walters, P.O. Box 675, Manassas, VA 22110. Ph (703) 361-3148.

RICHMOND - Bellwood Flea Market. 9201 Jess Davis Hy. Open 8-4:30 Sat. & Sun. (weather permitting) outdoors. Dealers fee: $4 - $8. Attendance fee: 40¢ each. Tables supplied - $1.50 each. Alvin Kline, 9201 Jeff Davis Hwy, Richmond, VA 23234. Ph: (804) 275-1187. Restrictions: no prepared food, livestock, firearms, or drug paraphernalia.

ROANOKE - Trail Drive-In Flea Market, Rt. 1, Box 157, on U.S. 460. Open every Sat. 175 dealers, $4 per space. 3000 avg. attend. James Swortzell or Tom Davis, Rt. 1, Box 157, Roanoke, VA 24012. Ph: (703) 32-0279.

ROANOKE - Lee Hi. Drive-In Flea Market, 1700 Apperson Drive. Open Sat. & Sun 8 am - 5 pm. Avg. dealers: 50. Outdoors. Dealers fee: $3. Admission free. Ralph L. Hoskins, 1700 Apperson Drive, Salem, Va. 24153. Phone (703) 389-5556. Restrictions: no food to sell as we have a modern snack bar.

STAUNTON - Verona-Virginia Flea Market, on U.S. 11. Open year round. Thur. thru Sun. 50 to 150 sellers, rent by the week, one table $7.50, booth $12. Rocky Simonetti, Box 317, Verona, VA 24482. Ph: (703) 886-9640. We sell largely to dealers.

STRASBURG - Strasburg Emporium. 306 East King Street. Open Fri., Sat., Sun. Indoors and out. Ph: (703) 465-3711.

THORNBURY - Easter Sales & Auction Co. Outdoor Flea Market. Open every Sat. & Sun. 8am till ? Auction Sat. 7 pm. Ph: (703) 582-5755.

WAYNESBORO - Skyline Drive-In Flea Market, Rt. 250 West. Open Sat. and Sun. 8 am to 4:30 pm. Seller's fee $2 on Sat., $3 on Sun. 25¢ admission. (New Market) A.T. Kline, Jr., 4501 Stanbrook Dr., Richmond, VA 23234. Ph: (703) 942-5130 or (804) 275-1187.

WASHINGTON

CHEHALIS - Sunbird Shopping Center, 1757 National Ave. Open Wed. thru Sun. 11 am to 7 pm. (9 pm on Fri.) 100 to 150 sellers, $3 to $25 for sellers fees. Dick Silstrom. Ph: (206) 748-3337.

CHENEY - Cheney Flea Market, 1011 1st St., Cheney Wa. 99004. Open Sun. - Thur. 9-6. Fri. & Sat. 9-8. Dealers fee: $5 day or $25 wk. Tables supplied. Free admission. Janet R. Davidson. Phone (509) 235-4347. No food items which would compete with grocery stores. Res. sug.

EVERETT - Puget Park Drive-In Flea Market. I-5 at 128th S.W. Interchange. Open every Sat. and Sun. and Holidays, April thru Oct. 9:30 to 4:30. 200 to 250 sellers, $6 for the weekend. 5 to 8000 attendance. 50¢ admission per car load. Clark Thomason, Box 1723, Bellevue, WA 98008, Ph: (206) 827-8241.

GRAHAM - Weekender Swap Meet, 6200-296th E, off Mt. Hwy (Rt. 7) 8 miles from Spanaway. Open every Sat. & Sun. Room for 500 sellers. Sellers fee $3 on Sat., $4 on Sun. For more info: Dick or Ginger Itaag, Ph: (206) 847-9675. New Market.

KENT - Kent Flea Market, 515 E. Smith. Open every Thurs. thru Sun. 9 am to 6 pm. Dealers. 12 to 14 sellers. $5 per day, $12 for the wknd, $40 for the month. Joe La Plante, 19040 S.E. 243, Kent, WA 98031. Ph: (206) 852-5463.

LONG BEACH - Del Vonne's Flea Mkt. are fun, at the Grange Hall, 1981 dates: May 2-3, Sept. (call for dates). Del Vonne Roberts, P.O. Box 24, Garibaldi, Or. 97118. Ph: (503) 322-3250.

PROSSER - Prosser Flea Market, 611 6th St. 50 sellers, $4 per day, $7 for the two days. 3000 attendance. Ph: (509) 786-2626.

RENTON - Renton Swap Meet & Flea Market. 550 Edwards St. Open Sat. & Sun. 10-5. 50-60 dealers. Att: 1500-3000. Robert Goetz, 150 S.W. 7th St., Renton, WA 98055. Ph: (206) 255-2099 or 228-6811. Res. sug.

SEATTLE - Spectrum Swap 'N' Shop, 17229 15th Ave. N.E., Seattle, WA 98133. Open Sat. & Sun. Avg. dealers: 50, indoors. Dealers fee: $10. Att. fee: none. Avg. daily att: 400. Mgr. Jim Schmitt, 28602 13th Ave., So. Federal Way, WA 98003. Heavy equipment restricted. Res. sug.

SEATTLE - Granite Curling Club Flea Market. 1440 N. 128th St. Open May 1st to Sept. 1st. (Fri. nite & all day Sat.). Dealers fee: $8. Tables supplied. Avg. att: 1000 plus. Andy Calderwood, 11715 Palatine Ave. North, Seattle, Wa. 98133. Phone 362-8378. Res. req.

178

SEATTLE - Angle Lake Flea Mart, 19832 Pacific Hwy., South. Open Thru. thru Sun. Indoors. Dealers fee: $11 all week. Free att. Avg. att: 800-1000. John Brewer, 13710 139th Ave. S.E. Renton, Wa. 98055. Phone 878-8161 (business) 255-2039 (home). Restrictions: firearms and porno materials. Res. sug.

SPANAWAY - Overniter Swap Meet. 6611 296th E. Open every weekend. Outdoor. Forest Haag, 6611 296th E., Graham, WA 98338. Ph: (206) 847-9675. Overnite parking.

SPOKANE - Engles Flea Mkt. N. 9014 North Division at the Y. Open 10-5 daily.

SPOKANE - The Emporium, 1906 E. Sprage Ave. 10-5 Tue. thru Sun.

WEST VIRGINIA

FAIRPLAIN - Fairplain Flea Market, on Cedar Lake Dr. Open June 30th thru July 4th, 1981. 125 dealers, $5 per day. Oris Tolley, P.O. Box 25, Kenna, W. Va. 25248. Ph: (304) 372-3039.

HURRICANE - Flea Market, held Sundays at Hurricane, 23 mi. W. of Charleston on Rt. 60. Dorothy Cyrus, 314 Kentucky Ave., St. Albans, WV 25177. Ph: 727-9939 or 562-5412.

PRINCETON - East End Flea Market, 301 Old Oakdale Rd. Open Tues., Wed., & Sat. 30 dealers pitdoors. Att: 2000. Lloyd Nichols, 301 Old Oakdale Rd. Princeton, W.V. 24740. Ph: (304) 425-7292.

WINFIELD - Winfield Riding Club Flea Market. Sat. & Sun. At the intersection of Rt. 34 and Rt. 35. Dealers: $3. Cliff Fisher. Ph: (304) 757-9040.

WISCONSIN

ADAMS - Adams Flea Mkt. Hwy. 13 south. Open April to Sept. Dealers: 20 indoors and 350 outdoors. Dealers fee: $3.75. Admission free. Avg. att: 400-500. Claude Komo, Rt. 1 Box 380, Adams, Wisc. 53910. (608) 339-3606. Overnight parking and camping facilities nearby. Lunch sold on grounds.

CALEDONIA - 7 Mile Fair, Inc., 2720 W. 7 Mile Rd. Open April 1 thru Oct. 31. Avg. dealers: 1000. Indoors winter season, outdoors: 1,000. Dealers fee: $7. Admission $1. Avg. att: 20,000. Scott Niles, P.O. Box 7, Caledonia, WI 53108. Phone (414) 835-2177. Restrictions: no food. Indoor - Nov. thru March. Call for location.

EDGERTON - Wisconsin Field Fair Flea Market, U.S. 90 and Hwy. 59. Open Sat. and Sun. Wayne A. Hemenway, Rt. 4 Box 204 F, Edgerton, WS 53534. Ph: (608) 884-3994 day or 884-4178 eves.

ELLSWORTH - Landry Auto Center Parking Lot, Route 1. Open Sat. 10-5. Sun. 9-5. Dealers fee $5 for 1 day, $8 for 2 days. Cal & Terri Landry, Route #1, Ellsworth, Wisc. 54011. Phone (715) 273-5659. Res. sug. Camping overnight permitted.

GREEN BAY - Brown County Fairgrounds. Open every Sat. 6 am to 5 pm. 100 sellers. $3.50 per space. 25¢ admission. Bob Zurko, P.O. Box 187, Shawano, WI. Ph: (715) 526-9034.

HAUGEN - The Barn, Hwy. 53. Open every Thur. thru Sun. 8 am to 5 pm. Indoors 4 by 8 tables available $4 per space. Vern or Louise Gabriel, Sarona, WI. Ph: (715) 234-2615.

KENOSHA - Mid City Outdoor Theatre Flea Market, on Hwy. 32. Open on Sun. May thru Oct. Over 100 sellers, $3 per space. 2 to 3000 attendance.

LADYSMITH - Community Auction Flea Market, Hwy. 8 between Ladysmith and Bruce. Open at 6:30 am on the following dates: October 5, 20, and 30. Auction at 10 am. Largest flea market in northwestern WI. Ph: (715) 532-3661.

LYNDON STATION - Resthaven Tavern Flea Market, South Hwy. 12-16. Open Sat. & Sun. Fee: $1 day. Resthaven Tavern, Lyndon Station, WI 53944. Ph: (608) 253-5241.

MENOMONEE FALLS - Starlite Swap O Rama, Starlite Drive-In, N. FonDuLac Ave., Hwy. 145 and 41. Open Sun. May-Nov. 80 to 100 sellers, avg. atten. 1500-2000. $4 fee. Swap Shop, Inc., 5630 Elston, Chicago, IL 60646. Ph: (312) 774-3900.

MERRILL - Bargain Bin Flea Market, Hwy. K, south of Merrill. Every Sat. and Sun. 9 am to 5 pm. May 15th thru Sept. 26. 30 to 100 sellers, $3.50 per day or $5 for the wknd. Attend. 1000 and up. Free admission. Rt. 5 Box 186, Merrill, WI. Ph: (715) 536-8002.

MILWAUKEE - 7 Mile Fair, 11 miles south of Milwaukee on I-94, exit 7 mile Rd. Open Sat. and Sun. April thru Oct., dawn to dark. Outdoors. 1000 to 1200 sellers. Niles, P.O. Box 7 Caledonia, WI 53108. Ph: (414) 885-2177.

MILWAUKEE - Expo Hall, Red Carpet Inn. Open on Sat. & Sun., Oct. thru March. 400 to 500 sellers, $12 per space for the wknd. 75¢ admission. Niles, P.O. Box 7 Caledonia, WI 53108. Ph: (414) 725-4231.

OSHKOSH - Flea Market, Downtown behind Penneys on Main St. Write or phone for dates and sellers fees. Gloria Smith, 1193 Lorette Ave., Menasha, WI. Ph: (414) 725-4231.

SHAWANO - Shawano County Fairgrounds Flea Market. Open on Sun., May thru Oct. also Sat. in June, July and Aug. 250 sellers. $4.50 per space. 35¢ adm. Bob Zurko, 1131 St. Agnes Dr., Shawano, WI 54304. Ph: (414) 499-2169.

SHAWANO - Red Owl Flea Market, Hill & Main St. Open every Tues. May thru Sept. 10 to 12 sellers. Free to sellers and buyers. Red Ownl Store. Ph: (715) 526-5111.

SLINGER - Little Switzerland's "17 mile Fair". 105 Hwy. 99. Open every Sun. fromJune 1 till Oct. 150 dealers outdoors. Att. 4000. Dorothy Greene, 1651 Mayfield Rd., Richfield, WI 53076. Ph: (414) 628-2705. Res. sug.

SPOONER - Millard's Wheel-In Flea Market, Hwy. 53 & 63. Open on Fri. 9 am to 4 pm. Ph: (715) 635-3801.

ST. CROIX FALLS - Pea Picking Flea Market. Hwy. 8 & 35. 5 miles east of St. Croix Falls. Open Sat., Sun., Holidays. Indoor and out. Fee: $5 day. Att: 2,500. Leonard Sommers, Rt. 2, Box 145, St. Croix Falls, WI 54024. Ph: (715) 483-9460.

WAUSAU - Crossroads Mall Flea Mkt., 1810 Stewart Circle. 1981 Dates are May 2 and again in Fall - call for dates - 150 dealers. Indoors. $8 fee. 4500 avg. att. Ken Ruether, P.O. Box 247, Schofield, WI 54476. Ph: (715) 359-9500.

WYOMING

CASPER - Flea Market, 306 N. Durbin (Eagle's Hall), Ph: (307) 234- 2480. Mailing address, 1112 W. 22nd, Casper, WY 82601. Indoor facilities, bimonthly, 1st Sun. after 3rd Fri. 30 dealers, 1250 attendance. Dealer's fee $5.

CANADA

ALBERTA

CALGARY - Swap O Rama, Calgary Exhibition & Stampede Park. Open every Sun. 150 dealers, $7.50 per space. 4500 to 5000 avg. atten. 50¢ adm. adults. Indoor and out. No. 2105-1200 6th St. S.W., Calgary, Alberta, Canada T2R 1H3. Ph: (403) 263-8210.

EDMONTON - Swap O Rama, Edmonton Exhibition Grounds. Open every Sun. New Market opened May 1977. Ph: (403) 424-2333.

BRITISH COLUMBIA

RICHMOND - Delta Drive-In Theatre Shop 'N' Swap, 340 Number Five Rd. Ph: (604) 278-9076, mailing address, P.O. Box 94050, Richmond, British Columbia, V6Y 2A2. Outdoor facilities, every Sun. 9 am to 4 pm. 150 dealers, 3000 attend. Attend. fee 25¢, dealer's fee $4.

VANCOUVER - Haney Legion Hall. Open every Sun. 9:30 am to 4 pm. Indoors. 30 sellers. $9 per table, $6 each add. table. Reg Langley, B.C. Ph: (604) 630-5426.

VANCOUVER - Swap O Rama, held at P.N.E. Grounds (Hastings & Renfrew). Open every Sun. 700 dealers indoor and outdoor. Daily atten. 12,000 to 15,000. Spaces $5, tables can be rented. Overnites ok. Murray Moxley, 1657 Nanaimo St., Vancouver, B.C. V5L 4T9. Ph: (604) 251-4498.

ONTARIO

GRAND BEND - Pinery Flea Market, 3 miles So. of Grand Bendon Hwy 21. Open Sun. 10 am to 5 pm. May thru Sept. Sellers fee $5 outside, $10 inside. 50¢ admission. Bob Sandercott, 13 Main St. Grand Bend, Ontario. Ph: (519) 238-8382.

STITTSVILLE - Gibson's Stittsville Flea Market on Hwy. 7. Open every Sun. 170 to 300 sellers (seasonal), sellers fee 19¢ a ft. indoors, $5 outside. 2000 to 4000 attend. John Gibson. Ph: (613) 836-5612.

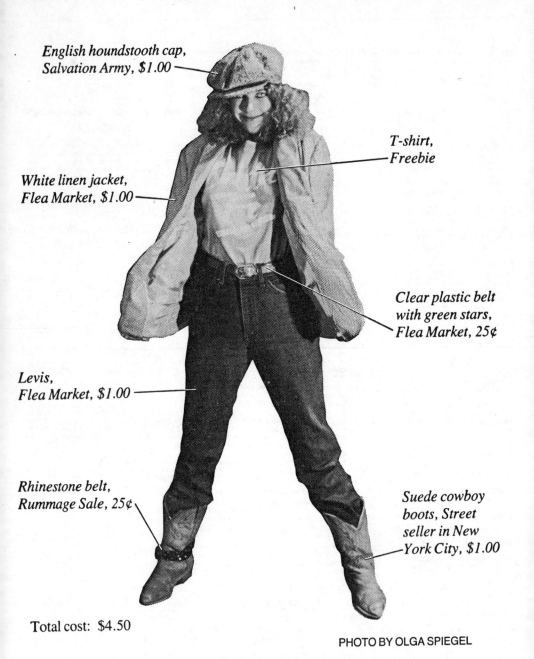

English houndstooth cap,
Salvation Army, $1.00

T-shirt,
Freebie

White linen jacket,
Flea Market, $1.00

Clear plastic belt
with green stars,
Flea Market, 25¢

Levis,
Flea Market, $1.00

Rhinestone belt,
Rummage Sale, 25¢

Suede cowboy
boots, Street
seller in New
York City, $1.00

Total cost: $4.50

PHOTO BY OLGA SPIEGEL

Cree McCree is a free lance writer and photographer, and a martial arts instructor. She became a professional flea in 1975, and has taken her cheap chic boutique to flea markets across the country. Most recently, she has set up shop at the Canal Street Flea Market in New York City.